Digital Humanities

Digital Humanities

Knowledge and Critique in a Digital Age

DAVID M. BERRY AND ANDERS FAGERJORD

polity

The right of David M. Berry and Anders Fagerjord to be identified as Authors of this Work has been asserted in accordance with the UK Copyright, Designs and Patents Act 1988.

First published in 2017 by Polity Press

Polity Press
65 Bridge Street
Cambridge CB2 1UR, UK

Polity Press
350 Main Street
Malden, MA 02148, USA

ISBN-13: 978-0-7456-9765-9
ISBN-13: 978-0-7456-9766-6 (pb)

A catalogue record for this book is available from the British Library.

Library of Congress Cataloging-in-Publication Data

Names: Berry, David M. (David Michael) author. | Fagerjord, Anders, author.
Title: Digital humanities : knowledge and critique in a digital age / David
    M. Berry, Anders Fagerjord.
Description: Cambridge, England ; Malden, MA : Polity Press, [2017] |
    Includes bibliographical references and index.
Identifiers: LCCN 2016048324 (print) | LCCN 2017010938 (ebook) | ISBN
    9780745697659 (hardback) | ISBN 9780745697666 (pbk.) | ISBN 9780745697680
    (Mobi) | ISBN 9780745697697 (Epub)
Subjects: LCSH: Digital humanities.
Classification: LCC AZ105 .B395 2017 (print) | LCC AZ105 (ebook) | DDC
    001.30285--dc23
LC record available at https://lccn.loc.gov/2016048324

Typeset in 11 on 13pt Adobe Garamond Pro by
Servis Filmsetting Ltd, Stockport, Cheshire
Printed and bound in the UK by CPI Group (UK) Ltd, Croydon, CR0 4YY

For further information on Polity, visit our website:
politybooks.com

For Lorna M. Hughes and Andrew Prescott

Contents

Acknowledgements

This book would not have been written without the support and assistance of a large number of colleagues who have in various ways contributed to the project. So, first, we would like to individually thank our respective supporters.

David would like to thank Mansfield College, University of Oxford, for electing him a Visiting Fellow during 2015/16, which offered a hugely supportive and scholarly environment in which to complete this book – and especially Pam Berry, Tony Lemon and John Ovenden, with whom he enjoyed many Wednesday evening Formals. David would also like to thank colleagues in the School of Media, Film and Music at the University of Sussex and the members of the Sussex Humanities Lab: particularly Caroline Bassett, Tim Hitchcock, Sally Jane Norman, Rachel Thomson and Amelia Wakeford, and, in the Computational Culture strand, Beatrice Fazi, Ben Roberts and Alban Webb. David is also grateful to the University of Sussex for support for the Sussex Humanities Lab and for digital humanities and computational media at Sussex – particularly Michael Davies, Debbie Foy-Everett and Alan Lester. He would also like to give thanks for the continued support of colleagues: Christian Ulrik Andersen, Armin Beverungen, Ina Blom, Melanie Bühler, Michael Bull, Mercedes Bunz, Natalia Cecire, Andrew Chitty, Faustin Chongombe, Christian De Cock, Natalie Cowell, Michael Dieter, Kathryn Eccles, Wolfgang Ernst, Leighton Evans, Gordon Finlayson, Paul Flather, Jan Freeman, Matthew Fuller, Steve Fuller, Alex Galloway, Craig Gent, David Golumbia, Ground Coffee House in Lewes (particularly Beth, John and Rick), Andres Guadamuz, David Hendy, Lorna M. Hughes, Tim Jordan, Athina Karatzogianni, Raine Koskimaa, Alan Liu, Paul Lodge, Geert Lovink, Thor Magnusson, The Mansfield College Porters, Chris Marsden, Ursula Martin, Derek McCormack, William Merrin, Peter Nagy, Jussi Parikka, Luciana Parisi, The Pelham Arms, Alison Powell, Andrew Prescott, Ned Rossiter, David De Roure, Lucinda Rumsey, Darrow Schecter, Paul Solman, Bernard Stiegler, Nathaniel Tkacz, Transmediale, Iris van der Tuin, Craig Vear, Pip Willcox and the many, many people he may have forgotten to include. Additionally, David would like to thank his Ph.D. students: Yilmaz Aliskan, Emma Harrison, Isla-Kate Morris and Carina Westling for their continued discussions. Many thanks also have to be expressed to Anders Fagerjord who has been a wonderfully collaborative and thoughtful co-writer. Finally, David would also like to thank his partner, Trine Bjørkmann Berry, and their children, Helene, Henrik Isak and Hedda Emilie, for accepting the disruption to family life from writing yet another book.

Anders would like to thank all his fantastic colleagues at the Department of Media and Communication at the University of Oslo, particularly Terje Colbjørnsen, Charles Ess, Bente Kalsnes, Lucy Küng, Maren Moen, Marius Øfsti, Terje Rasmussen, Tanja Storsul, Espen Ytreberg, the members of the band Stimulus Response, and Gunnar Liestøl, who introduced him to digital humanities more than two decades ago. His Ph.D. students Joakim Karlsen and Kim Johansen Østby have also introduced him to new areas and ideas, for which he is truly grateful. The Department of Information Science and Media Studies, University of Bergen, let him share an office space there for several months when this book was being written, and he would like to give thanks for the hospitality and support extended by Rune Arntsen, Kurt Gjerde, Stein Unger Hitland, Leif-Ove Larsen and Terje Thue. While there, he also enjoyed many fruitful discussions, including those with Dag Elgesem, Jostein Gripsrud, Lars Nyre, Eirik Stavelin and Bjørnar Tessem. He would also like to thank his many friends and colleagues for continued support over the years, including Espen Aarseth, Cheryl Ball, Jay Bolter, Taina Bucher, Martin Engebretsen, Gail Hawisher, Steve Jones, Anders Olof Larsson, Anders Sundnes Løvlie, Andrew Morrison, Cuiming Pang, Jill Walker Rettberg and Scott Rettberg. Finally, he would like to thank David Berry, who first came up with the idea for this book and invited him to take part, something he has enjoyed immensely.

We would both like to thank the team at Polity, who have been very supportive throughout the writing process. We would also like to thank Marcus Leis Allion for his wonderful cover design and for agreeing to take on the project. We are grateful to all the colleagues who have supported the writing of this book, and especially those who hack and those who yack in the digital humanities.

1   Introduction

This book is about the digital humanities, an exciting new field of research that emerged at the beginning of the 2000s.[1] As digital technology has swept over the world, the humanities too have undergone a rapid change in relation to the use and application of digital technologies in scholarship, although the perceived effects of this are sometimes not always completely visible on the surface of the constituent disciplines. The internet, hand-held network computing devices such as smartphones and tablets, and even 'smart watches' have become so ingrained in our lives that it is difficult to remember how we managed without them. Similarly, databases and image archives, applications and digital tools have begun to make a large impact on both the kinds of resources that are available to humanities scholars and the methods we use. Humanities research has been irrevocably transformed, as indeed have everyday life, our societies, economies, cultures and politics. These changes are echoed in new ways of thinking about culture and knowledge, and, in light of this, the humanities are actively augmenting and rethinking their existing methods and practices. 'Digital humanities' as a term and a movement has, since its first use in 2001, been taken up by many scholars and universities, and, perhaps more strikingly, by most major funding bodies, but remains contentious and contested.[2] Nonetheless, as a term, it helpfully situates humanities research that is self-consciously digital in its orientation, and assists in giving a sense of the kinds of research practice that are increasingly being shared and incorporated into humanities scholarship.

One need not talk to many humanists, however, before one learns that this label is an umbrella term for a variety of diverse practices, which often have a history that is older than that of the digital computer. Some voices also echo the opinion that digital humanities is somehow alien to the tradition of humanities, and may even be a threat to its values. In this book, we touch on some of these controversies and debates and seek to contribute to understanding of them and the ways in which they offer helpful critique, and, sometimes, anti-technology polemic.

This book builds on the theoretical and empirical work already done by fields such as media and communications, and connects them further to the field of digital humanities, particularly to develop and deepen the notion of a 'critical digital humanities'. In our increasingly postdigital age, whether something is 'digital' or not is no longer seen as the essential question (see Berry and Dieter 2015). There are fewer 'humanities issues' and distinct 'technical issues' that can be neatly bifurcated. The question of whether something is or is not 'digital' will be increasingly secondary as many forms of culture become mediated, produced, accessed, distributed or consumed through digital devices and technologies. Thus, the argument of this book is that the digital humanities must be able to offer theoretical interventions and digital methods for a historical moment when the computational has become both hegemonic and post-screenic. With 'post-screenic', we gesture to a move away from the computer screen or visual interface as the key site of interaction. We think of the 'digital' as a previous historic moment when computation as digitality was understood in opposition to the analogue, rather than complementary, as we argue in this book. Instead of thinking in terms of digital vs analogue, the specific affordances of each form should be understood and used together – for example, paper archives combined with faceted search, or photographs analysed with statistical thematic analysis, etc. Thus, under our contemporary conditions, the modulations of the digital or different intensities of the computational are manifested as a postdigital moment. This includes thinking about the politics of disconnection and how the idea of slowing-down digital projects to 'disrupt digital networks [might] be akin to what the slow food movement is to fast food: an opportunity to stop and question the meaning of progress' (Mejias 2013: 159). The digital humanities, as a field, is unique in being positioned between technology and culture and can therefore think critically about how these cadences of the computational are made and materialized. But, perhaps more to the point, digital humanists as builders of these kinds of systems often have a sophisticated understanding of technologies, algorithms, software processes and their implementation, and consequently can contribute important insights into how humanistic technologies can be developed.

Technology is often identified as something *done* to the humanities (and the university more broadly) – that is, from outside the institution. Whether through economic pressures (cuts in funding, new teaching pressures, marketization, 'do more with less') or technical pressures (digital transformations in publishing industries, new technologies of management and control, Bibliometrics, Google Scholar, etc.), the result is that the humanities have sometimes felt under siege or have been called into question, and been questioned about their viability, relevance or purpose in the twenty-first century.

Our book is positioned in the middle of this debate. We aim to trace some of the genealogies from 'computing in the humanities' into digital humanities (trace, as a full history would require a whole other, much longer book). We seek to show the wide variety of practices, methods and inquiries that identify with digital humanities, and even some that, although may not identify as digital humanities, can offer useful contributions to the field. We then discuss the possible impact, as well as the limitations, of computational tools and methods for humanistic research. Finally, we argue that the humanities must also build theoretical understandings of computation in culture, just as much as humanists and media scholars have explored the role of writing, of image, and of the printing press. Otherwise, the humanities will make themselves increasingly distant from a society so reliant on ubiquitous digital technology, which might be better called a postdigital society (see Berry and Dieter 2015).

In recent years, there has been a steady flow of research publication within the various disciplines where digital humanities work is being carried out. Many important texts discussing and debating the contours of digital humanities have been published, which have been of great impact (e.g., Schreibman et al. 2004; Berry 2012a; Gold 2012; Svennson and Goldberg 2015). Digital humanities is, broadly speaking, the application of computation to the disciplines of the humanities. But, as these authors have reiterated, digital humanities is, and remains, a discipline very much under construction. Indeed, Pannapacker has been asked whether the term 'digital liberal arts' might be more useful (Pannapacker 2013), and Bernard Stiegler (2012) prefers the term 'digital studies', to widen the range of its research focus. Franco Moretti has also argued that 'the term "digital humanities" means nothing', explaining that 'computational criticism has more meaning, but now we all use the term "digital humanities"' (Moretti 2016). In any case, digital humanities is now very much identified with a certain digital 'way' of doing humanities research, which has been described as a computational turn in the humanities (see Berry 2011).

This ongoing contestation and debate means that 'the territory of the digital humanities is currently under negotiation' (Svennson 2010). This book therefore seeks to contribute to a wider mapping of these contours and possible futures, but argues for an additional *critical turn* in the digital humanities that would serve further to strengthen and embed its position in the academy.[3] We believe there is a need to offer a tentative map of this growing field and a guide to the future trajectories of the discipline, and this book is an attempt to contribute to developing this important cognitive resource. By drawing such a map of the digital humanities, we also discuss and critique its strengths and weaknesses, through a critical digital humanities, where the use of computers and computer culture within the field, and more broadly within society and culture, is itself under scrutiny.

There is no single understanding of digital humanities as such, and we can find a lot of different definitions from practitioners who use the term in multiple ways depending on their fields. Indeed, digital humanists are 'already united in their dislike of their own label, their dogged insistence that everything that's being done has been going on since 1982 (or 1949 or 1736)' (Meeks 2012). There is also the suspicion that the digital humanities represents a 'management-friendly' means of disciplining faculty or that digital humanists are selling out the very principles of the humanities in their use of new-fangled technology. Changing to the term 'digital humanities', as Hayles argues, was meant to signal that the field had emerged from the low-prestige status of 'a support service into a genuinely intellectual endeavour with its own professional practices, rigorous standards, and exciting theoretical explorations' (Hayles 2012). However, this has not quietened the sense that digital humanities has controversial implications for the humanities and the university. Indeed, we agree, but we will argue throughout the book that digital humanities is an important contributor to the humanities and to developing 'computational' thinking more generally. Whether this will strengthen the existing contours of the humanities or result in a radical reconfiguration remains to be seen.

The 'digital humanities' can be usefully contrasted with what Sterne (2015: 18) has called the 'analogue humanities', a term he uses as a heuristic for thinking about what the humanities are and how they contrast and intersect with the digital humanities. He argues: 'the analog humanities refers to a nexus of methodological, technological, and institutional conditions across the humanities that have only come into clear focus in retrospect. They refer to the cultural and material infrastructures on which humanists depended and still depend. They were (and are) not uniform across fields. Just as "there is no single vision of the digital humanities, nor can a single vision be possible" . . . we could say the same for the analog formations of humanistic scholarship' (2015: 19).[4] This definition is useful in that it points to the importance of materiality and cultural techniques in relation to the epistemology and practices specific to a field of inquiry. Whilst it might overstate the disjuncture between 'analogue' and 'digital', it draws attention to the way in which epistemology and practice change in relation to changes in media of storage, processing and transmission.[5]

We argue that even the non-digital will become bound up in the preservation possibilities offered by the digital. So the newly digital archive as documentation of the passing of time becomes increasingly critical, both as a source of historical understanding and as a site of identity and culture. It also becomes increasingly encoded in a form of digital knowledge representation (see Folsom 2007). Indeed, we now live within a time of computational abundance which we might think of in relation to the question of being 'postdigital', in as much as we are rapidly entering a moment when difficulty will be found in encountering culture outside digital media (Berry and Dieter 2015). Or perhaps any excess outside the digital, which has been termed the non-digital, will largely itself be displayed through the digital ephemera of society, and ironically kept only within computational databanks, if it is preserved at all.

The way in which culture, education and computation are colliding is usefully demonstrated in the example of students looking to study in higher education. In response, the universities focus on the curation of 'high-quality content' and capturing the paths that students follow to find that educative content. As many academics are realizing, students are increasingly finding out about university programmes and courses via Google and other private companies, which can target specific ads at them to create stronger links between education and consumerism in the minds of students. This is in addition to the intensive drive to produce metrics and 'indicators of performance' in relation to a sector that is increasingly finding that its students are being actively transformed into consumers through governmental and legislative changes. There are also new markets and providers in this area, for example Apollo Education Group (the owner of University of Phoenix and BPP University), and corporate education is now worth an estimated $155 billion. So it is not just a case of computation changing the content and forms of knowledge examined within the university. Computation is also making possible the changing of the university itself, its structures, and its relationship with students, aided by funding regimes driven by private and public actors, and by new regimes of monitoring, accounting and managerial control.

These new technologies also accelerate certain kinds of instrumental practices, such as modularization, mass education, private providers and new kinds of student (in the UK sometimes referred to as three broad market segments).[6] New kinds of management are made possible, which can be combined with qualitative and quantitative monitoring and assessment – such as Britain's REF (Research Excellence Framework) – and student feedback can be used directly to monitor academic 'performance'.[7] Indeed, as Gold (2012) argues, 'at stake in the rise of the digital humanities is not only the viability of new research methods (such as algorithmic approaches to large humanities data sets) or new pedagogical activities (such as the incorporation of geospatial data into classroom projects) but also key elements of the larger academic ecosystem that supports such work'. This is creating a new visibility for the university and the existing practices of scholarship, collegiality, management, regulation, teaching and research (see Besser 2004 for a discussion of the digital library). As Gold further explains, 'whether one looks at the status of peer review, the evolving nature of authorship and collaboration, the fundamental interpretive methodologies of humanities disciplines, or the controversies over tenure and casualized academic labor that have increasingly rent the fabric of university life, it is easy to see that the academy is shifting in significant ways' (2012: ix). We might further add that computation is directly implicated in the possibility of implementing the changes through management information systems and technologies of monitoring and control that, in their granularity, are completely novel in the university.

In the UK, this is demonstrated by a new student tuition fee regime and changes in student recruitment patterns. A new vocationalism is detectable in students (and certainly in university management discourse), with employability required to be baked into undergraduate courses. This is increasingly connected to the digital, communications, media skills, etc., and sometimes understood as '21st-century skills'. Indeed, Silicon Valley is also turning its attention to the $1.3 trillion education 'industry'. The university system costs many students a lot of money through tuition fees, and obtaining a small fraction of this money provides a significant sum. The 'squeezed middle' universities are rightly very concerned about having their core programmes and educational mission hollowed out by private 'challenger' institutions, who are often more willing to exploit these uncertain times in education.

For example, Coursera (for-profit), Udacity (for-profit), edX (not-for-profit) and many others involved in MOOC (Massive Open Online Course) 'education platforms' often cherry-pick the most lucrative teaching from universities and repackage it, leaving the public universities to pick up the more expensive, less popular or unfashionable subject areas. These types of education platform are not just tools: they also promote an internal reorganization of the university as it seeks to compete with market-driven private providers, but also the digital media delivery that is central to MOOCs' organizational logic. Indeed, MOOCs provide a model, based around mass education, ease of delivery (for example, 15–minute lectures) and highly polished packaged modules – so that, in many ways, they threaten to drain the most popular courses out of university teaching and into their systems, leaving behind expensive-to-teach and fragile subject areas. The excitement over MOOCs appears to have cooled somewhat and their purported participatory or democratic potential is increasingly rearticulated in terms of finding a smaller number of previously unidentified academically gifted students.[8] Indeed, there has been a shift towards mostly vocational training and the notion of 'augmenting' traditional teaching, but the fact remains that this technical imaginary created by MOOCs, etc., has had a tremendous effect on how universities see themselves and their relationships with wider publics, governments and students. The pressure from MOOCs has also forced universities to spend vast sums of money defensively and, in many cases, needlessly, on 'learning technologies' that either fail or are little used, and on marketing, public relations and customer relationship management (CRM) systems.

Within this highly volatile situation, the digital humanities occupies a privileged location as both a highly informational discipline and one which appears at first glance to be closely aligned with the worst aspects of computerization and marketization of the university. In contrast, in this book we argue that digital humanities can offer a critical and theoretical contribution to the key debates around this digital technology and the humanities, and in particular to exploring the new trajectories offered by the changes in the university. By outlining those exploring 'differing modes of engagement, institutional models, technologies and discursive strategies' (Svennson 2010), and the issues that need to be critically interrogated and linked to the wider questions associated with critical approaches to digital humanities, new media and digital methods more generally, this book also argues for the digital humanities to become more keenly involved in the kind of cultural criticism called for by Liu (2012).

We further believe that the digital humanities should continue to extol the traditional values of the humanities, such as concerns for history, for aesthetics, for language and culture, and for philosophical understanding of human life and thought. Indeed, it is a field that is well anchored in the long history of independent liberal arts universities, and without any *necessary* connection to neoliberal capitalist ideologies or instrumentalism in education. In fact, as we go through the important debates surrounding the use of computation in the humanist disciplines, we will see that the main concern always is the disciplines themselves, and not performativity, markets or a move to being subsumed under computer science. Where the digital humanities have the power to transform the humanities is where the field opens new scales in research questions that always have been the concern of humanities scholars, but within a newly digital and computational context. As Busa argued in 1980 – and this remains relevant today – 'the use of computers in the humanities has as its principal aim the enhancement of the quality, depth, and extension of research and not merely the lessening of human effort and time' (1980: 89).[9]

A first necessary insight is to reject the idea that digital technology is invading the humanities. Computers were used for humanist ends from very early on in their history, and not only, as one might think, as mere storage for large libraries of text. Early computers were primarily built to calculate, and human text was used (alongside artillery firing tables and nuclear fission simulations) for such calculations, for example in machine translation (arguably the beginning of computational linguistics) and the creation of concordances (hailed by many as the first true digital humanities projects).[10] Only when computers became more accessible and had more memory were they used to store and retrieve books and other texts. Another strand of humanist use of computers began in the second half of the 1960s, when new, advanced computer displays were used for experiments with hypertext and multimedia as new forms and genres of expression. In our book, we discuss the importance of these genealogies, combined additionally with another: the understanding of computing not from a computer science perspective, but from the perspective of philosophy (Berry 2011).

Having established this background, we attempt to paint a picture of the current state of the digital humanities, not by listing uses of digital technology in disciplines from archaeology to zoosemiotics, but by identifying some shared common principles. While it may have been possible a decade ago to go through the various disciplines to look at the internal debates and uses, there are now too many important projects discussed in too many specialized journals and books for us to treat them with any justice in a book such as this one. Instead, we direct our attention to digital materiality, looking at common ways of representing texts and other objects in computer systems, and how they are processed computationally, together with the practices associated with it.

Digital humanities is a field that often requires a team of people with diverse backgrounds. It is not uncommon that humanists form teams with experts in database programming and computer visualization and statisticians. We have aimed to make this book readable for a general humanities audience, which inevitably has made us leave out many of the finer details in any specialized area. This book will not teach you how to create a relational database or program an advanced algorithm (and you will not learn how to interpret archaeological findings or a Victorian novel either). For those finer details, there is a wide literature available (see, for example, Schreibman et al. 2004; Berry 2012a; Gold 2012; Svennson and Goldberg 2015). What we hope to do is to make visible the common principles, to prepare the ground for an informed discussion of those principles and the modes of engagement they allow. As we now see how digital technology opens new avenues for humanist scholarship, it is also a moment in time when we may go back and look at the earlier, 'analogue' humanists and realize how they also have been dependent on the technologies available to them.

Thinking and writing are always tightly related, and changes in humanist practice bring about changes in research writing. We do now see a new kind of research literature appear, online, distributed, hyperlinked and using multimedia and integrated links to online databases. These new developments in research writing are very much informed by hypertext and multimedia research, which we might see as a further contribution to a genealogy of digital humanities around the question of new forms of publication, open access and participatory knowledge practices (see Berry 2008; Jordan 2015).[11]

As research changes, writing changes, and also institutions change in order to accommodate these new possibilities better. We believe it is time for digital humanities to deepen its critical understanding of computer technology and its associated practices. That is the final purpose of our book: to collect the early threads of a critical digital humanities, and discuss where they may lead us in the future. The humanities have always been concerned with the contemporary tools for thought and communication, and today networked computers of all sizes are the main media for a working humanist. This is a question not only of histories, literatures and media but also of new philosophies for the twenty-first century, which need to assess critically the role of code and computing in contemporary thought.[12]

The field of digital humanities has tended to focus on tools and archives in relation to database collections of texts, artworks, scholarly works, dictionaries and lexicographic corpora. Digital humanists introduce methods that are new to the humanities, such as computer statistical analysis, search and retrieval or data visualization, and apply these techniques to archives and collections that are vastly larger than any researcher or research group can handle comfortably. Indeed, it is often claimed that 'digital humanities practitioners need to possess a certain quotient of technical knowledge to be considered digital humanists' (Koh 2014: 98). Too often that knowledge, often hard and painfully won through technical projects and programming, encourages the digital humanist onto the pathways already laid by computer science and other technical disciplines.

Many of these digital humanities collections and archives are available on the web or in digital databases, and the material they contain is more openly available. For example, historians can 'sit in their offices and search through old records and valuable manuscripts kept in faraway places', and art historians can 'compare high-resolution digital photographs of paintings from collections in different countries' (Boonstra et al. 2004: 26; Greenhalgh 2004: 32). But this networking of digital archives does not necessarily undermine the notion of shared community in digital humanities. Civility is a very important value, to the extent that sometimes it is claimed that 'to be a digital humanist is to be "nice": collegial, egalitarian, nonhierarchical, and able to work well with others' (Koh 2014: 95), concepts that go back to the collegial roots of the university itself.[13] Whether or not digital humanities offer a radically new way of working with source materials, its focus on collegiality and community are important humanistic principles in a digital age that is often cast as primarily about performance and efficiency.[14]

As we've seen, digital humanists are sometimes targeted as unwelcome messengers of the coming changes to culture and humanistic study. The digital humanities is then seen more often as a threat in relation to the future of the university and the humanities. Digital humanities can be seen as a connected humanities, able to create new kinds of employees, skills and knowledges appropriate for a 'new economy'. It also sometimes appears to be a little too close to the kinds of instrumental logics that are seen with great scepticism by humanities scholars. As Grusin (2013) wrote: 'is it only an accident that the emergence of digital humanities has coincided with the intensification of the economic crisis in the humanities in higher education? Or is there a connection between these two developments?' Is it possible to draw a distinction between the optimism of the 'digital' humanities and the downbeat tone of the 'crisis' humanities (see McGann 2014).[15] This is something we will return to throughout the book.[16]

There is a strong association with 'making things' in the digital humanities, which has been linked (both by digital humanists and others) with current concerns over 'marketable skills'. Digital humanities questions and explores many issues, from digital storage and retrieval of all kinds of texts, sounds and imagery, to networked communication, to digital pedagogy. And here, of course, we mean computational media of all kinds, using digital media skills such as programming, design, web coding, database management and so on. It is therefore hardly surprising that its detractors see digital humanities as yet another move by neoliberalism/managerialism within the university. Digital humanities raises important questions about how to deploy instrumental rational techniques and practices within the humanities, sometimes insightfully and sometimes with disquieting implications for the humanities more widely. From questions about 'knowledge representation' to digital methods and research infrastructures, Drucker (2012) rightly asks, 'can we engage in the design of digital environments that embody specific theoretical principles drawn from the humanities, not merely work within platforms and protocols created by disciplines whose methodological premises are often at odds with – even hostile to – humanistic values and thought?' Indeed, as she explains, this 'question is particularly pressing in light of the absorption of these visualization techniques, since they come entirely from realms outside the humanities – management, social sciences, natural sciences, business, economics, military surveillance, entertainment, gaming, and other fields in which the relativistic and comparative methods of the humanities play, at best, a small and accessory role' (Drucker 2012: 86). These are important and pressing questions that reinforce the need for digital humanists to connect strongly with their disciplinary colleagues in the wider humanities, both to assess the direction of travel and to refresh and energize their research programmes.

Often the phrase 'more hack, less yack' is used in digital humanities to refer to their preference for a more technical orientation, such as programming, rather than theorizing about it. This is a very strong tendency in the digital humanities community, and often articulated in terms of the value of 'building things' at the expense of what is often seen as unnecessary 'theory'. The construction and making of digital systems, archives, interfaces, visualizations and so on are often over-valorized, and the technology can very easily become the focus of a research project in digital humanities. Humanities scholars can also be easily dazzled by the technology, but also by the audience that these humanities–technical projects can attract – in contrast to the almost complete lack of interest among journalists and the public in most traditional humanities research. We argue that this is a limited and self-defeating aspect of digital humanities which urgently needs to become more self-reflexive and, yes, theoretical in its approaches, to widen its intellectual depth and breadth. Without a keen critical reflexivity, digital humanities is failing in its normative potential to contribute to the wider humanities, above and beyond its instrumental contributions.

Even a cursory glance at digital humanities communities reveals a technophile bias.[17] Social media backchannels, blogging, visualization, programming and new hardware are all actively used. This translates into a heavy focus on tech in digital humanities, both discursively and in project terms. Social media usage is perhaps the most obvious example of this, where a lot of digital humanities discussion takes place. Often at conferences, the digital humanities 'backchannel' is a key way of following the conference's digital humanities threads (some of which are never articulated outside of Twitter and Facebook, e.g. at the Modern Language Association). The early adopter mentality also translates easily into a 'progressive' discourse, contrasted with the 'old-fashioned' traditional humanities. These dichotomies are both real and imagined; productive and unproductive. Indeed, often the outputs of digital humanities research, such as code, archives, technical books, etc., are not conceived as scholarly output for tenure, and so on. This is a key source of contestation for both tenured and what are called 'alternative academics' (or #altac academics) – that is, holders of non-faculty professional positions in the university who still create and contribute to research activity (see Nowviskie 2010). But this computational turn has also been interpreted as a general move away from theoretical and hermeneutic concerns by the humanities, and a turn away from critical engagement (see Berry 2011; Cecire 2011b). As Lovink argues, 'digital humanities, with its one-sided emphasis on data visualization, working with computer-illiterate humanities scholars as innocent victims, has so far made a bad start in this respect. We do not need more tools; what's required are large research programs run by technologically informed theorists that finally put critical theory in the driver's seat. The submissive attitude in the arts and humanities towards the hard sciences and industries needs to come to an end' (Lovink 2012).

In other words, we can and should build humanistic tools and methods from a base that is informed with the norms and values of humanistic principles (see Feenberg 2002; Berry 2011). That is, to echo Drucker, to move 'humanistic study from attention to the *effects* of technology (from readings of social media, games, narrative, personae, digital texts, images, environments), to a humanistically informed theory of the *making* of technology (a humanistic computing at the level of design, modeling of information architecture, data types, interface, and protocols)' (Drucker 2012: 87). In the context of writing algorithms and building digital systems, this means that we need to consider the specific historical constellation of ideas and practices within which we experience algorithms and in which they are made and remade. We need to critique the idea of an ahistorical view of algorithms and the metaphors and analogies that are necessary to explain, but are not sufficient for understanding, algorithmic forms. This is particularly important when computational approaches fetishize the use of 'scale' and data as the new intellectual horizon, for work, action and intellectual inquiry, such that Big Data replaces the more important forms of critical reflection in the humanities.

For example, a key issue revolves around the questions raised by data mining and data analytics. Data mining requires researchers to explore the underlying database, the system data flows, problems related to cross-platform data and their architectures and Application Programming Interfaces (APIs) and related computational technologies and problematics. The increasing corporate use of sophisticated software systems to filter, curate and sift through the data for customer, web, user and so forth requires the development of pattern-matching algorithms that can operate on large data collections of routine information. Of course, this information is not then necessarily presented in textual form – rather, it is visualized, which makes it more amenable for visual pattern recognition by the user. These techniques are crossing over rapidly into the humanities. This creates a very different experience for the reading of or working with texts or other humanities artifacts. Because of this, important questions need to be addressed in relation to how seeing through computation changes what we see and what counts. As Svennson explains, computers in humanities computing often take on the role of 'calculating engines . . . the use of computers as a tool may be an ideology of cognition and functionalism' (Svennson 2010).

There is some justification in these concerns. These issues have been characterized as the difference between the 'dark side' and the 'light side' of the digital humanities.[18] Grusin argues, 'it is largely due to their instrumental or utilitarian value that university administrators, foundation officers, and government agencies are eager to fund DH [digital humanities] projects, create DH undergraduate and graduate programs, and hire DH faculty, it is also the case that this neoliberal instrumentalism reproduces within the academy (in both traditional humanities and digital humanities alike) the precaritization of labor that marks the dark side of information capitalism in the twenty-first century' (Grusin 2014: 79). And, as Johnson further explains, 'the "dark side" is that there are places we don't see, push out, abuse, erase' (Johnson 2016). Whilst Grusin's dark–light binary is obviously problematic in that it is far too abstracted from the reality of much digital humanities work, it is nonetheless helpful for situating some of the debates around pressures on the humanities that are being vocalized against developments in the academy. The digital humanities are sometimes seen as the site of a bureaucratic technocratic logic, 'minimum publishable units' ('MPUs'), a divided academy between tenured and non-tenured (#altac), and so forth. Thought to be closely linked to technical concerns, digital humanists often communicate both in a technical language (e.g. MOOCs, backchannels, XML) and through a different medium (e.g. social media and blogs). The funding available also tends to become more technically oriented and seems to have radically different concerns from that of traditional humanist scholarship. Hence, Grusin further claims that 'digital humanities reproduces structurally both within itself and among the humanities writ large the proliferation of temporary, precarious labor that has marked late twentieth- and twenty-first-century global capitalism' (Grusin 2014: 87).

As shown by the unabashed rise in importance of statistics and computational techniques for the humanities more widely across the higher education sector, and both the increase in funding streams and the emergence of digital humanities centres, labs, self-designated researchers and disciplinary apparatus, it is clear that the digital humanities is a growing field. One can think of the way in which Big Data analysis of cultural data, such as social media streams and Facebook networks, has so easily become a tool for the advertising industry to use sentiment analysis to nudge customers and sell products. By 'Big Data', we mean data that 'pushes at the limits of traditional relational databases as tables of rows and columns, and requires new ways of querying and leveraging data for analysis . . . [and] big data is big to the extent that it exceeds and changes human capacities to read and make sense of it' (Amoore and Piotukh 2015: 343). Unsurprisingly with the creation of new funding streams (such as through the American and British research councils NEH and the AHRC), universities have begun to reorient towards this new research agenda with new programmes, research projects and centres, and the development of new disciplinary apparatus. These concerns over the use of technology and the changes in funding seen to link it to wider society resonate back within the academy where the varieties of computation can be conflated into fears of neoliberal attempts to use technology to discipline the academic world.

It is certainly the case that the 'programming industries' in Silicon Valley are interested in creating new forms of institutionalized 'expertise', and the university is another site of knowledge creation that seems ripe for 'disruption'. Part of these companies' strategy is to use data-mining and Big Data techniques to collect the tacit knowledge of users and their 'data exhaust' and store them in databases and data lakes. These databases, combined with heuristic algorithms, create 'applied knowledge' and are capable of making 'judgements' in specific use cases, including the instrumentalization of humanities knowledge. But we want to argue that computational systems and practices can and should be created by humanists for humanists. This is crucially where digital humanities, with its focus on academic development and uses of technology, is exemplary and offers the possibility of a countervailing model for how computation might serve the humanities, rather than the other way around. As McGann argues, 'to date, the digital technology used by humanities scholars has focused almost exclusively on methods of sorting, accessing, and disseminating large bodies of materials. In this respect the work has not engaged the central questions and concerns of the disciplines. It is largely seen as technical and pre-critical, the occupation of librarians, and archivists, and editors. The general field of humanities education and scholarship will not take up the use of digital technology in any significant way until one can clearly demonstrate that these tools have important contributions to make' (McGann n.d.).[19] It goes without saying that these contributions have to move beyond the purely instrumental and mechanical automation of processing of humanities materials.

Computation has compressive effects and generates flattening metaphors, and the visual language of computation tends towards an encounter, maximized perhaps by its tendency towards spatiality, to transform time from a diachronic to a synchronic experience and often into a discrete output. For example, history itself may be re-presented through the screen through a number of computation functions and methods that make it seem geometric, flat and simultaneous, which can be creative and generative as a contribution to humanities scholarship. Indeed, Hitchcock has argued that 'academic historians have yet to effectively address the implications of the online and the digital for their scholarship, or to rise to the challenge that these resources present' (Hitchcock 2013: 20). The danger is, however, that a sense of history then becomes a sense of real-time interactions, not so much distant and elusive, whether as cultural or individual memory, but here and now, spectacular and vividly represented and re-presented. These temptations are widespread when using computation as problems of fields are backgrounded and history and difference can be given a 'presentist' focus. Using new digital methods, related to studying 'old' historical archives, raises similar problems when the rich complexity and materiality of an archive is translated into a digital form. Hitchcock argues that this has 'resulted in the substantial deracination of knowledge, the uprooting, or "Googleization", of the components of what was once a coherent collection of beliefs and systems for discovering and performing taxonomies on information' (2013: 14). But it is important to note that this problem is not inevitable – rather, it requires that humanities scholars ensure that they are closely involved in the technical work or that they can safeguard the archive and curate the way in which it is translated and encoded.[20] But this will not be easy, in terms either of learning these skills or of getting disciplines actively to contribute to capacity building around these issues. Prescott signals his frustrations with some academics when he argues 'the only time that the corduroyed Colonel Blimps of the British historical establishment have grudgingly bestirred themselves from their deep slumber to engage extensively with digital matters was when they belatedly realized that changes in open access might upset the cosy financial arrangements that provided a life-support system for ailing learned societies, and a hasty rearguard action was mounted to try to preserve the status quo' (Prescott 2014: 340).

To be able to 'confront the digital', as Hitchcock (2013) suggests, requires that humanists take digital technology more seriously. This involves thinking through the theoretical and philosophical questions raised by protocols, databases and codework, in as much as fused constructs of encoded information, technology and media are used to construct new forms of archive. Indeed, the ineluctable co-presence of code both operationally behind the scenes and phenomenally in a work's experiential form, is still to be explored adequately in digital humanities.

Part of this has to involve being attendant to technical projects' history, presented through databases, code and algorithms, and ensuring that, rather than the 'code' leading the project, the humanist is always ensuring the responsiveness of the specification and design of the technical system – even when this creates further headaches, as inevitably it will, for the programmers and project managers. These are important aspects for understanding computation in this postdigital world and a key factor in getting a grip on the challenge of critical thinking within a computational milieu (Berry and Dieter 2015).

This means moving away from a comparative notion of the digital, contrasted with other material forms such as paper, celluloid or photopaper, and instead beginning to think about how the digital is modulated within various materialities with specific affordances. Thus, the contrast between strictly 'digital' or 'analogue' no longer makes sense. Indeed, we need to think in terms of *modulation of the digital*, a distribution across an axis which shows a valence of more or less computation (Berry 2014), which gives rise to the expectation of the always already computational of everyday life.[21] So it is here that we get our first glimpse of the possibility that the digital humanities offers for a critical reading of culture and society that connects to the changing ways in which culture is produced, consumed, critiqued and disseminated in complex computational societies.

Thus, critical notions of quantitative and qualitative dimensions of *Compute* (or abstract computation) will be increasingly important for thinking about culture, economics, society, politics and everyday life (Berry 2014). Tracing power will in many cases be tracing Compute, in terms both of the reservoirs of Compute managed by gigantic computational stacks, and of the places where Compute is thin and poorly served. By 'stacks', we mean the corporations that increasingly rely on computational 'technology stacks' for profit and power, such as Google, Apple, Facebook, Amazon (GAFA) and Twitter, but also the computational imaginary formed through the notion of these stacks as a diagram (Berry 2014; see also Bratton 2014; Terranova 2014).[22]

Computation as already always part of life heralds the moment that the digital as *digitization* is already perhaps drawing to a close, and that new challenges lie ahead for thinking about the way in which the computal saturates our culture, institutions and everyday life in varying degrees of modularity and intensity. This growth in computation has put citizens at an obvious disadvantage in a society that has historically tended not only to disavow the digital as a form of knowledge or practice, but also to ignore computational thinking or skills as part of the educational requirements of a well-informed citizen. For example, Glenn Greenwald, the journalist who broke the Snowden surveillance revelations, was previously unaware of the importance of understanding encryption and cryptography for the citizen of a digital society (Greenwald 2013).

Another aspect that is relevant for the humanities as computer power has increased is the tendency to hide computation within simulations of traditional containers, such as e-books, through techniques of skeuomorphism or glossy algorithmic interface design, such as flat design – rather than learning and teaching computational practices as such. This, perhaps, has the advantage of enabling new computational forms to be used and accessed without the requisite computational skills to negotiate the new literary machines of computation, such as the underlying logics, structures, processes and code. However, it also means that, in many cases today, we are unable to read what we have written, and are not always the writers of the systems that are built around us (Berry 2011; Oliver et al. 2011; Allen 2013). This illiteracy does not seem to be the ideal condition for the emergence of an informed and educated citizenry to engage with the challenges and dangers of a fully softwarized postdigital society. It also points to the urgent need for a critical and engaged *Bildung* for the postdigital world, if it is not to become precariously post-democratic. This includes notions of digital literacy, interface criticism, computational thinking and transcending the boundaries between humanities and computation.

Other disciplinary areas are also challenged by the increase in digital archives, tools and methods – such as the social sciences – and links need to be strengthened between them and the digital humanities (see Berry 2012a; Gold 2012; Svennson and Goldberg 2015: 1). For example, many of these issues have been researched and continue to be addressed in the discipline of media and communications. By 'media and communications', we mean the interdisciplinary study of communication media, through approaches from both the social sciences and interpretative methods drawn from the humanities, but also drawing on economics, psychology, political economy and other disciplines. Closely connected to the cognate area of cultural studies, and building on its insights, media studies has explored popular culture, taking popular forms of media seriously. Media studies has sought to examine web sites and blogging, and social network sites, through a notion of 'social media' which tends to be broadly conceived as a further medium within the field. Additionally, there is a sociological wing to media studies which explores how people engage with digital media, in terms both of the consumption of media, and of their use of media in everyday life. The more humanities-oriented, interpretative wing uses traditional media studies techniques to examine how imagery and text work together (in what are sometimes referred to as 'multimodal texts'), and also narrative structures of hyperlinked texts and new digital publication forms. But also, as broadcast media have become digital media, many of the taken-for-granted notions of media studies have come under reconsideration.

We think it is important also to look to the field of software studies, where good work is being done in terms of opening the black box – the technical notion of objects which have opaque or impossible-to-read internal states but readable surfaces – of technologies. By using the term 'software studies', we want to link to the argument that Lev Manovich made in *The Language of New Media* (2001): that media studies in the digital age should become 'software studies'. Indeed, in the past five years, this field has begun to emerge in its own right. Software studies presents the question of computation and digital technologies as a research object and therefore uses a number of techniques to 'read' algorithms, for example through a close engagement with code and software as text, understanding software, and critically examining algorithms' affordances, structure and political economy. Software studies covers a wide number of approaches to the digital, from theoretical interventions to more empirically oriented techniques and methods. There is also an engagement with the specific aesthetics articulated and used in software – for example, code as poetry – but also with how interfaces structure and mediate experience, and how algorithms encode power (see Kirschenbaum 2004).[23] Many of the approaches and theoretical insights would enrich the digital humanities with new theoretical concepts and problematics.

This book explores the traditional concerns of knowledge representation, digital methods, research infrastructures and archives. This cluster certainly identifies the major contours of the field, but, as we shall see, privileges a particular approach to digital humanities concerned with knowledge representation via the development of tools and archives which can be usefully augmented by critical work, from the fields mentioned above. We supplement this by looking at the more recent turn to materiality and cultural critique as a way of doing and making digital humanities research – thus expanding the traditional disciplinary concerns of digital humanities and deepening its critical reflexivity about the work and methods of its subject area.

We illustrate this with a pictorial representation of the layers of abstraction in figure 1. This gives the reader an idea of what we are calling 'the digital humanities stack'. This type of diagram is common in computation and computer science to show how technologies are 'stacked' on top of each other in increasing levels of abstraction. Here, we use the method in a more illustrative and creative sense of showing the range of activities, practices, skills, technologies and structures that could be said to make up the digital humanities, with the aim of providing a high-level map. This is clearly a simplification, and is not meant to be prescriptive; rather, for the newcomer to the digital humanities, it helps with understanding how the varied elements that make up the digital humanities fit together. Whilst others

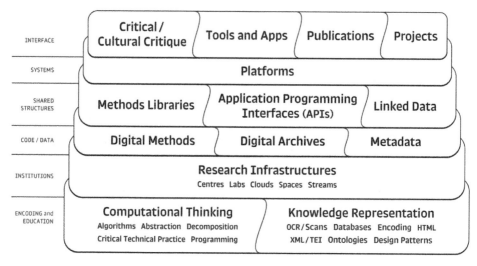

Figure 1. The Digital Humanities Stack

may criticize the make-up and ordering of the stack that we present here, nonetheless, it more or less provides a useful visual guide to how the rest of the book is meant to contribute towards understanding digital humanities – that is, it is both descriptive and prescriptive. So this diagram can be read as the bottom levels indicating some of the fundamental elements of the digital humanities stack, such as computational thinking and knowledge representation, and then other elements that later build on these. It would have been our preference for the critical and cultural critique to run through more of the layers, but in the end it made for a more easily digestible visual representation if we didn't over-complicate the diagram. As this is a version 1.0 of the digital humanities stack, we look forward to reworkings of it, and complication and re-articulations.

As this diagram indicates, new metaphors will need to be developed to help us to understand how the computational changes our taken-for-granted notions of size, complexity and analysis in the digital age. For example, one way of negotiating the problem of scale raised by the digital – that is, the big and the small – which has been suggested by Hitchcock, is the notion of a 'macroscope', a term which was created in '1969 by Piers Jacob, and used as the title of his science fiction/fantasy work of the same year – in which the "macroscope", a large crystal, able to focus on any location in space-time with profound clarity, is used to produce something like a telescope of infinite resolution. In other words, a way of viewing the world that encompasses both the minuscule, and the massive' (Hitchcock 2014).

He quotes Börner: 'macroscopes provide a "vision of the whole", helping us "synthesize" the related elements and detect patterns, trends, and outliers while granting access to myriad details. Rather than make things larger or smaller, macroscopes let us observe what is at once too great, slow, or complex for the human eye and mind to notice and comprehend' (Börner 2011).[24]

Technologies have an increasing centrality to many forms of research in the humanities, but also raise dangers of instrumentalization, and a political economy linked to large opportunities to apply for research funds and investment. In our view, digital humanities could be an ideally placed discipline for exploring these wider concerns. But it is also important for mapping the way in which the micro-levels of scholarly analysis are changing, whether in terms of digital scholarly editions, preservation or encoding. In other words, digital humanities should become more reflexive about itself as a discipline and the approaches it brings to bear on its research objects.

To explore digital humanities, we offer some historical context and the terrain on which the discipline has been active in chapter 2. Digital humanities has been variously termed the 'next big thing', 'young', 'energetic', 'theological', 'political', '#altac', 'transformatory', etc.[25] Some scholars, such as Stanley Fish (2012), argue that digital humanities 'is theological because it promises to liberate us from the confines of the linear, temporal medium in the context of which knowledge is discrete, partial and situated'. These and other contrasting views on digital humanities demonstrate that, indeed, digital humanities has grown into a wide and varied field. In fact, most humanities disciplines now have scholars who use computation as an important resource in their research. What we believe is shared among them is what Jeanette M. Wing has called 'computational thinking' (2006, 2008): a certain way of thinking in abstractions and automation that is suited for computer algorithms. In chapter 3, we provide an overview of some of the common elements of computational thinking. Most of these are derived from computer science, but we also use examples from digital humanities throughout. Implicitly, this also acknowledges the interdisciplinary nature of digital humanities: it is always a marriage of insights and methods from computer science with methods, questions and theories from the humanities. *Automation* is the first and most basic thinking skill; most computer projects earn their power from the computer's ability to perform repeated tasks quickly and with precision. This further implies the ability to formulate a problem at the right level of *abstraction*, and to be able to *decompose* a complex problematics into smaller, computable parts. We also discuss the nature of *algorithms*, and delve into one of the core debates in digital humanities: does one need to code? We argue that, while most humanities scholars probably will not take part in coding complex systems, learning a programming language and the associated *aesthetics of code* will deeply enhance one's understanding of computing as a cultural phenomenon. Basic coding should be considered part of a digital literacy, we argue, and needs to form part of humanists' training in order for them to be able to build, criticize and deploy these complex computational systems, but it is not a panacea and multiple approaches to humanities work are to be welcomed and encouraged.[26]

Chapter 4 takes up the data that algorithms and abstractions compute: the different representations of knowledge used in digital humanities. The success of digital humanities is founded on large archives of historical material, and these are in turn made possible by the different ways historic, tangible material is coded into digital formats that may be used for computation. For each kind of material, there is a split between the representation of the objects' sensory appearance, such as alphabetic text, formats for images, sound, 3D models, etc., and representation of metadata about each object. In databases of language and literary works, knowledge representation has taken the form of markup languages such as SGML (Standard Generalized Markup Language) and XML (Extensible Markup Language), which have developed into advanced, standardized yet adaptable schemes. In archaeology and other disciplines, geographic information systems (GIS) link information on artifacts and events with geographical coordinates and databases on landscapes, vegetation, urban development, etc. Together, the sensory representation and the metadata form a computer model that can be manipulated by automated algorithms. New methods are used to investigate these representations, including techniques such as data mining, cluster analysis, computer simulations, automatic content analysis and exploratory data visualizations. These and other techniques raise questions of the epistemology of the humanities. While the research questions may be similar to those in the 'analogue humanities', the constitution of what counts as an interesting answer may have changed so profoundly that it no longer is compatible with the traditional epistemology of the humanist disciplines.

In chapter 5, we look at the importance of research infrastructures in supporting digital humanities, but also to think about the conditions of possibility for humanities scholarship more widely. As Anderson argues, 'collection-holding institutions act as creators, curators, and bearers of knowledge about their holdings; technical development seeks not only to capture and represent digital information and content but also the processes by which that knowledge is created and continues to be created as it is analysed and used; researchers act not just as users but also as "readers", of both the collection-holding institutions and of the holdings, possessing both archival and artifactual intelligence, and weaving narratives based on interpretive and analytical research methods and processes' (2013: 21). This is a good way to think about research infrastructures: not only as material things that are built to hold, store, maintain and preserve research and archival material, but also as processual – that is, they make possible various forms of action on, access to and transformation of primary scholarly sources, to facilitate new forms of scholarship.

'Digital methods' is explored in chapter 6. Digital methods is a concept coined by Richard Rogers to describe methods that deal with data that are 'born digital' – that is, texts and works that are created to be read online, or data registered while people do their everyday activities in digital media. Furthermore, the methods are taken, or at least inspired, by those applied by large corporations in the digital economy (Rogers 2013).[27] Digital methods are concerned particularly with the use of computational techniques to extract, scrape, collect or capture digital data from various, usually internet-based, sites and services. Digital methods form a set of scholarly approaches that by using algorithms and code, mine large datasets that Amazon, Google, Twitter and other companies have made accessible via public interfaces (APIs), often to shed light on research questions from humanities and social sciences. Thus, different registers are combined in ingenious ways to be able to find information on topics they were not designed to cover. In this book, we aim to widen the scope of digital methods, and also include other movements that belong in the 'born digital' realm. The first is software studies, as previously discussed, and as taken up by several other scholars who are interested in how computer software is the premise for modern media, arts and culture. Computer code is either studied in itself as cultural technology (or even as poetry), or reverse engineered from the results, to uncover the workings of the algorithms that put together our news, our connections via social media, and our literature and artworks. The second realm of humanist study of digital work lies in the archives of works that are not digitized, but created digitally. Not surprisingly, these texts do not adhere to the best practice standards of scholarly archives, and the archival and retrieval processes pose tremendous problems that, for a large part, are still unsolved, putting future archives at risk.

Chapter 7 looks at digital scholarship and interface criticism to think about how the results of digital humanities research are displayed, published and made available and accessible. As the datasets of digital humanities reach millions of records, quotations and tables give way to high-resolution graphical displays. Visualizations are the user interfaces to computer data, and follow the computer science design patterns such as layering of hardware and software, and the separate code entities of model, view and controller. Taking the concept of interface further, we argue that digital humanities, in what Steven Johnson (1999) called the age of 'interface culture', needs to take a critical view on the concept of interfaces. Interfaces are described in design literature as 'intuitive' and 'transparent', with discussion of design trends such as 'flat' versus 'skeuomorphic'. These simple characteristics tend not to stand up to a critical examination. As interfaces are manifestations of ideologies and policies that governed their design, and as culture is digital, a critical interface studies is helpful if the humanities are to be relevant for the postdigital era. The chapter contains several examples of possible trajectories for such work: one is a style history of web interfaces, a work begun by Engholm (2003) and Liu (2004); another is critical studies of interfaces as texts, in the form of both close and distant readings (that is, not actually reading the books and looking through the archives themselves but relying on algorithms and computers to do this for us). Taylorist assumptions of usability tend to be somewhat simplistic, and while more modern notions of User Experience (UX) try to incorporate aesthetic notions (under such terms as 'hedonic quality'), there is much to be added to this from traditions such as art history, literature, and media studies. Finally, we discuss critical design as a research approach: scholars such as Stuart Moulthrop and Gregory Ulmer have for decades, in both theory and practice, advocated the design of alternative computer media as a form of cultural critique that adds to our understanding of interfaces in culture and interfaces as culture. Last in this chapter, we discuss digital research publishing, in which researchers over two decades have produced scholarly hypertext and multimedia works that cannot exist in print.

Finally, in chapter 8 we open a more speculative and theoretical discussion of possible future directions for the 'digital humanities' by connecting to the notion of a critical digital humanities and the social, cultural, economic and political questions of a recontextualization and social re-embedding of the digital humanities within a social field. We call this a critical digital humanities, and it comprises questions such as: how is knowledge transformed when mediated through code and software? What are the critical approaches to Big Data and digital methods? Does computation create new disciplinary boundaries? We argue that the computerization of humanities tends to change concepts and ideas as they are adapted to computational models. But the digital is not only about humanities research, it also permeates culture at large, and understanding digital technology and computational techniques is necessary to understand the human condition in a postdigital age. Historical perspective has always been important for the humanities, and a critical understanding of the digital must begin with a critical history of computation and programming techniques. Questions of privacy and personal data are also part of this history. This is a question not just of government surveillance, as exposed by Edward Snowden and Wikileaks, but also of the digital trails we leave behind in the server rooms of Google, Facebook, Apple, Amazon and other corporations. Central to our discussion is the concept of compute (Berry 2014) an abstract unit of computation, as both potential and actuality. This includes an examination of the politics of computation, particularly in relation to the building of systems and their contestation – what we are calling 'unbuilding'. This includes the question of personal visibility in postdigital culture, both as empowering a sense of self, and as a problematic sense of having one's image captured and being captured as a subject. The panoptic *Geist* of digital media gives rise to counter-cultures of cryptography and jamming, aiming to retain a private self in the age of digital surveillance and Big Data. We argue that to be private is also the possibility of being part of a crowd: not standing out, but being one of many. These are issues that strike at the heart of humanities, questions over what it is to be human, how one understands the distinctions between human thought and the ability to exercise one's reason. Digital humanists bring expertise to bear on technology, culture and history, whose contribution to public culture and to debates over our shared life is something that digital humanists should seek to intervene in, continuing the conversation with the wider humanities.

2 Genealogies of the Digital Humanities

In its early days, humanities computing tended to concentrate on supporting humanities-technical projects through the application of technical knowledge and experience. This sometimes meant that it seemed as if the 'real' humanities scholars drove the intellectual side of the project and the humanities computing technicians implemented it.[1] Even though the digital humanities is a relatively recent disciplinary formation and it draws its history from 'computing in the humanities', or 'humanities computing', it also incorporates a number of strands both theoretical and technically oriented from across a range of disciplinary areas (see Schreibman et al. 2004; Berry 2012a; Gold 2012).[2] Scheinfeldt (2008) argues that 'the digital humanities family tree has two main trunks, one literary and one historical, that developed largely independently into the 1990s and then came together in the late-1990s and early-2000s with the emergence of the World Wide Web'.[3] This is a useful way to understand the debates and arguments that are manifest in the field and, to a remarkable extent, map onto this division. In this chapter, although we focus mainly on digital humanities, it is important to remember the complementary development of and interconnectedness with work in digital history (see Gregory 2014).

The foundational work in digital humanities was generally concerned with the application of the computer to the textual materials of the humanities (see Feeney and Ross 1993): what has been described as treating the 'machine's efficiency as a servant' rather than as a 'participant enabling of criticism' (McCarty 2009). The term 'digital humanities' is of much more recent origin, and the field's previous incarnation was humanities computing, which was strongly associated with tools and archival work, to the extent that humanities computing soon became understood as a service department providing specialized computing support work and technical assistance to other humanities departments (see Flanders 2011; Nyhan 2012).

The workings of digital technologies, systems, encodings, processes and projects have been a key concern of digital humanities from its very beginning. This is broadly known within the digital humanities as knowledge representation (see Sowa 2000; Schreibman et al. 2004: xxv). This is also connected to the remediation of culture that digitization presents and that 'the whole of our cultural inheritance has to be recurated and reedited in digital forms and institutional structures' (McGann 2014: 1). Indeed, Schreibman et al. (2004: xxvi) argue that the process of knowledge representation 'requires humanists to make explicit what they know about their material and to understand the ways in which that material exceeds or escapes representation', and the fact that the process digital humanists follow 'to develop, apply and compute these knowledge representations is unlike anything that humanities scholars, outside of philosophy, have ever been required to do'. Whilst we might take issue with the claim that other humanities scholars were not reflexive about their categories and knowledge frameworks, it is, however, true that the explicitly calculable requirements of much digital humanities work on encoding encourages a very different relationship with knowledge and information. This calculability is linked to the discovery of 'patterns and connections in the human record that we would never otherwise have found or examined', making an implicit reference to the scaling-up in the quantity of data that computation makes possible (Schreibman et al. 2004: xxvi). As Ramsay (2004: 195) argues, 'dealing with patterns necessarily implies the cultivation of certain habits of seeing . . . [and] of all the technologies in use among computing humanists, databases are perhaps the best suited to facilitating and exploiting such openness' towards seeing.[4] This is taken together with the aggregation, analysis and presentation of particularly visual forms of analysis, such as data visualization, charts and so forth (see Warwick 2004: 375; Drucker and Nowviskie 2008). This points to the key aspects of acquisition, encoding, processing and representation that make up what we might think of as the digital humanities workflow. It is this explicitly technical orientation that informs both digital humanities and the way in which it tends to reflect on its activities.

It is helpful to think about these issues in terms of a genealogy of the digital humanities that tends to shun its historical antecedents, and hence think through some of the ways in which it has been previously articulated – but also to think through analytical classifications, such as that introduced by Stephen Ramsay, who discussed digital humanities 'type 1' and 'type 2' (Ramsay 2013b), or by David Golumbia, who proposed 'narrow' or 'broad' digital humanities (Golumbia 2013). We also want to set up the context for the later argument that digital humanities needs to widen and deepen its cultural critique (Liu 2011), and introduce design and the medium-specific work of software studies and media studies (Berry 2014).[5] Indeed, digital humanities has also developed a public engagement role and, as Liu argues, digital humanities is 'ideally positioned to create, adapt, and disseminate new methods for communicating between the humanities and the public', but also to 'create technologies that fundamentally reimagine humanities advocacy' (Liu 2012: 496–7). Today, the field is much more multi-faceted and, as we argue in this book, the potential for cultural critique of computational culture offers new possibilities for the field of digital humanities (Liu 2012: 496–7). In this book, we want to move beyond linear narratives of digital humanities development and make connections between digital humanities and other disciplinary formations, both historically and in terms of important influences. We also want to link these to the contemporary milieu in which digital humanities is expanding rapidly and connecting to other areas and approaches. But, first, we briefly turn to look at the foundation of the digital humanities, as computing in the humanities.

Digital humanities often refers back to a disciplinary 'origin story' associated with humanities computing and its 'founding', which has become something of a taken-for-granted explanation of where digital humanities emerged from. This tends to be articulated as stemming from the work of Roberto A. Busa, a Jesuit priest and professor of philosophy. Busa developed a list of concordances of St Thomas Aquinas's work using IBM computers in 1949, resulting in the 56–printed-volume *Index Thomisticus* as an analysis of the work of Thomas Aquinas (Schreibman et al. 2004; see also chapter 4 below).[6] For this reason Busa is often seen as the starting point for thinking about the history of digital humanities, sometimes giving the impression that Busa was working in a vacuum. It is laudable therefore that Busa himself argues, 'although some say I am the pioneer of the computers in the humanities, such a title needs a good deal of nuancing . . . isn't it true that all new ideas arise out of a milieu when ripe, rather than from any one individual?' (Busa 1980: 84).[7]

In the case of Busa, there is a clear link made between the affordances of computation and humanities work.[8] Thus, very early on, a connection was made between brute-force computation as a tool of humanities research and the transformation of historical or literary documents into a computerized archive or database (see Nyhan 2012). As McCarty documents, in 1965 the last handmade concordance was published (by Ione Dobson, about Byron), and in 1966 'the American scholar Joseph Raben founded the first professional journal in the field, *Computers and the Humanities* (CHum).' (McCarty 2003: 1226). The connections between the human-generated work and the move to automated systems for collecting and collating humanities materials is useful for thinking about the shift from a predominantly print culture to a digital one. This could be said to have necessitated a new conceptual language of tools and archives. This early conceptual distinction between tool and archive, program and data, continues as an important conceptual shorthand for the field. Indeed, computation was strongly linked to its new storage capacity and the possibility of comprehensive archives and databases as a result of digitization, together with the computational power of textual searching, filtering, concordance production and manipulation that was made possible. This led to the creation of support systems and semi-standardized software for the archiving and maintaining of textual repositories (Hockey 2004: 10).

Tools and archives continue to be key concepts for understanding the technical contributions of the field but they also point towards a disciplinary specificity of digital humanities through a sense of 'community' around these tools and archives. This has remained remarkably consistent in the years since Busa's early work and has marked the field in particular ways. For example, Koh (2014) argues that 'the social contract of the digital humanities is composed of two rules: 1) the practice of *civility*, or "niceness"; and 2) *possession of technical knowledge*, defined as knowledge of coding or computer programming. These rules are repeatedly cited within the digital humanities community, but they are at the same time contested and criticized' (2014: 94). These basic norms are key for creating the fundamental elements for social interaction and organization. The cultural norms of technical knowledge in terms of knowledge, representation and elements of programming (understanding, if not necessarily doing), combine with the shared meaning generated through collective interpretative schemas that inform and define their interaction. In many ways, as the taken for granted of 'humanities computing' has changed into digital humanities, it was inevitable that the expansion of disciplinary concerns would generate new challenges and sources of conflict and contestation. Indeed, there has been a great amount of internal debate and contestation in the field recently, for example. Scheinfeldt (2008) has argued that we are in '[a] moment of change right now, that we are entering a new phase of scholarship that will be dominated not by ideas, but once again by organizing activities, both in terms of organizing knowledge and organizing ourselves and our work . . . collaborative encyclopedism, tool building, librarianship'. In practice, however, digital humanities has not developed a static set of ideas and concepts which can enable organization building in this manner. Rather, it continues to be an extremely flexible area for debates over knowledge, computation and the humanities, as evidenced by recent work such as Allington et al. (2016). In our opinion, this is a sign of growing strength in the digital humanities.

In digital humanities, the notion of scholarly work tends to be wider than in normalized forms of academic output, such as monographs and academic papers. Rather, digital humanities scholars are keen to stress their non-standard concerns with producing encodings, digital versions, databases, ontologies, metadata and visualizations as new forms of academic knowledge production made possible by computation. This aspect of digital humanities is much discussed in the field due to its implications for academic standing, tenure and promotion. This links very clearly to digital humanities' own self-perception as an 'outsider' field, and, whatever the merits of these claims, it is interesting that computation has, for the most part, been more influential at the encoding phase of knowledge production. Of course, this is changing as computation as a reading medium gains ground through both web technologies and mobile devices, and new forms of digital screens, and hence on the form of the reading public in relation to the monograph or academic paper. However, it cannot be denied that digital humanities has been at the forefront of identifying and problematizing the way in which the materiality of paper is both crucial to, and a problem for, the humanities as a whole.

The introduction of computing to the humanities has not traditionally been met with enthusiasm by researchers and scholars. There have been debates on the use of computers in the humanities ever since they were introduced and 'even today there are pockets of stubborn resistance against computing. At the same time, we can see that, although basic computing skills of word processing, e-mailing and web browsing are nowadays omnipresent among humanities scholars, their methodical and technical skills for computerised research are fairly limited' (Boonstra et al. 2004: 13). Disciplines such as linguistics have been somewhat more welcoming to computation, and have worked with computation for a considerable period of time from the 1950s, although until more recently it has tended to be more 'occasional' than methodologically central (see Feeney and Ross 1993; Kaltenbrunner 2015: 3).

Indeed, some other important milestones in the digital humanities were the electronic editions of Christian Latin texts produced by the CETEDOC research centre in Louvain in the 1970s, the founding of the previously mentioned professional journal *Computers and the Humanities* by Joseph Raben in 1966 (Gilmour-Bryson 1987), and the Philadelphia Social History Project (PSHP) (Hockey 2004: 5; Kladstrup 2015). But also the 'first international professional body, the Association for Literary and Linguistic Computing (ALLC), was founded in 1972, followed by the Association for Computers and the Humanities (ACH) in 1978, and the Association for History and Computing in 1987. The *ALLC Bulletin* began in 1973, becoming *Literary and Linguistic Computing* (LLC) in 1986' (McCarty 2003: 1227).

However, there was generally not a large amount of work done on computing from within the humanities themselves due to lack of interest and expertise – indeed, 'scholars in the humanities had to rely on help mainly from computer linguists. A great deal of the activity therefore centered around source-editing' (Boonstra et al. 2004: 26). This particularly textual dimension remains strong within the disciplinary focus of the digital humanities and makes clear the links with the humanistic disciplinary object of analysis.[9] As Hockey explains, 'a glance through the various publications of this period shows a preponderance of papers based on vocabulary studies generated initially by computer programs . . . of interest for some kind of stylistic analysis or for linguistic applications' (Hockey 2004: 9–10). This remained so with the foundation of the Association for Computers and the Humanities (ACH) in the 1970s, a major professional society for the digital humanities that supports and disseminates research and cultivates a professional 'community' through conferences, publications and so forth.

An early counter-example emerged in Germany where, in 1975, German historians and sociologists founded the Quantum-group in order to explore, in close collaboration, possibilities and problems with the use of historical and process-produced data. This was 'driven by a feeling of uneasiness in empirical sciences with data based on surveys only, and by the turn of historians away from ideographic and narrative approaches. It was aimed at closing the gap between the German situation and the upswing of quantitative history elsewhere' (Boonstra et al. 2004: 26). Its journal, *Quantum Information*, later changed its name to *Historical Social Research* (*Historische Sozialforschung*) and this grew into a broader publication that covered subjects which related to history and computing, whilst nonetheless focused on the computational aspects of historical research (see Boonstra et al. 2004: 26).

Nonetheless, the larger linguistic and literary influence on digital humanities can be felt in the field's relation to the Text Encoding Initiative (TEI), published as a set of guidelines in 1994. TEI is essentially a markup language drawn from SGML (Standard Generalized Markup Language), similar to XML. TEI was the 'first systematic attempt to categorize and define all the features within humanities text that might interest scholars' (Hockey 2004: 12). Much of this work of humanities computing was focused on building archives, infrastructure and digital tools and included the idea of 'comprehensive' and 'exhaustive' archives using XML, usually as TEI markup, in textual works, and the creation of metadata around physical artifacts. With the rise of the internet and the World Wide Web in the 1990s, together with its own markup language HTML, there has been some divergence between the TEI and other encoding practitioners but in any case, as McGann argues, 'organizing our received humanities materials as if they were simply information depositories, computer markup as currently imagined handicaps or even baffles altogether our moves to engage with the well-known dynamic functions of textual works' (2004: 199–201).

The encoding aspect of digital humanities remains crucially important and, as Cordell has argued, 'you may find encoding or archival metadata development boring or pedantic – certainly some do – but you cannot pretend that encoding is less a part of the digital humanities than coding' (Cordell 2014). These encoding practices can also be traced back to earlier work in textual computation but also innovative email discussion lists like The Humanist set up in 1987 by Willard McCarty (McCarty 2003: 1227; Hockey 2004: 11). As McCarty documents, 'conversing in groups such as Humanist, as well as one-to-one, provides an obvious means for establishing a loose, dynamic sense of the field and the relative importance of contributions to it'. For example, McCarty explored the possibility of a research agenda particular to humanities computing, first articulated as 'methodology', then later as a concern with 'models' and 'simulation' (see McCarty 2004, 2009, 2013a). Indeed, this has been mirrored in Kirschenbaum's (2013) notion of 'methodological outlook' and his focus on forensic approaches to media (Kirschenbaum 2008). This is sometimes articulated as an 'exploratory methodology, where the researcher or student is encouraged to explore materials, datasets or issues in an experimental fashion' (Svennson 2010).[10] This notion of experimentation is a key issue and relates also to the notion of a humanities lab that we will examine later.

The importance of knowledge representation within the digital humanities remains an absolutely key thread that continues to inform debate and contestations over what a digital humanities project is, for example regarding the rise in use of XML and the TEI. This notion of knowledge representation as the encoding of cultural forms in a computational wrapper, usually a form of metadata such as a Shakespeare play encoded into XML (see the Folger Shakespeare Library for exemplary versions of this), is very particular to the digital humanities. Even today, this interest in encoding objects remains a core part of the identity of digital humanities and its activities (Fitzpatrick 2012: 13). Indeed, on the importance of encoding, Cordell (2014) wrote, 'any vision of digital humanities that excludes or dismisses the close and careful work of digital preservation, editing, and publication is simply false' (see also Deegan and Tanner 2004: 488–93; Smith 2004: 577). We might also add that any history of the digital humanities that does not identify this element is also seriously misrepresentative of the field's development. Indeed, as Renear argues, TEI is itself now a research community around the subject of encoding, and connects together many professions, disciplines and institutions across the globe. Its practitioners define themselves through a shared interest in encoding, concepts, tools and techniques. They tend to concentrate on textual discourse, with the focus on improving general theoretical understanding of textual representation, and the practical goal of using that understanding to develop further methods, tools and techniques to support practical applications in publishing, archives and libraries. TEI practitioners have sophisticated understanding of knowledge representation systems (such as formal semantics and ontology, object orientation methodologies, etc.), and offer new ways of theorizing them (non-hierarchical views of text, antirealism, hypertext and so forth) (see Renear 2004: 235).

Since 2001, humanities computing has become known as digital humanities, a relatively new term but one which draws on this older history of computing in the humanities. Unsworth remarked in 2001 that the reason for naming the first digital humanities programme at Université Laval, Québec, was because 'the name of the program ("Digital Humanities") is a concession to the fact that "Humanities Informatics" (which would probably be a more accurate name) sounds excessively technocratic, at least to American ears. The other obvious alternative – "Humanities Computing" – sounded too much like a computer support function' (Unsworth 2001).

In this book, we accept this definition and understand the field as concerned with a certain computational 'way' of doing humanities research, which we survey and explore. Indeed, Kirschenbaum (2012a: 9) describes the term 'digital humanities' as a floating signifier 'that increasingly serves to focus the anxiety and even outrage of individual scholars over their own lack of agency amid the turmoil in their institutions and profession', but which is nonetheless a 'scholarship and pedagogy that are bound up with infrastructure in ways that are deeper and more explicit than we are generally accustomed to'.[11] For example, debates and critiques over the nature of the discipline of digital humanities circulate encoded as '"DH" – variously also dh/DH/D_H/#dh as well as #transformdh and #dhpoco' (Kirschenbaum 2014: 51; see also Lothian 2011).[12] Nonetheless, even as the term 'digital humanities' has solidified and entered into more general usage, we are keen to acknowledge that digital humanities is, and remains, a contested term. But the question of the digital humanities is not solely a symbolic or discursive one. Digital humanities is also symptomatic of wider changes taking place in the university as it increasingly informates its systems and begins to introduce computation into wider use. These infrastructural changes and requirements for undertaking research are key to deeper understanding of the positive benefits the digital humanities can bring to the culture of the humanities in research universities.

McCarty (2003) has usefully conceptualized digital humanities as a concern with the building of 'methodological commons' and, through these resources, enabling other possibly 'less digital' scholars to pick up and use the tools and archives to enable the search for 'patterns' and develop techniques of 'modeling' and transforming humanities into much more of an 'experimental field'. By modelling, McCarty (2004) points to the 'heuristic process of constructing and manipulating models, a "model" [he] takes to be either a representation of something for purposes of study, or a design for realizing something new' (2004: 255, emphasis removed).

Using a metaphor of a mercantilist market, he argued that the 'humanities computing specialist acts as merchant trader of these intellectual goods, seizing opportunities for importing and exporting them as the occasion warrants . . . From his or her perspective, the various disciplines serve as laboratories in which these goods are exercised, probed, and improved upon' (McCarty 2003). McCarty categorizes the forms of approach used in digital humanities through the search for 'patterns' across digital humanities 'branches': (i) algorithmic: development of software for the analysis of source materials, to focus on mechanical elements in the analysis of data, as well as to allow large quantities of data to be processed and the specified patterns in them found; (ii) metalinguistic: computationally rigorous linguistic analysis; (iii) metalanguages by which computationally elusive entities may be tagged in texts and thus reliably processed; (iv) representational: focuses on arranging, formatting or otherwise transforming the appearance of data.

In this construction, digital humanities 'is an epistemological practice of its own, not needing the *imprimatur* of theory to proceed', and 'need not wait on the emergence of a theoretical framework, . . . its semidirected, semicoherent activities are no discredit, rather the norm for an experimental field' (McCarty 2003; cf. Berry 2012a; Sterne 2015). This draws on Hacking's notion of an epistemology by intervention (e.g. using a microscope, staining, injecting). But it also disavows a theoretically informed practice, whether historically or otherwise. As McCarty argues, 'research questions for humanities computing arise from [one's] involvement [in various disciplines] and so a research agenda and all that goes with it' (2003). However, this formulation leaves the research questions *for* the digital humanities to be defined elsewhere. McCarty describes this as 'serving client disciplines, which tend to initiate collaborations, set the agenda for research and take academic credit for the result' (McCarty 2012: 117). Hence, digital humanities becomes a shared set of methods, tools, archives, across the humanities, without a disciplinary focus of its own, beyond that of building better tools and archives (creating tools for 'intervening'). Thus, 'digital humanities', although a contested term, becomes used by a growing number of researchers to describe the broad kinds of research work they undertake, or even a tactical or discursive construction (Kirschenbaum 2013, 2014).[13]

Consequently, there remains a theoretical and disciplinary anxiety in digital humanities, expressed by McCarty (2010) as 'our little and fragile field: [it has a] tendency to industrialization'. While digital humanists may develop tools, data and metadata critically e.g., debating the 'ordered hierarchy of content objects' principle; disputing whether computation is best used for truth finding or, as Samuels and McGann put it, 'deformance' (1999) – 'rarely do they extend their critique to the full register of society, economics, politics or culture' (Liu 2012), or indeed to the very tools with which they undertake their research activities. The key to the argument of this book is not that one should choose one or the other, but rather that the discipline is strengthened by having scholars that specialize in and can move between digital humanities projects and digital humanities theory.

Until quite recently, digital humanities projects have involved using the machine to support research practice rather than as a critical tool in its own right (McCarty 2009). The computer as archive or search tool has been relatively accepted by the humanities as a means to undertake research. But these tools and resources haven't generally been accepted as scholarship in and of itself, and certainly there has not been enough work on absorbing and developing the approaches that enable the digital aspect of the digital humanities to be used as a means of critique, in and of itself. Indeed, when it comes to critical work in the humanities, the gold standard remains the monograph. Thus, there continues to be a boundary between the kinds of work produced between these worlds of humanities (academic) and the technical (tools). This division of academic knowledge from support echoes that found in industry where information management functions are often separated into a service function for the corporation. Among the oddities of this conception are that there is often already a computing support department in most, if not all, universities and that the digital humanities are usually inhabited by academics and research-oriented staff. This historical division may help explain some of the way in which certain activities were rewarded as academic (monographs/promotion), and others were seen as 'merely' academic-related or technical (tools, archives). But it is notable that computer science has successfully distinguished itself from other computing functions within the university and produces its own form of knowledge output that is understood as discipline-specific.

In digital humanities, both its recent and historical instantiations have tended to concentrate on text-focused work which has given the field a focus and a scholarly concern that makes its work recognizably digital humanities (see Schreibman et al. 2004: xxiii). That is not to say that digital humanities work is purely textual in nature – far from it, as many projects demonstrate – however, we could argue that text has a paradigmatic function in digital humanities work. Nonetheless, the discussion over the sustainability of these kinds of digital humanities has been a constant refrain, particularly in relation to the fragility of digital works, especially located on webservers and cloud-based platforms (see Pitti 2004: 471–3).

In a previous work, Berry (2012a) argued that we might analytically divide the digital humanities: 1st Wave – Computing in the Humanities, computer archives and tools (1940–2001); 2nd Wave – Digital Humanities (DH), interfaces and the born digital (2002–9); 3rd Wave – digital humanities (dh), materiality and cultural critique (2009–). The aim of this division is not to create closed concepts; rather, the aim is to develop analytical time periodization that is paradigmatic, or exemplars around which digital humanities work can be clustered during specific moments. Indeed, there was a lot of cross-over between these different modes of digital humanities activities, and they continue to inform each other.

This division broadly follows Schnapp and Presner's (2009) identification of the first two waves of digital humanities. The first, in the late 1990s and early 2000s they argue, tended to focus on large-scale digitization projects and the establishment of technological infrastructure. The second wave, which they inevitably call 'Digital Humanities 2.0', was, they argue, generative, creating the environments and tools for producing, curating and interacting with knowledge that is 'born digital' and lives in various digital contexts (see also Davidson 2012: 476). These are different models for thinking about the trajectory of digital humanities projects and for helping us to understand the temporal and methodological grounds for the various aspects of digital humanities projects that continue to be debated in digital humanities today.

Davidson further argues that 'Humanities 2.0 [or multimodal humanities] is distinguished from monumental, first-generation, data-based projects not just by its interactivity but also by openness about participation grounded in a different set of theoretical premises, which decenter knowledge and authority' (Davidson 2012: 711). This trajectory 'can be traced by comparing Unsworth's 2002 "What Is Humanities Computing and What Is Not", with Schnapp and Presner's 2009 "Manifesto 2.0". At the top of Unsworth's value hierarchy are sites featuring powerful search algorithms that offer users the opportunity to reconfigure them to suit their needs . . . By contrast, the "Manifesto" consigns values such as Unsworth's to the first wave, asserting that it has been succeeded by a second wave emphasising user experience rather than computational design' (Hayles 2012: 44).

Berry has argued that digital humanities should orient itself towards a third wave of digital humanities that is critically reflexive about its engagement with computation / the digital as an object of research, as part of the problematic of humanities scholarship in the digital age (Berry 2012a, 2014). This is broadly in line with Alan Liu's work, which suggests that digital humanities is ideally placed to work with new-media scholars and particularly with the questions raised by cultural criticism and engagement with wider publics. Berry has argued elsewhere this could represent a positive turn towards a more critical digital humanities. Drucker similarly argues that the 'challenge is to take up . . . theoretical principles and engage them in the production of methods, ways of doing our work on an appropriate foundation. The question is not, does digital humanities need theory?, but rather, how will digital scholarship be humanistic without it?' (Drucker 2012: 94).

In order to help explain the historical conjunction of digital humanities as different from cognate but nonetheless distinct fields, Ramsay (2013b) argued that there were two types of digital humanities. Type 1 digital humanities saw digital humanities as archives/tools, 'building', 'more hack, less yack'. The 'hack', as it is sometimes called, 'refers to the concept of making: this might include developing a game, prioritizing a pedagogical practice that includes teaching students how to develop a tool, coding an archival project, soldering circuits together for an art installation, or developing a new tool for scholarly publishing' (Ramsay 2013b). This is often contrasted, both in the literature and in everyday discussions of digital humanities, with the view that '"yack" is perhaps . . . recognizable to most humanities scholars. It refers to the acts of theorization by writing or speaking, usually in solitary exercises, or at times on a conference panel or scholarly collaboration' (Barnett 2014: 74).

Ramsay argues that Type 1 digital humanities (DH) is 'united not by objects of study, per se, but by a set of practices that most regarded as intimately related: text encoding, archive creation, text analysis, historical gis, 3d modeling of archaeological sites, art historical cataloging, visualization', and general meditation on what all of these new 'affordances might mean for the study of the human record' (Ramsay 2013b). He explained that 'Type 1 DH is [a] community' and 'in early 2001, this community fatefully decided to call itself "digital humanities"', as humanities computing sounded like a 'campus technical support group'. Ramsay argues that 'digital humanities' is 'useful because it distinguished our activity from media studies'.[14]

With Type 2, on the other hand, Ramsay argues that 'I don't know exactly how it happened . . . Media studies practitioners were digital humanists; people who had devoted several decades to digital pedagogy were digital humanists; cultural critics who were interested in Internet culture were digital humanists; and digital artists of a certain variety were digital humanists.' The resultant confusion of disciplinary identity, for

Ramsay 'sounds like the recreation of the humanities itself after some technological event horizon' (Ramsay 2013b). Type 2 digital humanities, then, is a more expansive notion, including media theory, cultural critique, media and communications, etc.

Ramsay has also reconceptualized the key approaches to digital humanities that are being informed by the notion of 'more hack, less yack' as 'building things' – sometimes standing in for the requirement that one 'codes' to be a digital humanist. Critiquing this distinction, Golumbia (2013) termed them the 'narrow' (DH) or 'big tent' (dh) digital humanities. He did this to draw attention to the limited way in which digital humanities tended to be used, but also to how it would be deployed differently depending on the circumstances of its use – thus, for funding applications the narrower definition would tend to be used, but when called upon to reflect on social and political questions, a wider notion might be deployed (see also Koh 2014: 103). Golumbia argued that there are important implications for digital humanities regarding widening of the research field to other disciplinary and critical research broadly understood.[15]

Without failing to acknowledge the excellent critical work that is going on in the field of Digital Humanities (see Schreibman et al. 2004; Gold 2012), we argue that more support for critical work in digital humanities from funders, and indeed from digital humanities projects, is needed. This could take the form of better support for critical/reflexive dimensions in digital humanities-funded projects – not just connecting to interdisciplinary work in computer science/engineering and so on, but also with more critical scholarly academics (see Gold 2012). These are important issues because they help us, as digital humanists, to think through the nature of our work, particularly in relation to how that work is conceptualized and understood, but also the metaphors and analogies that are invoked in that understanding. The self-definition of digital humanists sometimes treads on the uneven lines between metaphor and problematic constructions of the future of the humanities – for example, Jockers argues: 'what is needed now is the equivalent of open-pit mining or hydraulicking . . . Close reading, traditional searching, will continue to reveal nuggets, while the deeper veins lie buried beneath the mass of gravel layered above. What are required are the methods for aggregating and making sense out of both the nuggets and the tailings [. . .] [to] exploit the trammel of computation to process, condense, deform, and analyze the deeper strata from which these nuggets were born, to unearth, for the first time, what these corpora really contain' (Jockers 2013: 9–10).[16]

Across the scholarly spectrum, as well as wider society, new levels of expertise are called for, usually grouped under the notion of 'data science', a thoroughly interdisciplinary approach sometimes understood as the movement from 'search' to 'correlation'. The digital humanities can bring this expertise in humanities processing together with large data sets, such as those found in Big Data, or data lakes. Critical approaches can supplement these new digital methods and explore how technologies are organized into complex assemblages which create the conditions under which new knowledge and practices are developed – material digital culture. Across the multiple levels of their operation, basic principles of computation are applied, such as: modularity, iteration, abstraction, optimization, etc., to understand how normative decisions are delegated and prescribed. Digital humanities can also explore the governmentality of these structures, and how they connect to wider questions in society, and so on (Rouvroy 2009). Information has time value, and soon can lose its potency. This drives the growth of not just Big Data, but real-time analysis – particularly where real-time or archival databases can be compared and processed in real-time. Currently, real-time is a huge challenge for computational systems and pushes at the limits of existing computal systems and data analytic tools.

In a technical sense, this is the emergence of what we might call 'really big data' applications represented by 'batch map/reduce' – such as Hadoop and related computational systems – and 'real-time map/reduce', whereby real-time analytics are also made possible on data – represented currently by technologies like Google's Dremel (Melnik et al. 2010), Caffeine (Higgenbotham 2010), Impala (Brust 2012), Apache Drill (Vaughan-Nichols 2013) and Spanner (Iqbal 2013), etc. This is the use of real-time stream processing combined with complex analytics and the ability to manage large historical data sets, for example audio-visual archives, massive text sets, web archives, etc. The challenges for digital humanities are considerable at this scale, requiring peta-scale computational architectures so that the data can be held in memory, but also the construction of huge distributed memory systems enabling in-memory analytics, combined with developing complex algorithms and technical skills that create the research infrastructures to support and develop these resources for humanities scholars. With the requirement to build, manage and critique these systems, one can readily understand why a physical lab can be an important part of the supporting infrastructure of computational work in the humanities.

The digital humanities is described here as an historical, material and critical approach, understanding that the key organizing principles of our experience are produced by ideas developed within the array of social forces that human beings have themselves created. We agree with Moretti when he argues that 'to make the humanities relevant you need something much bigger than the digital humanities. What the humanities need are large theories and bold concepts' (Moretti 2016). We think that the digital humanities could have something important to contribute towards thinking about and developing our understanding of the role of the human in an increasingly digital present – it could and should develop large theories and bold concepts. This includes understanding computational conditions of possibility for developing and supporting research infrastructures, and appreciation of the complexity of describing and encoding knowledge representation, creating and maintaining tools and archives as a critical reflexive subject and as an agent dynamically contributing and responding to these structures and practices. How might one structure a humanities education that contributes to the personal development and intellectual maturity of humanity, educate citizens, etc.? What are the key questions and challenges in the computational age and what might a humanities undergraduate or postgraduate programme look like when informed by these insights?

We now turn to some of these questions, firstly in terms of what we might call the conditions of possibility for developing the knowledge and understanding for critical and reflexive work in the digital humanities – something we are calling computational thinking.

3   On the Way to Computational Thinking

Working with digital humanities requires a new kind of critical approach to computational thought, which we call *computational thinking*. In this chapter, we will explore this kind of thinking and how it can be developed. We can think of this type of cognitive practice as related to a type of knowledge developed through a computational *phronesis* – that is, not merely a form of technical knowledge (*techne*) but the form of practical wisdom that emerges from action. It includes the ability to reflect on computation and computational practices as a whole. This form of computational thinking is therefore necessarily linked to a set of practices, or what we might call literacies, related to technical, and particularly algorithmic or computational, know-how.

Here we use the term 'know-how' drawn from Ryle (1945), to gesture towards the already embodied, practical reasoning that takes place through the activity of knowing how to do things, which is what Ryle calls 'knowledge-how'. This Ryle contrasts with the notion of 'knowing-that' or 'knowledge-that', which is more fact-focused and involves a capacity to recall knowledge without the explicit reasoning capacity required to generate the knowledge in the first place. This notion of knowing-how is very rich for thinking about digital humanities, in terms of both the 'hack' aspect of knowing how to use computers in humanities scholarship, and the 'yack' aspect of knowing how to think about what it is we are doing when practising digital humanities. Ryle argues:

> philosophers have not done justice to the distinction which is quite familiar to all of us between knowing that something is the case and knowing how to do things. In their theories of knowledge they concentrate on the discovery of truths or facts, and they either ignore the discovery of ways and methods of doing things or else they try to reduce it to the discovery of facts. (Ryle 1945)

Digital humanities has often discussed what literacies are necessary as new regimes of computing emerge, often within the context of a particular programming language. This question returns again and again in the discussion of what citizens in a newly postdigital culture need to take an active part in. What do they need to learn? What should the future education comprise? This is often simplified to the question 'Should one code?' Those in favour of learning how to code often claim coding is not just a technical skill, but a skill that requires a certain kind of reasoning that is important for more than just producing a running program. Moretti, for example, explains that:

> it's that coding, and I see this in young grad students or younger colleagues, allows them to have a type of intelligence and intuitions that I don't have and will never have. It's an intelligence that takes the form of writing a script, but in the writing of the script there is also the beginning of a concept, very often not expressed as a concept, but that you can see that it was there from the results that the coding produces . . . [U]niversities that have a digital humanities program, minor, major, should make sure that everybody gets a chance at having that type of intelligence. (Moretti 2016)

In this chapter, we want to frame these questions in relation to the notion of computational thinking and explore the relationship between this form of thinking, related practices of computation and public culture.

Indeed, these questions have been echoed historically in relation to culture, and today in a *computational* culture they are rearticulated in relation to computational competences. In the register of art, for example, Brecht, previously, considered competence itself to be superfluous in relation to learning about art itself, in as much as providing an opportunity of access and therefore praxis opens the possibility of such experiences and understanding. He wrote, 'one need not be afraid to produce daring, unusual things for the proletariat so long as they deal with its real situation. There will always be people of culture, connoisseurs of art, who will interject: "Ordinary people do not understand that." But the people will push these persons impatiently aside and come to a direct understanding with artists' (Brecht 2007: 84). Whether the 'people' are ready to deal directly with computation is an interesting question, and in many cases they already are doing in our era of ubiquitous digital media. Nevertheless, it is certainly the case that the majority of people today have had only a perfunctory introduction to the technologies on which they are so reliant in everyday life. Indeed, this is echoed at the level of the university where, historically, insufficient attention to computational education has been provided. We think this is a productive starting point but it is not sufficient in as much as it focuses perhaps too heavily on the instrumental dimension of computation. By thinking through these elements, we also want to start to supplement and broaden them so that they include humanistic modes of thought and practice. Together, we think these can form the basis for developing both a foundation for digital humanities practice and a condition of possibility for critique and critical work in the field.

Computational thinking is usually described as deploying the principles from computer programming and computer science in problem spaces. One may apply computers to new fields, or use programming principles without computers, as when creating routines or workflows. The term was originally developed within an education discourse: Jeanette M. Wing (2006, 2008) and many others believe strongly that this kind of abstract thinking will be an essential skill in the coming decades, and argue that it should be part of the curriculum in general education. Cuny, Snyder and Wing have defined it as 'the thought processes involved in formulating problems and their solutions so that the solutions are represented in a form that can be effectively carried out by an information-processing agent'.[1] Wing later formulated computational thinking as 'automation of our abstractions' (2008).

In an attempt to provide an overview of the skills that make up computational thinking, Wing (2006) lists many concepts from computer science: for example, recursion, type checking, aliasing, abstraction, decomposition, separation of concerns, modelling, invariants, etc., while insisting that computational thinking is 'conceptualizing, not programming' (Wing 2006: 35). Selby and Woollard (2013) have surveyed the debate following Wing's initial article, and propose that: 'computational thinking is an activity, often product oriented, associated with, but not limited to, problem solving. It is a cognitive or thought process that reflects the ability to think in abstractions, the ability to think in terms of decomposition, the ability to think algorithmically, the ability to think in terms of evaluations, and the ability to think in generalizations' (2013: 5).

We want to take you through some concepts and practices we think are crucial to developing critical computational thinking. This list, by its nature, is intended to be open-ended, and not meant to be comprehensive, by any means. Rather, we want to gesture to some key areas that could be usefully drawn upon in thinking about how to teach, embody and practice computational thinking. In turn, we will look at automation, abstraction, decomposition, algorithms, learning programming languages, and the aesthetics of computation, and then draw these elements together to think about how these might be combined into a form of computational thinking. These contribute to research practices today in a similar way to how humanities scholars are thought to have used archival thinking, or 'archival intelligence to make best use of archival finding aids and the materials contained within' (Anderson 2013: 11). Researchers in the past have had to learn how to use classification systems, libraries, archives and other resources, and they have to engage with different actors, such as librarians, archivists, technicians and curators. Similarly, computational thinking contributes to a form of computational intelligence that facilitates the use of these new digital resources, but also access to older resources that may have been remediated – that is, digitalized, placed in a digital catalogue or turned into sources of new meta-data.

First, we might observe that *automation* is the core of computing. Before the electronic computers, humans performed calculations following standardized routines, and were called 'computers'. Indeed, Busa's early work with the *Index Thomisticus* used electric punch-card machines to automate a process, and not electronic computers in the modern sense. Human researchers selected a line from one of Thomas's works to be punched on a card, machines made as many copies of the card as there were words in the line, added them to the total stack, and sorted the stack (Busa 1980; see chapter 4 for more on Busa).

Franco Moretti demonstrates the usefulness of automated work without the use of computers in his book *Distant Reading* (2013). In one of the studies, he teamed up with his graduate students and read 128 early detective stories from the last decade of the nineteenth century. Knowing the solution of the murder mystery, they looked for clues to its solution earlier in the text, and categorized them according to a simple scheme. By abstracting away all other parts of the stories, Moretti and his students could study how one particular genre trait developed over a period of time. This was not a coincidental abstraction; the presence of clues is by many considered to be the most important family trait of the detective genre. It then came as a surprise to Moretti to find that the presence of clues was *not* widespread in the sample, and, furthermore, that the device did not spread and become more popular over time in the sample either. Here the students acted, in effect, as human calculators or computers, distributing the load of analysing the corpus of books under consideration. Similarly, Manovich and his colleagues have used Amazon's Mechanical Turk service for image recognition: they pay a large number of human operators to look at images and code what they depict, and these codes are then treated statistically (2014).[2]

Humanist research can, and will often, involve meticulous repetition of small analytical steps, indicating that automation is not in any way foreign to the humanities. When tremendous amounts of work need to be done, they can be delegated to an automaton, whether human or electronic, which performs a tiny task over and over millions of times. Word searches in large collections of text is one of the most powerful tools for digital humanities, both for locating all the places a term is used and to count the appearances of a word to create statistics. Word searches and counting are also the basis for the computational revolution in linguistics. It is not difficult to perceive how one could take note of every instance of every word in a corpus in a very long list, and then next to each word add the other words appearing in its close context, such as the sentence. When this long list is created, one can count how many times each word is used together with all other words it appears together with. The necessary steps are all very simple to perceive, but one realizes quickly that it is an enormous task, even for a quite small corpus. Automating the same process to a computer, however, not only makes it achievable, but has produced tremendous results in corpus linguistics. Automation may also succeed in producing usable results where mathematics fails. Engineers frequently need to simulate the reliability of complex systems, systems that cannot be modelled with probability or existing statistics. Instead, they use 'Monte Carlo processes', where the simulation is run a large number of times with random input (the use of random numbers is in itself one of Wing's (2008) examples of computational thinking).

While automation is not, as we have shown, alien to traditional humanist research, computational thinking is the ability to reflect routinely on where the computer may be applied to humanities work in order to automate a process or a collection of processes. This ability to recast the humanities work within a workflow that can be broken up into discrete elements subject to an automation is a core constituent of the ability to create and manipulate humanities data in the digital humanities.

Next, we look at the notion of *abstraction*. Computer science did not, of course, invent abstraction, as Selby and Woollard (2013) have also pointed out, nor is it a domain to which computer science has a special claim. All sciences and all humanities think in abstract terms. But in order to automate, computer science thinks in special kinds of abstractions, which are also applicable to other domains.

Computer abstractions are 'extremely general because they are symbolic, where numeric abstractions are just a special case', Wing (2008) argues, adding that abstractions in computing are richer and more complex than in mathematics and physical sciences. At the same time, she is using a quite simple notion of abstraction: to 'ignore the details that are uninteresting for the problem at hand'. This very instrumentalism is also at the core of computational thinking in the humanities. Scholars turning to computers look for ways to represent their materials so they can be computed, and are amenable to further computation.

Like Wing (2006, 2008), we would like to highlight the *layering* of abstractions as a cornerstone of computational thinking. Any use of computers will incorporate more detailed (low-level) descriptions and models of the problem area than standard close-reading methods, and more high-level abstractions. Models are combined into hierarchical aggregate models in order to compute complex problems. Moving down to lower levels is what is done when decomposing a problem. Interestingly, while this is to move closer to a problem, it does not mean to move away from abstraction – in fact, a problem may be rendered more abstractly when broken down into the tiniest of steps. In the opposite direction, higher-level abstractions, such as algorithms, may be recreated in many different systems, and thus be regarded as abstractions of similar structures across many realizations. Our suggested *digital humanities stack* (see the Introduction) is an example of thinking with layers. As more abstract forms are layered on previous elements, a qualitative change in the way in which computational resources are used and manipulated is achieved. Books represented in markup languages such as HTML or TEI (see chapter 4) are good examples of abstraction in computational thinking. At the base layer, all the letters, all the punctuation, and every space between words in a book are represented as characters. At a layer above, the organization of words into larger segments is then represented with codes for paragraphs, headlines, and chapters and/or chapter titles. What is represented on the printed page using headlines and extra blank space (as when a chapter begins on a new page) is in the computer represented with codes. At a different level of abstraction are codes for semantic units, such as the marking of quotes from other works, lines of dialogue, or, in critical editions, alternative versions of the same passage, taken from different versions of the work.

Markup codes, especially those developed by the Text Encoding Initiative (TEI), have always had a practical objective: they are created to allow for a future automation. By coding the structural and semantic elements, the same stored digital text can be printed or shown on a screen in many different typographies and layouts, using automatic layout rules. The same codes can also be computed to create abstract models of the text, such as setting up a table of contents, or computing the number of lines spoken by a certain character, or how many times a certain word is used in different inflections through a work. Markup thus employs abstraction on different levels, which again are open for a large and diverse set of different computational uses of the marked-up texts. This is computational thinking in its very basic form: a correct set of abstractions allows for a large number of different automations. This is why knowledge representation and encoding as a set of practices are a hugely important part of digital humanities.

The question of modelling has been much debated in the digital humanities (cf. McCarty 2016). Markup is not a model in itself, but it is a way of encoding text data to allow the digital humanist to create computerized models. By marking up the text according to the hierarchical pattern of title, chapter, sub-heading, paragraph and text, the encoder prepares the text so a model outline can be computed. Other aggregate models of the text are also possible, producing various statistics that may be studied and further calculated to know more about the total text in question.

Next, we consider *decomposition*. The power of computing comes from performing tiny tasks over and over again, so breaking a big problem or task into smaller parts that can be solved in succession is a crucial computational thinking skill. All of computing is layered, and all uses of computers are orchestrated repeated uses of a very small number of logic functions, such as AND, OR and NOT. Programming languages automate sequences of uses of these expressions into common operations, such as mathematical operations, if-then-else operations, loops, and memory storage and retrieval of different kinds of variables. How finely a problem can be decomposed is a question of computational literacy. A computer programmer can see how a problem may be decomposed into computer language routines, and also standard algorithms or procedures. Modern languages and programming environments come with large libraries of routines and classes that may be reused in combination. On the other end of the continuum, the humanist is needed to define the problem area and the possible solutions to it. The first step in decomposition is to operationalize the research question: transform a large field of interest into a definite question and a procedure to answer it. The procedure is what (at least in many disciplines) is known as the research method, and is akin to an algorithm. The fact that the computer in the end needs to be programmed should thus not be read as a dividing line between the programmer and the non-programming scholar. Decomposition as methodical and logical task-oriented thinking is something all scholars and researchers are trained in.

For example, musicologists at the University of Oslo have studied with different methods how music streaming services are used in Norway. In the qualitative study, people were asked to keep diaries of their listening habits in certain periods, and were later interviewed about how they selected the music, and in what situations they put it on. The problem of total music use was thus decomposed into time fractions, and the study was delegated to the informants, who recorded their use. Afterwards, the recorded diary and interview information was analysed (Hagen 2015). Such a decomposition is not too different from the computerized quantitative studies performed by other researchers in the project, in which the aggregated streaming logs for the entire Tidal music streaming service were divided according to whether each unique listener was listening to a single song by an artist or an entire album, how listening habits correlated to large concert events and music festivals, and when during the day listeners enjoyed which genres (showing that heavy metal music peaks in the early afternoon, while most jazz numbers are streamed around midnight) (Maasø 2014).

Next, we look at the notion of *algorithms*. Decomposition, abstraction and automation come together in computer programming, and this may be formally described as an algorithm or collection of algorithms. That is, a structured sequence of steps create an output from an input through the mechanical application of a series of operations constrained by logical operators and conditionals. Computational thinking involves an understanding of how algorithms are built, and arguably also familiarity with a few standard algorithms.

An algorithm is usually defined in a manner similar to this (from *Encyclopaedia Britannica*): a 'systematic procedure that produces – in a finite number of steps – the answer to a question or the solution of a problem' (Algorithm 2015). While the word 'algorithm' derives from the Muslim mathematician Al-Khwarismi's name, the concept is as old as mathematics itself, as any procedure to solve a certain problem would be an algorithm. As computers are intrinsically layered, computer algorithms are always located at a certain level of abstraction. A mathematical algorithm will, for example, involve basic mathematical operations such as rules for addition or division, for which specialized algorithms will be used, but these are buried in the libraries of programming languages, and seldom find their way into the flowcharts routinely used to map out new algorithms by programmers, who can assume that that detail is abstracted away.

An abstractly stated algorithm for computers may also be programmed in many ways. For example, Joseph Weizenbaum's famous ELIZA program, which was written to respond to any English input with a typed response simulating a Rogerian psychotherapist, was programmed in the language MAD-SLIP on an IBM 7094 computer at MIT, and published only as a general description (Weizenbaum 1966). Weizenbaum first described how sentences were parsed: 'An input sentence is scanned from left to right. Each word is looked up in a dictionary of keywords. If a word is identified as a keyword, then (apart from the issue of precedence of keywords) only decomposition rules containing that keyword need to be tried' (1966: 38). Then he moved on to details of how certain keywords required unique treatment: 'It is very often true that when a person speaks in terms of universals such as "everybody", "always" and "nobody" he is really referring to some quite specific event or person. By giving "everybody" a higher rank than "I", the response "Who in particular are you thinking of" may be generated' (Weizenbaum 1966: 39). Weizenbaum also provided a basic flowchart of the keyword detection, and some specific algorithms for weighing keywords. As ELIZA only ran on the MIT IBM 7094 system, several others programmed similar systems based on Weizenbaum's publications, the most widespread being a 1966 version in LISP by Bernie Cosell, on which

Richard Stallman appears to have based his version for the GNU EMACS. Jeff Shrager's BASIC program written in 1973 and reprinted in many popular computer magazines was also based on Cosell's program (Shrager 2015). Similar programs exist for many systems today, including mobile phone versions and a Java applet that can run in web browsers. These multiple versions will necessarily be different as they run in different languages: Cosell's LISP version was 2500 lines of code, while Shrager's BASIC program is only 250 lines of code, and other versions fall between the two in length. Are these the same algorithm? The answer will again depend on the chosen level of abstraction. In their details, they are not strictly identical, but they are similiar enough to be considered versions of the same. More importantly, in most cases they generate the same responses to the same input, so, to a user, they appear to be the same program.

Computational thinking is also the skill of looking to put well-known algorithms to use. Computer science and related fields have over time built up a large repertoire of often-used algorithms held in libraries, that are often reused in digital humanities with interesting results. Wing's (2008) example is the use of 'shotgun sequencing' which has revolutionized genetics. The shotgun method is in itself an example of using random numbers and decomposition, two of Wing's (2006) principles of computational thinking. Very long DNA sequences are broken into random overlapping bits, and each bit is sequenced in a separate process, in practice using many computers to sequence all the bits. The sequenced bits are spliced together by a different algorithm looking for overlapping ends. In the humanities, algorithms from genetics have, for example been used in literature studies to hypothesize stemmas (chronologies of when different manuscript versions of the same work were written) of medieval manuscript versions of Chaucer's *Canterbury Tales* (Spencer et al. 2003), and to map out common genre features in romance novels published by Harlequin (Elliott 2015). This ability to move algorithms between different problem domains is one of the exciting research opportunities opened up by digital humanities.

Applying algorithms from other fields normally requires cross-disciplinary teams, as few scholars have the necessary expertise in both mathematics and a humanist discipline. As Moretti (2016) observes, 'digital humanities is introducing within the humanities, group work, systematically', and the development of digital platforms, tools and methods is certainly improved if the cross-disciplinary insights of larger teams of researchers are brought together in a group, pulling in the relevant expertise and skills as necessary. This is why many digital humanities projects are made up of interdisciplinary teams that bring trained specialists to bear on particular research questions. This is sometimes referred to as 'big humanities', referring to this shift from the lone scholar to research teams and (often) Big Data, combined with computational tools applied to new scales of humanities research.

The use of algorithms for humanist research may at times turn into its own sub-field. Finding and refining algorithms to solve a certain well-defined problem may be rewarding to many scholars. What may happen, though, is that the research interest changes from solving a traditional humanist research problem (e.g., who was the author of a work) to an algorithm problem (which algorithm is most effective in establishing the author of a new text – cf. Hoover 2004), and then again into a mathematics problem (why it is that the most effective algorithm performs so well – cf. Argamon 2008). We can see parallel developments in the field of Artificial Intelligence and computer science.

It seems that we tend to model our understanding of the human mind on the computers and algorithms we have created. Bolter's (1984) observation that the computer is the overarching metaphor in our time is echoed by several other writers. Chun (2011) has contended that, while early computers were constructed based on the then-current theories of how the human mind functions, the situation was soon flipped: subsequent theories of the mind used the electronic computer as a metaphor. In his account of the history of Artificial Intelligence (AI), Phillip Agre (1997) explains that, in order to create systems that generated output that seemed to be the result of intelligent consideration, AI researchers created narrow, technical definitions of everyday terms. He argues:

> a word such as planning, having been made into a technical term of art, has two very different faces. When a running computer program is described as planning to go shopping, for example, the practitioner's sense of technical accomplishment depends in part upon the vernacular meaning of the word . . . On the other hand, it is only possible to describe a program as 'planning' when 'planning' is given a formal definition in terms of mathematical entities or computational structures and processes. (Agre 1997)

What begins as an attempt to model human behaviour – or, rather, human behaviour as a result of intelligent reasoning – quickly turns into a quest to solve narrow technical-discursive tasks. The goal becomes that of demonstrating a working solution to a technical-discursive problem, which then may be reused. Thus, when 'a term such as "planning" or "constraints" or "least commitment" has been introduced into the field through a first implemented demonstration in a particular domain, AI people will quite naturally shift that term into other domains, drawing deep analogies between otherwise disparate activities' (Agre 1997).

This is clearly also a danger for the humanities when their work is seen through the optic of computational approaches. Hence, it is important that digital humanities remains focused on the research questions that are drawn from the humanities, even whilst working in and through computational approaches.

While AI research has inspired modern theories of reason, intelligence and language outside the areas of computer science (see, for example, Eco (1976)), it remains remote from mainstream psychology or philosophy, perhaps exactly for the reasons outlined above. AI models of reasoning are created within the problems of the field, and there is no a priori guarantee they can be exported to other areas.

This is important to bear in mind in an age in which popular social media appear to 'learn' about each individual user, and recommend books or music based on association rule learning (introduced by Agrawai et al. 1993), comparing one user's consumption with that of others. If we surrender the defining power of concepts such as 'taste' (Amazon), 'news' (Google News), 'relevance' (Google search), 'interest' (Flickr) to computer programmers, we are also conceding centuries of humanist insight. It will, on the other hand, obviously be futile to wish away Amazon's recommender system, Facebook's 'News Feed', or YouTube's recommended videos, and those humanists who shy away from these channels run the risk of becoming marginal and losing contact with modern culture. The current interest in machine learning makes it increasingly likely that many more of these services will appear and be ever more sophisticated. The only way left for a relevant and critical humanities is to understand and criticize the apparently intelligent or knowledgeable algorithms and to suggest alternatives based on humanist traditions. As Hayles (2015) argues, when discussing the rise of the 'cognitive unconscious' – that is, technologies that 'carry out cognitively sophisticated actions' (504): 'at stake is the centrality of meaning in the humanities, the interpenetration of human consciousness with the cognitive unconcious, and the openings these developments create to re-think the role of the humanities' (2015: 505).

It took only a decade for social media to change completely the everyday media habits of the Western world, and, with them, arguably important parts of modern culture. Economic power has shifted from the media corporations of earlier media to younger companies like Facebook, Google, Apple and Amazon. Agenda-setting power is shifting from newspapers and television to social media. In what appears to be a democratic shift, tweets on social media and links to stories and videos ('shares') on Facebook or Weibo can transform the agenda of public debate. Algorithms largely govern this attention, however. Facebook realized in 2006 that the combined output of all the friends of an average Facebook user would overwhelm him or her, and they introduced the EdgeRank algorithm to users' news feeds (Facebook 2011). EdgeRank scans all available messages from all the friends of a user, easily adding up to over 1,000, and selects some of them, based on tens of thousands of variables describing each post and its poster (McGee 2013; Patterson 2015). Bucher (2012) has argued that this sifting function will necessarily influence a user's behaviour on Facebook. To stay 'visible' to their friends, users will learn what kinds of posts elicit response from their Facebook friends, and thus adapt to the algorithm. It appears that, to be able to act on one's own life situation in a social media culture, one needs to think algorithmically, and for a humanist it will become increasingly important to think critically about algorithms and their implications. This algorithmic shaping of behaviour is a key ethical question for computational disciplines (see Berry 2012b).

Now we return to the question of *learning to program a computer*, which is increasingly thought of as an empowering practice in relation to our highly computational age. By programming, one not only gets a more detailed and less mystified understanding of the computer, but also the pleasure of creating a program that actually does something. Even the simple and traditional 'Hello World' exercise both explains how strings are stored and how screen output is created, and gives the budding programmer the pleasure of making action happen. Programming is probably the only way truly to master computational thinking, as that kind of reasoning is characterized by viewing the world as problems that may be solved by computer programs.

Many humanities writers have been discussing at length how the computer's construction from the very bottom layers not only determines what it can be used for, but also determines culture in a digital age. The infamous 'zeroes and ones' at the base of digitization have been the attention of much scholarship (see, e.g., Kittler 1995; Chun 2011; Dexter 2012). Much less has been written about higher levels of representation, and Manovich's (2001) insight that the representation in the computer being numerical is more important than the actual number system (or alphabet, cf. Finneman 1999) has not been adequately addressed by scholars. It is tempting to ask why the binary numbers should be more consequential than, for instance, the hexadecimal representations actually found in low-level computer programs. Berry (2011) suggests a more holistic view of the multiple layers of computer code when he divides computer code into different 'ideal types'. Code as an abstract will be realized as 'delegated code' when manifested as source code in a particular computer language, and as 'prescriptive code' when compiled into binary code for the computer to run. Understanding these crucial distinctions is very important for thinking in the digital humanities.

Much energy goes into discussing the benefits of different programming languages and deciding which one to teach. Although this is important, it should not overshadow the purpose of teaching computational thinking principles. As Leon argues, 'the goal should be to develop enough knowledge to manipulate the material you have in order to answer your scholarly question, not so that you have this abstract sense of capacity to build things as a programmer, unless that is necessary to answer your questions' (Leon 2016). Indeed, we should acknowledge and appreciate the differences between computer languages, which are there for a reason – usually linked to a specific requirement of a problem domain. Computer languages are of different levels, again demonstrating the layering of abstractions so typical of computational thinking. For example, the web site 'If this then that' (http://ifttt.com) allows users to connect different web services with the grammar of a simple 'if' test. It can serve as an example of a very high-level language, integrating thousands, if not millions, of lines of lower-level computer code in the web site itself and the services it plugs into. All these operations are abstracted away from the user, who only sees the simple if–then statement. JavaScript is a lower-level language, still relatively easy to program, and also reliant on many levels of applications and code to run. To program a native application for a popular device, whether stationary or mobile, requires lower-level code and much more consideration of computational detail. Languages that have been useful in digital humanities projects, such as PERL or PHP, are examples of languages that require more consideration of the kinds of variables one uses, but have different benefits to humanist projects: available tools to manipulate text strings for the former, easy access to popular database tools for the latter.

Lower-level thinking is required in building up research databases of digitized material. The encoding system, such as TEI, the database structure, etc., need to be carefully planned not only to enable effective data retrieval, but also in order to get data in: a good database structure makes it easier to build and maintain a database, which, after all, is the main work of any research collection. The shape of the research collection is also dictated by the ontology used to structure the database – which can have huge implications for the later use of the database, and, indeed, subsequent attempts to change a database structure can be a real headache. Hence, within the digital humanities, sensitivity to both the humanities materials, which have to be thoughtfully curated, and to the technical design and implementation have to be a dual aspect of the work, and serve to illustrate the complexity of working in this field.

Layering in code is also the principle in object-oriented programming. Born from attempts to model workplaces in computers (Dahl and Nygaaard 1966; Holmevik 1996), object-oriented programming languages allow the programmer to create models out of self-contained objects. Each object holds both its data (fields) and its methods (the algorithms that perform calculations on the data). A program thus describes the objects and how data are exchanged between them. Objects are in many languages described as abstract classes, of which instances are created. That means that several instances of (born from) the same class can exist simultaneously, having the same fields and methods. Classes can have sub-classes that inherit some fields and methods from the parent class, while some are unique to the sub-class. This inheritance concept is another example (or may we say instance?) of computational thinking as layering, combined with a focus on modularization (or decomposition). A problem area is thought of as a model of the world, which is divided into abstract modules that form the classes of objects. Some subjects alter the minds of students, and learning object-oriented programming is such a thought-changing experience for many. While it may be a tough concept for the beginner, as soon as one masters the basic concepts, it may change how one perceives the world. As Jay David Bolter (1984) has argued that every age uses a central technology as the main metaphor for its explanations, we believe that objects, classes and instances will be used as metaphors in many theories in years to come.

In recent years, this modularization has been taken a step farther as very large computer systems have been built using the patterns of service-oriented architecture (see, e.g., Fox and Patterson 1994). Examples using this approach include Amazon and Facebook. In such architecture, a system is built of interconnected, but separate, subsystems, described as 'services'. A log-in system may be one service, a checkout system another, and a database may be a third. Services connect only via formal APIs – one system is not allowed to reach into the data of another system in any other way. Proponents of service-oriented architecture argue that the resulting system is more flexible – as the different services may be written in different languages and on different technical platforms – and more robust, as one service can continue to run even if another fails. These ideas are influencing digital humanities as it starts to articulate its systems in terms of platforms and research infrastructures, especially in terms of interoperability of systems and the sharing of data, for example through the notion of linked data, which enables data to be referenced by other systems across a range of different databases and to be combined and aggregated into new forms.

The digital methods initiative (DMI) is an example of a similar high-level approach, whereby researchers create scripts to harvest data for research purposes from the large databases of corporations such as Google, Twitter and Amazon. As we discuss later, to assemble web services in this manner requires an ability to see what kinds of questions may be answered with these tools, and, among those questions, pose the ones that are interesting for one's research. This is computational thinking in practice: to translate one's questions and concerns into models and routines that can be solved by a computer.

Now we want to look at the notion of *aesthetics* in relation to computational and digital forms. Programmers often view program code as aesthetic objects, much in the same way as mathematicians see beauty in elegant equations. An algorithm is considered to be 'beautiful' when it is simple and clear, yet powerful, just as equations in mathematics or physical science are considered the most beautiful when they are simple, but have great power of proof or prediction: '[W]e not only want algorithms, we want *good* algorithms in some loosely defined aesthetic sense . . . its simplicity and elegance, etc.' (Knuth 1973: 7).

Computer code is not just abstract, however – it is written to solve a task, and 'elegant' solutions are appreciated, as they mean efficient code. Chaitin explains that 'a program is "elegant", [if] it's the smallest possible program for producing the output that it does' (2006). A few lines of code that can produce significant effects are therefore considered elegant, especially if the technique used is novel and less obvious. Producing high-efficiency, beautiful code is considered a demonstration of the smartness and creativity of the programmer.

Computational thinking is, as Wing (2011) argues, also a part of engineering thinking. An elegant program may thus not only be elegant as written code, it may also use resources effectively. Of two programs that perform the same task with similar correct results, the fastest will normally be preferred, or the one that uses less memory, bandwidth, CPU power or other scarce resources. It may even be an ethical task to create a piece of software that can run on old computers that can be acquired cheaply by a university (or a person) in the Global South.

It is also considered a virtue to write down code so it is easy to read for people other than the programmer, from the names used for variables that are understandable to humans, to the layout of the code on the screen, using line breaks and indents to make the program's structure visible. One of the best showcases of code aesthetics is perhaps the yearly competition in 'obfuscated code', in which contestants submit programs that are illegible to humans, yet perform a useful task when compiled. This competition is, of course, a humorous comment built on the same aesthetics (see Berry 2011 for a discussion of obfuscated code).

Code is even treated as literature in some circles, for example in the 'code poetry' movement, whose members read and write computer code as poetry (see Berry 2011). A poem written in code may be executable (and would by many be considered more elegant), but not all are. We see this movement as a potential area of study in a third wave of digital humanities, in which scholars turn to the computer to understand its role as a human system of communication and a cornerstone of our current computational culture.

Training in computational thinking therefore inevitably touches on developing an appreciation of elegant code. This aesthetic mode of reading computation contributes to the practice of digital humanists even when they are not writing code. Indeed, this way of seeing made possible by computation helps train the capacity to see effective solutions to research interests articulated through computation and formal analysis. An understanding of code aesthetics fosters better systems, where the different parts are clearly described and delineated, so it is robust, reliable and can be altered, added to or reused by others. It was thought in the classical humanist tradition that training in logic and grammar developed clear and logical thinking. There may be much in this view, and we contend that to think in terms of code aesthetics similarly will foster clear thought, especially for digital humanists.

We have given a few examples of skills that computational thinking relies on, such as automation, abstraction, layering modeling, decomposition and algorithms. These skills are best nurtured, as we have argued, by practising actual programming in one language or another. To code is, of course, not a panacea for all the ills of society. It is becoming increasingly clear, however, that programming skills make one able to interact with and guide one's life in an increasingly computational culture that relies on digital technologies for many aspects of everyday life. Being able to program, one becomes able to operate, and to define how the computational will function in relation to individuation processes. It helps us to see where computation is manifest in everyday life. We will discuss these issues for the remainder of this chapter.

Many argue that computerized processes are increasingly taking over low- and middle-income jobs, and will create a huge disruption in the average future workplace, and that this development is overlooked by many (see Cowen 2013; *Economist* 2014). Computation can be understood as a milieu that is never *seen* as such, even as it surrounds us and is constantly interacting with and framing our experiences. Indeed, Stiegler (2009) argues that:

> *that which is most close*, is that which is *structurally forgotten*, just as water is for a fish. The milieu is *forgotten*, because it effaces itself before that to which it *gives place*. There is always already a milieu, but this fact escapes us in the

same way that 'aquatic animals', as Aristotle says, 'do not notice that one wet body touches another wet body': water is what the fish *always* sees; it is what it *never* sees. Or, as Plato too says in the *Timaeus*, if the world was made of gold, gold would be the sole being that would never be seen. (2009: 13–14)

Today, computation is increasingly not seen, obscured or ignored by virtue of its everydayness. Not only that, culture is itself transformed as the epistemic function of code grows when previous media forms are transformed into a digital substrate, being turned into software (or 'softwarized') in the process, and so the possibilities for using and accessing that culture change too. Without such competences, Berardi argues, 'the word is drawn into this process of automation, so we find it frozen and abstract in the disempathetic life of a society that has become incapable of solidarity and autonomy' (Berardi 2012: 17). For Berardi, cognitive labour would then have become disempowered and subjected to what he calls 'precarization' (2012: 141).

These developments are not limited to industrial workers. Within the field of digital humanities, there is a tension between new forms of working within the humanities, alongside the creation of new forms of hierarchy and precarity in relation to full-time academic staff versus short-term contract labour and managerial monitoring. As Flanders observes, 'increasingly, the use of project management tools to facilitate oversight and coordination of work within IT organizations has also opened up the opportunity to track time, and this has fostered an organizational culture in which detailed managerial knowledge of time spent on specific tasks and on overheads is considered virtuous and even essential' (Flanders 2012: 303).

These practices are often then applied to para-academic work in the digital humanities creating an accounting culture around academic work and bringing strategic–rational behaviour and instrumental rationality into academic ways of undertaking scholarly work, as Flanders describes:

> the spreadsheet . . . tracks the project, [the] unit of funding (time, product) could be spent to purchase an equivalent quantum of time or product from some other source: from a vendor, from an undergraduate, from a consultant, from an automated process running on an expensive piece of equipment. The precise quantification of time and effort permits (and motivates) a more direct comparison of work according to metrics of productivity and speed and permits a managerial consciousness to become aware of all the different ways of accomplishing the same task with available resources. (Flanders 2012: 304)

These are not merely theoretical concerns but are of utmost importance for digital humanists to be aware of, if they are not to allow these new forms of Taylorist practices to colonize the humanities. Digital humanists cannot pretend that contemporary contestation over automation, proletarianization and precarity are not relevant to their practices and discipline. Rather, as the vanguard of many of these new technologies and techniques, it is paramount that they are able to balance these powerful and new methods with the continuities required for ensuring that the ways of knowing developed in the humanities are preserved even as they are extended. This awareness and responsibility is later articulated in this book as critical digital humanities, but here we can signpost this by noting that critical technical practice is similarly important for the computing and informational disciplines.

In response, Berardi calls for an 'insurrection', in as much as 'events' can generate the 'activation of solidarity, complicity, and independent collaboration between cognitarians', that is, 'between programmers, hardware technicians, journalists, and artists who all take part in an informational process' (Berardi 2012: 142–3). Whether such an insurrection is possible or desirable we put to the side at this juncture, but note that this event generated by computation cannot just be ignored.

Digital humanities is uniquely positioned to contribute to the debates in this area, and also to pedagogies to teach computational technologies, allowing students to see the computation in our culture (see Berry 2012a; Reid 2012: 357; Waltzer 2012: 337). Indeed, Kirschenbaum argues:

> the digital humanities today is about a scholarship (and a pedagogy) that is publicly visible in ways to which we are generally unaccustomed, a scholarship and pedagogy that are bound up with infrastructure in ways that are deeper and more explicit than we are generally accustomed to, a scholarship and pedagogy that are collaborative and depend on networks of people that live an active 24–7 life online. (Kirschenbaum 2010)

This includes a commitment to open access, computational techniques of both reading and meta-reading of texts, and the translational opportunities afforded by statistical and algorithmic production of data and information visualizations. These are often articulated in terms of public humanities, critical concerns around democratizing knowledge, forms of open access, and a wider contribution to public culture and civil society.

One important aspect of this is the development of new forms of literacy, if we can call it that, in relation to the computational, which is similar to what Berry (2014) has called *iteracy*. It is also connected to developing notions of reflexivity, critique, and emancipation in relation to the mechanization of not only labour, but also culture and intellectual activities more generally. Understanding the machine, as it were, creates the opportunity to change it, and to give citizens the capacity to imagine that things might be other than they are.

This is important in order to avoid a situation whereby the proletarianization of labour is followed by the capacity of machines to proletarianize intellectual thought itself. That is, to avoid machines defining the boundaries of how, as a human being, one must conduct oneself, as revealed by a comment from a worker at a factory in France in the 1960s who observed that, 'to eat, in principle, one must be hungry. However, when we eat, it's not because we're hungry, it's because the electronic brain thought that we should eat because of a gap in production' (Stark 2012: 125). Delegation to the machine of the processes of material and intellectual production abstracts the world into a symbolic representation within the processes of machine code. It is potentially a language of disconnection, a language that disables the worker, but simultaneously disables the programmer, or cognitive worker, who no longer sees another human being, but rather an abstract harmony of interacting objects within a computational space (Berry 2014). This is, of course, a moment of reification, and, as such, code and software may act as an ideological screen for the activities of the market, and the harsh realities of neoliberal restructuring and efficiencies, the endless work,[3] made possible by such softwarization. By developing a disciplinary sensitivity to these wider concerns, through, for example, cultural critique, digital humanities can, in addition to producing new forms of knowledge and practice in the humanities, also contribute to a critical reflexive citizenry that can use its computational understanding in civil society, politics and academic knowledge generation for the public good.

One can look at computational thinking as Wing does, as a skill that needs to be developed, and in many ways it is. It is also a way of approaching challenges so that computers and code can be employed effectively, which is nurtured through use of computers. But, just as much as computational thinking is a set of discrete methods and skills, as Wing and others argue, it is a mode of thinking that may completely transform how one thinks about knowledge and argument. Computational thinking has the potential to create a computational epistemology. Fitzpatrick (2011) envisages a not-so-distant future where we realize that the idea of individual research publishing (with its associated system of merit and status) was tied to an era of paper publishing. Networked computers open up to a different era, in which global networks of researchers collaborate on common problems, adding their works to a database that holds their shared knowledge, not unlike how Wikipedia contains considerable knowledge without having single authors. Acord and Harley (2013) and Pochoda (2013) have voiced similar views, but also demonstrate that the current system intrinsically has considerable forces working against such a development. But even if Fitzpatrick is not exactly right, it should be very clear now that those who wish to act critically in an age of computational thinking and computational epistemology need to understand at least some of the workings of the computer. While we do not wish to take part in a simplistic 'hack or yack' debate, we believe we have shown that a critical understanding of computing at its different levels is a prerequisite for a digital humanist, and that this only can be built through active involvement with actual computer systems, combined with the theoretical insights provided by both material practices and philosophical reflections on the limits and implications of, and transformations made possible by, computation.

4   Knowledge Representation and Archives

As we have seen, the digital humanities, at its most straightforward, is the application of computational principles, processes and machinery to humanities texts. When we refer to 'texts', we widen the notion to include all material cultural forms, such as images, books, articles, sound, film, video, etc. Much of the early work of the digital humanities was focused on getting traditional humanities texts into a form whereby they could be subject to computational work, for example through digitization projects, new digital archives and databases, and the 'marking up' of texts to enable computational analysis. However, digital humanities has also had to come to terms with new forms of digital collections and archives, such as the web itself and the archives made from it (e.g., the Internet Archive). Archives and databases may often be made up of data about data – so-called 'metadata' – and computational materials illegible to humans.

Even though 'digital humanities' as a term is relatively new, it serves as a continuation of the earlier form of 'computing in the humanities'. Much of the previous work had been concerned with building archives, infrastructure and digital tools for humanists to undertake research. As part of this, the ideas grew of building 'comprehensive' and 'exhaustive' archives, using XML and TEI markup (1980s+) in textual works, and creating metadata around physical artifacts which would create a much more computable form of humanities corpus to enable the application of new computing-inspired methodologies.

Humanist research is about human-made texts and images, and, ultimately, about knowledge that is objectified and represented in language or image. Computers do not read and understand, but they have other powers we can make use of. A digital file may be copied in an unlimited number of reproductions that are identical to the first. It may be compressed and sent over the internet, and can be accessed from all over the globe. It is also distributed: while an original artwork will fade, and nitrate film may even combust, digital copies are much easier to preserve: they are just copied again. As digital copies are mathematical representations, we further use the computer to repeat calculations and operations at lightning speed: 'The digital humanities also try to take account of the plasticity of digital forms and the way in which they point towards a new way of working with representation and mediation, what might be called the digital "folding" of memory and archives, whereby one is able to approach culture in a radically new way' (Berry 2012a: 2).

In order to harness this power in humanist research, a digital representation of the research material must be created, or, as Willard McCarty (2004) has argued, a digital *model*.[1] When the model is in place, algorithms can search and calculate on them. 'To an observer B, an object A* is a model of an object A to the extent that B can use A* to answer questions that interest him about A', Minsky wrote (1965). The model is not the object itself, but a representation of those aspects of the object that concern the researcher. McCarty explicates what this means in digital humanities, stating that a computer model demands 'complete explicitness and absolute consistency' and that 'the modeling system must be interactive': the researcher must be able to manipulate the model. The model may be the actual text – the words – of a work, or it may be a facsimile, an electronic photo or recording. Alternatively, the model may consist of metadata, information about a work. For example, the ELMCIP Knowledge base is a catalogue of electronic literature, where thousands of works are listed with title, year, author (and the author's nationality, gender, place of residence and birth year), publisher, language, medium, exhibition history, etc. (ELMCIP 2015). Although the database does not contain any actual works, it acts as a model of the field of electronic literature, which may be studied by researchers interested in the aspects that are recorded. Inescapably, any computer model will be reductionist, so while models make calculations and computer-based research possible, they also leave out important details. As these details have been the focus of humanists for centuries, many scholars oppose digital humanities. For those trained in close reading, a distant reading may seem less interesting. However, the coarser distant reading makes it possible to gain other kinds of knowledge and answer other questions. This is far from saying that close reading should be replaced by distant reading, but it may be supplemented by it. Rather, it is important to remember that methods, by necessity, cannot capture all details of their digitized collections. (In the ELMCIP database, the first concern is the criteria for addition: What is the database actually modelling? Which works are included, which are not, and how can one know whether the model is 'complete' in any common use of the word?) A computer model necessarily treats all texts as similar in many respects. The focus of classical humanities has been the details of what makes each text unique.

As previously mentioned, an early work in digital humanities was a concordance of works by Thomas Aquinas. The *Index Thomisticus* by Roberto Busa was made with a model assuming that Thomas Aquinas's language can be divided into definitive word stems, *lemma*, under which all inflections are sorted. Under the lemma *sum*, we find the inflected words *sum*, *es*, *fui*, *fuisti*, *essem*, *esses*, *fore*, *futurus*, etc. (Busa 1980; Winter 1999), and, under each word, every phrase in which it is found. In some instances, two or more words are 'homeographic' – they are written the same, although they are separate words, and need to be grouped under different lemmas. Finally, some compound expressions of several words were combined into one lemma, such as *mortuus est* (Winter 1999). The resulting concordance allows a scholar to study how Thomas used any word throughout his work, without having to read it all in sequence. As Busa reflects, no little amount of scholarship was involved in preparing the definitive list of lemmas, and he contends that it was necessary to push Latin semantics to a level of rigour it never had achieved before (Busa 1980).

Similarly, on 4 July 1971, Michael Hart typed the United States Declaration of Independence into the Xerox Sigma V mainframe computer at the Materials Research lab of the University of Illinois, and announced to other users where the file could be accessed.[2] Some have called this the first electronic book (Hart 2008; Lebert 2008), and it was the first text of Project Gutenberg, later founded by Hart. What he typed in was the same letters, forming the same words, as found in the first printed version of the Declaration, printed by John Dunlap on 4 July 1776, after a manuscript written by Thomas Jefferson, which has since been lost. Which document should be considered the 'original' Declaration is a matter of debate, and much scholarship has gone into locating and preserving the early versions of this text, such as Jefferson's rough draft with corrections, or the handwritten copy on parchment (the 'Engrossed Declaration') from 2 August, with the signatures of fifty-six members of Congress.

In any case, Hart's electronic version is a model of the original text: by studying it, interested scholars may learn much about the words (and their meaning) in the original Declaration. They may not, however, learn about the look of the Dunlap version, the engrossed parchment, or Jefferson's draft. High-resolution images of these are available today from the web servers of the US National Archives, which constitute other models of the Declaration. They capture much more of the visual appearance, but their words are, on the other hand, not as easily treated by algorithms as those in the text file.

Writing as a tool for transcribing and fixing language has proven its immense powers over millennia. Digital text is a further development of this approach. Each letter of the alphabet is turned into a computer code, so strings of letters can be stored and recalled in the computer. But an important fault in many Anglo-American projects is the tendency to assume an English-language character set is to be used, which in today's globalized world is inadequate. While English uses the Roman alphabet, Spanish, French and Italian use various accents over letters. Scandinavian languages have added letters such as æ, ö and å, while the Polish alphabet contains the letters ą, ć, ę, ł, ń, ó, ś, ź and ż. Hart's Project Gutenberg uses the first standard digitization of letters, the 7–bit ASCII code ('vanilla ASCII'), which contains only English letters, and thus cannot encode Scandinavian or Polish alphabets.[3] And we have not even begun to discuss other scripts such as Greek, Thai, Japanese or Chinese (to mention only a few). Unicode was the first attempt at a true global standard, and the version released in 2015, Unicode 8, contains more than 120,000 characters in different alphabets and other scripts, although even here there are still absences and problems with the compressive effects of digital encoding. Indeed, today, many of the digitized documents are in ASCII code (such as those in the Gutenberg Project), which fail to capture many of the world's languages. One might therefore observe that a first consideration for a digital humanist is the question of which encoding of the letters – that is, which model of the letters – to use, as this will have significant consequences in later iterations of the project.

Writing has always been more than merely the sequence of character after character, word after word. The works that have come down to our time from the age of scrolls, such as Aristotle's treatises or the Bible, as well as most modern novels, flow from page to page, and may be 're-flowed' seemingly without much change. However, different writing surfaces do have different characteristics – their materiality – and these physical features influence the writer, and can be used by the writer for effects or additional information – for example, writing with pen and ink, as opposed to writing in a word processor, generates a different sensibility and skillset in relation to writing practice. In a codex or book, pages are important both for reference and for keeping track of the order of information contained in the book. So, for example, a new chapter will often begin on a new page or page numbers are used to locate passages. Marginal information, footnotes, illustrations and illuminations also relate to the page, and then we have not yet considered poems and other works where the placement of type on the page carries information. The William Blake Archive has had to tackle these questions from the outset (Eaves et al. n.d.), as Blake was an artist who worked in words and imagery together, a true multimedia pioneer in the age of woodcut and print. Both the Talmud and the Quran are traditionally printed with marginal notes built up over generations, which have to stay in a certain spatial relation to the main text.

Digital collections encode spatially oriented material to represent it in the computer, most commonly using markup and text encoding, a data model where metadata are included with the text. Historically, there have been two kinds of metadata: information about how the following text should be typeset (bold, centred, ragged, etc.), or information about what kind of textual element it is. Most theorists agree that the latter is preferable, as it is more flexible: one can easily program rules stating how each kind of element should be formatted in print or other output, while at the same time the information about the text's logical structure can also be used for many other purposes.

Most markup follows the principle Renear (2004) outlines as the Ordered Hierarchy of Content Objects (OHCO), whereby lines of a text are grouped into paragraphs, and these paragraphs into sections and chapters. The OHCO model crucially rests on the foundation that markup should describe the logical organization of a text, and not the visual presentation. Chapters are coded, but page turns or columns are not (in principle, although exceptions do exist).

There are many advantages to the principle of logical markup and the OHCO model, as Renear argues in detail (following DeRose, in DeRose et al. 1990), and he goes quite far in arguing that these principles are manifestly superior. We need to remember, though, that this is a data model that, like any model, is fit for some purposes, but not necessarily for all applications. The OHCO model implies that any text may be described as such a hierarchy, and that this description will be relevant for many or all purposes. It further implies that it is the structure of a text, and not its physical presentation on paper or screen, that is of interest to the scholar. A researcher may, however, be interested in how medieval monks spaced words in manuscripts, and compare this to modern typesetting, and thus need to code column breaks, page breaks, and maybe even line shifts. This could also be structured as an ordered hierarchy, of a different kind. While it is possible to mark this up together with the logical codes, the two cannot be part of the same hierarchy, as their categories will overlap. The difficulty of modelling these kinds of edge cases demonstrates that each data model (and associated encoding) will have specific strengths and weaknesses, and may even be inappropriate and misrepresent or undermine the very characteristics of an artifact or textual document that is being encoded.

Editors have always *marked up* manuscripts with pen and ink, inserting comments on edits, corrections and formatting on a written page. Digital *markup* derives from this tradition, but, early on, decided to mark logical categories and not presentation or layout. Standard Generalized Markup Language (SGML) was the first standardized markup language. It was developed by a committee led by Charles Goldfarb (who was one of the developers of IBM's earlier General Markup Language, GML), and published as a standard by the International Organization for Standardization in 1986. It is not a set of markup in itself, but a set of rules for how a rigorous markup vocabulary should be constructed (Renear 2004).

Tim Berners-Lee's HTML language for the World Wide Web was loosely based on SGML, although it allowed mixing presentation tags with logical tags. Wishing to address this perceived lack of rigour, the World Wide Web consortium agreed on the Extensible Markup Language (XML) in 1999, which is now widely used as a file format for many applications – for example, Microsoft Office – or for storing text to be used by applications, as is normal practice in many embedded or JavaScript programs for the World Wide Web. Even the Scalable Vector Graphics file format for storing vector-images created on a computer is an XML format. XML has two main characteristics: first, it is extensible, that is, all users are free to define their own sets of markup tags; but second, documents need to be 'well-formed', meaning that any marked segment must be fully contained in another segment, and there should be one top-level element containing the whole of the text.

XML is the recommended markup language of the Text Encoding Initiative (TEI), an international organization developed since 1987 by digital humanities scholars on both sides of the Atlantic, which, in 2016, had sixty institutional members. It 'is a consortium which collectively develops and maintains a standard for the representation of texts in digital form. Its chief deliverable is a set of Guidelines which specify encoding methods for machine-readable texts, chiefly in the humanities, social sciences and linguistics' (Text Encoding Initiative 2015). These guidelines are a set of XML schemas for marking up digital texts. All TEI documents have a header element where metadata are coded. The minimum information in the header is author and title, publisher, and a description of the text's source, but a large range of codes are available to describe how the text was encoded, more information about the text and how it was created, and its history of revisions. For the text itself, there are some codes available for all TEI documents, such as paragraphs and quotations. Coders may then choose to incorporate different modules for different genres, all equipped with codes to mark the text in impressive detail, or they may introduce new codes and modules. As the available modules are developed by the community, they mirror the genres of collections that have been created within the digital humanities: poetry, drama, transcriptions of speech, dictionaries, manuscripts, facsimile collections, critical editions and language corpora. There are also modules for special kinds of illustrations, such as tables, formulas and musical notation, and a special module to describe graphic models directly in XML, without the use of any other graphics formats.

Markup languages are powerful for many purposes, and have proven successful in many digital humanities projects, yet they are not without problems. For example, as previously mentioned, there is a particular difficulty with overlapping encoding markers. All markup languages stemming from the SGML tradition require that markup tags do not overlap. This is rigorous, and adheres to the OHCO principle, but does not necessarily hold true for all aspects of all texts. Not all texts are Ordered Hierarchies of Content Objects. Jerome McGann (2004) has pointed out that overlap is a symptom of a conflation of different ontologies. Language is an *autopoetic* system: any observation and critique of language will have to take place in language, thus feeding back on both the language and the critique. A model like the OHCO, however, is *allopoetic*, assuming that the observer has a place outside the observed phenomena, as when an astronomer watches the universe with a telescope. An allopoetic approach to textual study will ultimately be imprecise, according to McGann, as it misses the true nature of language. McGann's argument is important, but the question remains of how much of a problem this is in real-life applications. The OHCO model is well suited to many research projects, otherwise digital humanities would not have had much traction. McGann's own counter-example, a tool for multidimensional markup in textual analysis, is intriguing, but he only demonstrates its value in a very detailed reading of one single poem. While this certainly is a kind of digital humanities, it is of a very different kind from the projects for which markup was designed. His theoretical model, as well as his system, may not be of much assistance to digital critical editions and large-scale text analysis.

The TEI guidelines are, on the contrary, a rather impressive manifestation of the ambition and rigour of its community. Most, if not all, of the critical considerations we offer in this chapter have been recognized, and solutions have been sought. One example is the module for 'Representation of Primary Sources', which is a markup for digital images (facsimiles) of original texts in combination with electronic transcriptions. A more practical downside to this rigour is that there is increasingly more work required to code texts, as more and more detail could be described in markup. This is where many digital humanities projects have to make a decision about where to make a 'cut' regarding the level of detail and rigour of the encoding that is to be used in a project. Detailed encoding takes time, is prone to errors (such as can be introduced through the use of OCR (optical character recognition) software, for example), which need to be remedied, and is costly in terms of labour time. As Hitchcock (2013: 14) has argued in relation to the Burney Collection, 'the problem is that while we think we are searching newspapers, we are actually searching markedly inaccurate representations of text, hidden behind a poor quality image . . . and our uncritical approach to OCR is just one instance of a series of wider issues that are raised by our growing reliance on keyword search itself'. So choosing a standard encoding practice with careful scanning, translation and correction, although imperative, is not a panacea for making correct design decisions at an early stage of the project.

The debates over XML/TEI encoding within digital humanities are in many ways the public expression of digital formalism implicit in digital humanities projects. These can stem from an over-concentration on problems that computation can solve, and the reduction of other projects to this frame. This derives from a tendency to see humanities scholarship through what we might call the *strong-encoding paradigm* in digital humanities, which argues for knowledge representation to be the core activity in the field. Whilst not wishing to diminish the importance of good encoding and markup practice, in the strong-encoding articulation of digital humanities *as* encoding, everything else is supplementary. In contrast, we argue that weak-encoding is a more pragmatic approach to the importance of encoding more generally, as part of a good practice associated with a balancing of the quality of, and comprehensiveness in, encoding a project. To put this another way, we don't see the value of making the perfect the enemy of the good within the digital humanities. What is often not acknowledged in this position is the way in which it implies a reconfiguration of a disciplinary constellation of concepts to those drawn from computation, especially a database form of thinking.

The database is the most common kind of computer model: most (if not all) digital humanities projects use databases in some form. While databases yield enormous power to the users, each database is only as good as its design. Millions of records may be searched, filtered and sorted in less than a second, but there will only be the data specified in its rows and tables. A basic assumption behind all databases is that all the records are similar in that they may be described with the same attributes. Such a focus on similarity may have the effect of hiding the uniqueness of each record. The database's design binds the structure of data in advance, to add another column at a later time will require the whole dataset to be recoded, as the new variable must be added for each record. Any humanities project needs to consider carefully how it is creating its database model.

According to Alan Bilansky (2016), databases have changed scholarship. Before digital collections, a major obstacle for scholars in history or literature was not primarily accessing old literature, Bilansky argues, as it was available in microform, but knowing that it existed. The ability to search databases for key words and phrases allows for a completely different kind of reading, and Bilansky documents how it is now, in many fields, considered impossible to do research without access to literary databases. The database 'represents a new form of textuality, and scholars have come to rely on databases' affordances to develop new ways of reading' (Bilansky 2016). However, it is the search function that has been most revolutionary, not the database technology itself. Search, which he shows in many projects was added as an afterthought, has, almost unnoticed, changed many major humanist disciplines. That search was not part of the original design of archives such as the Early English Books Online and the Women Writers Project is another example of what scholars of Science and Technology Studies have documented again and again: new technology is routinely used in different ways from those its designers thought of. Any digital humanities projects will need to think cautiously through their technology and how it will support humanist projects.

It is very common, however, for digital humanities projects to begin to articulate themselves within a computational register, particularly when choosing technical systems, languages, data formats, etc. The need for a 'digital presence' on the web also complicates, and in some instances drives, a project, with many digital humanities projects becoming things that 'hang off' web sites. This technicism is more often that not articulated through technical concepts rather than humanities concepts. Partially this is drawn from the pseudo-precision that technical and computing concepts appear to bring and which can be attractive when thinking about projects, but also because the building of the system requires a technical, systemic framework for design and implementation. The former is a collapse of humanities scholarship too quickly into technical concepts; the latter requires care and critical reflexivity in the design and implementation of these systems. Of course, often the financial background to a project is a cause of this scenario: the clock is ticking after all, and, in computational projects, time is money. Additionally, the technical members of a team are often itching just to get started on the code, and often begin assembling too soon their personal technical toolsets and frameworks – which may or may not be appropriate for the project under development.

In this situation, it can be hard for the humanist to try to slow down the project development and suggest critical technical practice or the widening or problematization of key concepts and ideas in the implementation. The danger is, of course, that by disavowing the standpoint of the critical humanist, a 'digital humanities project' is created that is unsatisfactory to the wider scholarly community but also has a problematic technical implementation that is poorly designed and not scalable. This is, additionally, the cause of the problem of 'digital humanities islands', created when technical thinking causes the project to become insular and inward-looking during the building of the project. Technical projects are also often full of acronyms (THATcamps – The Humanities and Technology Camps), puzzling concepts and naming conventions, not to mention the programming source code itself.

Another critique – and from a different direction – worries that digital technologies have undermined and reconfigured the very texts that humanities and digital humanities scholars have taken as their research objects, and re-presented them as fragmentary forms, often realigned and interleaved with fragments from other texts. This interdiscursivity and intertextuality of the digital has, of course, been much remarked upon and even used creatively in the writing of new forms of digital and e-literature. However, in a new way, this process has, to follow Stiegler (2013), begun to undermine the 'long circuits constitutive of disciplines and universal knowledge, that is, theoretical knowledge'. By referring to 'long circuits', Stiegler is gesturing towards the way in which culture is held within material forms, such as books, films, archives and libraries, which need to be re-read and re-thought in order to form part of our cultural everyday. Without being in a 'circuit', these ideas and concepts are lost, as no-one is able to think them. From this, it follows that, if we overly rely on 'distant reading', the 'circuit' of culture no longer includes us, and we are essentially alienated from culture and hence from knowing these things for ourselves. The tendency for algorithms themselves to be used in humanities research poses just this question for the kinds of work traditionally associated with the humanities, namely hermeneutics, the interpretation of writing. If we no longer describe a method, such as the production of concordances within digital humanities to assist reading, but actually a logic of algorithms within computational media from which no 'long chains' are reconstructed from their shorter counterparts, then our understanding of culture is fragmented. This Stiegler diagnoses as a serious danger to societies as they deconstruct the very structures of education and learning on which they are built. As a remedy, he calls for the creation of counter-products that might reintroduce singularity into cultural experience and somehow disconnect desire from the imperatives of consumption.

Thus, we enter a time of a new illegibility, in which we might say that we can no longer read what we are writing – we increasingly rely on digital technology both to write and to read for us as a form of algorithmic inscription. Not only are there new forms of grammatization but we are entering a phase whereby the grammatization process produces symbols and discrete representational units which become opaque to us even as they are drawn from us through technical devices that monitor and track us. As Stiegler writes, digital technology engenders 'a process of the grammatization of flows, as a process of discretization – for example, of the flow of speech, or the flow of gestures of the worker's body – [this] is what makes possible . . . technical reproducibility and thus . . . control, and therefore, by the same stroke, the organization of short circuits inside the long circuits constitutive of transindividuation' (Stiegler 2009: 40).

Indeed, the question the digital poses to the humanities is addressed directly at what Lakatos (1980) would have called the 'hard-core' of the humanities, the unspoken assumptions and ontological foundations which support the 'normal' research that humanities scholars undertake on an everyday basis – for example the notion of a hermeneutically accessible 'text' as a constitutive and foundational concept. Digital humanities has attempted to address these issues with notions of 'close' and 'distant' reading, particular practices related to dealing with both small and larger numbers of texts. However, it remains somewhat ill equipped to deal with the hermeneutic challenges of computer-generated data which nonetheless contain some sense of internal structure, meaning and, in some instances, narrative, but which are structured in 'chains' that are not conducive to human memory and understanding.

This process of transindividuation, through practices such as a humanities education, creates the psychic structures for the possibility of thinking at all. They are constitutive of the development of the 'maturity' of the individual and the collective formation and education of ethics, intelligence and knowledge. It is through transindividuation, Stiegler argues, that the ability to 'think for oneself' is developed, and which he has used to outline 'what is a life worth living', a concern to which the humanities have traditionally been linked (Stiegler 2013). It is here, in its destabilizing and deconstructing moment, that Stiegler argues that the digital as presently constructed, undermines the development of attention, memory, concentration and intelligence. Hence the need to reconnect what we are calling computational thinking to the wider issues of a social milieu and the practices of digitality.

So far in this chapter we have focused on writing, but much of digital humanities is concentrated on digital collections of non-linguistic visual (and aural) material. Artworks are photographed or scanned with advanced digital equipment, and the resulting files are made available to researchers through interfaces of varying complexity and power. The latest technologies use very-high-resolution cameras, so important pieces such as the Bayeux tapestry may be examined millimetre per millimetre, or the interface may be zoomed out so one can fit the whole in the width of a laptop screen. Such a remote view could be seen as an impoverished experience, lacking what Benjamin called the *aura* of the actual object (Benjamin 2002), but, paradoxically, views that are impossible in the room with the actual tapestry become possible on a remote computer connected via the internet.

Facsimile representations serve at least three functions. They may safeguard the original works, as the digital copy may reduce the need to handle an old, precarious document, and as the digital version may be stored in the unhappy event that the original is damaged. Digital copies may also be handled remotely over the internet, so scholars no longer need to visit a library in another city or country to view a manuscript, for instance. The third use of facsimiles is enabling machine-assisted visual analysis of a large number of documents, as in Manovich's Cultural Analytics, which we will discuss in a little more detail below.

A different kind of visuals are those that are created as a result of research projects – for example, maps. Geographic information systems (GIS) are a combination of visualization software and databases. A GIS could be thought of as a digital map: the basic principle is that points in space may be represented on a map so the relation between the points is preserved. In most maps, the relation is a Cartesian relation between an x-axis and a y-axis, where x may be east–west and y north–south. The distance and direction between a point A and a point B may then be measured on the map. One basic difficulty is that, while the Earth is round (or spherical), most maps are on a flat surface (paper or a screen), so a kind of projection will be needed. Onto this Cartesian grid, lots of information may then be added in the form of different layers: buildings, land or sea, vegetation, roads, borders, elevation, sea depth, etc.

A GIS treats the map-drawing function separate from the database, however. Geographical information is stored in the database in the form of latitude, longitude and elevation, and vectors from these coordinates. In this form, a GIS stores information on elevation, vegetation, buildings, etc. Digital humanities projects typically connect another database with a GIS. A catalogue of objects may include a latitude and longitude, enabling them to be placed on the map. If the internal coordinate system is spherical, the computer may calculate the projection in real-time, so the user can change the projection while staying with the data. Examples may include where an object was found or where a language or folk music example was recorded.

Archaeologists were early adopters of Geographic Information Systems. Field archaeologists record as much data as possible about excavations. When a dig is excavated, it can't be done again: the layers that are removed cannot be put back for the next archaeologist. The only way to save the information that could be read from the site is to record as much of it as possible. In the 1970s, some began to store the field records in databases, and such databases were later coupled with GISs. Few (if any) humanist projects make their own geographic information systems; they rely instead on exist-ing systems, which are coupled with their own databases, using the location as an index key. Large systems with public interfaces (APIs), such as Google Maps and Open Street Map, have increasingly been used in recent years, and as these are so easily available, more scholars have begun to incorporate GIS.

Geographical systems allow for many new visualizations of material on maps, when large amounts of data are laid over a map of an area, and these may in turn be used for new kinds of analysis. These exciting possibilities are only as good as what is in the systems, however, in terms of both width (what is included) and how detailed the information is. As Eiteljorg (2004) puts it: 'available data – whether maps or data tables – may determine the questions asked, or, more worrisome, the ones not asked'.

3D objects, such as sculptures or historical objects, may also be repre-sented in digital form and stored in databases. The simplest form consists of a series of photographs around an object, which are then combined – 'stitched' together – in the computer, and mapped to a cylindrical form. An interface allows the user to turn the cylinder, giving the impression of a rotating object. If photographs taken from all sides of the object are combined, the object may be rotated freely in any direction. This kind of representation gives a good impression of how the object looks, but cannot be used for any purposes other than visual representation. For the visitor to a web site, this may be exactly what is wished for, but the researcher may have other wishes, such as measuring the model, or placing it alongside other models to form a tableau of a historical period. Instead, scholars use Computer Assisted Design (CAD) software for these purposes. CAD software allows one to create numerical representations of 3D objects, and these representations are used to create visualizations on a screen, which may be viewed from any angle (even from the inside out) and distance, and solids as well as curves and surfaces may be represented. Visualizations may also be output as prints on paper, or 3D models from a milling machine or a 3D printer.

Archaeologists make extensive use of CAD software, both when record-ing findings and sites, and to create models of the past: 'For some, the CAD model is the kind of record that a drawing once was – containing all the dimensional and geometric information known from surveying. For others the model is the starting point for reconstructing missing parts or phases, for making realistic images, or for envisioning larger ensembles, cityscapes, or landscapes' (Eiteljorg 2004).

To recreate not only the dimensions but also the appearance of objects that no longer exist, one has to paint the surface of the model to resemble the material depicted. Commercial CAD software includes a myriad of dif-ferent surface textures that can be added to the models, but these will by necessity always be approximations to the real material, and as CAD software is mainly designed for designers of new products, they are more likely to look shiny and new than decades (or millennia) old. To record existing objects, it is possible to add photographs to the CAD model, combining the photographic approach with the CAD model approach.

Another advantage of CAD models is that they may be exported and placed into other kinds of visualization software, even virtual reality (VR) applications.

For example, in a CAVE (a recursive acronym which stands for CAVE Automatic Virtual Environment) project at Brown University, artifacts from the excavations of Petra were placed in a 3D simulation inside a CAVE, a room with stereoscopic projection on four walls. For a user with 3D glasses, 3D objects appeared to be sitting inside the room, and she could even walk around them and study them from all sides. The Petra project had scanned found archaeological objects and created digital 3D models of them. As the CAVE was a model of the excavation site, each model was positioned in the place corresponding to where they were found at the site. By pressing buttons on the user interface, the user could remove whole layers, so deeper-lying objects would appear (Acevedo et al. 2001).

Another example is the SitSim project at the University of Oslo, which imports CAD models into Unity, a software engine created for game design. Instead of modelling a fictional game-world, the researchers recreate historical sites in Augmented Reality applications that can be viewed on mobile devices. In the Via Appia SitSim, users can walk down a stretch of the historic Via Appia in Rome, and the mobile screen will show what it looked like in Cicero's time in the direction the screen is pointed (Liestøl 2014).

Augmented reality (AR) or VR simulations of archaeological sites are examples of aggregate visual models that are used for further analysis. Visual analysis may be very consequential in itself for thinking about humanities research questions – anecdotal evidence is given by Moretti, who relates how he understood Horatio's role in Shakespeare's *Hamlet* the moment he looked at a network graph of all the characters in the play (Moretti 2013). Network analysis is an approach that can be used in digital humanities which studies phenomena as networks of relationships. These are described as *nodes* and *edges*, and together known as *graphs*. The nodes (also called *vertices* or *points*) are the basic units of the networks, often persons, but it could also be groups, works of art or other nonhuman entities. Relations between nodes are called edges (*arcs* or *lines*), and are drawn as connecting lines in a network diagram.

Link analysis is the first step in network analysis, and requires an association matrix: a matrix of the different entities, in which associations between them can be registered. The network graph can be drawn once the links are coded, but, in reality, this is no simple matter. Link analysis often requires expert knowledge of the area, and although there is much work in developing automatic methods, there are obstacles in link analysis, especially in large data sets. When the network is created, it can be analysed statistically in several ways.[4]

Network analysis as a method has become very popular in social science in recent years, using network theory to study social groups, undoubtedly inspired by the easy access to data sets from Facebook, Twitter, Amazon and others through their public APIs (see also chapter 6 on digital methods). The availability of network graphing software such as Gephi has also contributed to this. Not all researchers have the necessary mathematical background to understand the statistical methods in Gephi, however, and, a consequence of this, may produce descriptive and predictable results, or even pretty graphics with little actual content to the visualization.

Network theory has also been applied to narratology, in what is called narrative network analysis, the idea being to map large collections of texts using network theory. Networks are created to visualize characters and time in narratives. Moretti mapped *Hamlet*'s characters as a network, where each character was a node, and where two characters were related (adjacent) if they exchanged words in the play (Moretti 2013). Roberto Franzosi's analytical principle is to search for subject-verb-object (SVO) triplets (Franzosi 1998). Many works in narrative network theory have been used to map causality networks in narratives; others have mapped out political fields from large collections of newspaper articles. For example, Sudahar et al. (2015) searched a corpus of 2 million newspaper articles, selecting articles around election times, and then parsing the language to find actors and actions, and a network graph was drawn for the 100 most-mentioned actors and their relations.

Network analysis is a well-established field. Other forms of visual analysis are also widely used, e.g., Boonstra et al. list cluster-dendrograms, lifelines, calendar views, concentric circle diagrams and more exotic solutions, such as Lexis pencils and Perspective Wall views (Boonstra et al. 2004). A more recent development is 'cultural analytics'. It is akin to distant reading, and could be described as a form of 'distant looking'.

'Cultural analytics' is a term coined by Manovich and his Software Studies Initiative, which aims to bring computer-based research methods such as data mining, data visualization and visual analytics to 'cultural data' and the humanities. The aim is to develop methods to study culture in an age in which millions of images and videos are published on the net every day: 'Before, cultural theorists and historians could generate theories and histories based on small data sets (for instance, "classical Hollywood cinema", "Italian Renaissance", etc.). But how can we track "global digital cultures" with their billions of cultural objects, and hundreds of millions of contributors?' (Manovich 2009: 5). In parallel to digital humanities projects that study large collections of texts, cultural analytics uses computerized image analysis of collections of thousands of images; in both approaches, samples can be harvested online via the API of sites like Instagram, or from archival collections. Cultural analytics models consist of quantitative measures of each image. Computer algorithms measure aspects of each single image, such as the color distribution, average tone, or aspect ratio. Image recognition software is used to detect common objects, such as pieces of architecture, or whether there is a human figure in the image and, if so, how it is posed, the angle between the head and shoulders, and much more (Tifentale and Manovich 2015). The resulting database model is then turned into visual models. The most remarkable of these use graphic arrangements of miniature versions of the images, for example. In the visualizations of different photo collections in New York's Museum of Modern Art (MOMA), miniature versions of thousands of photographs are sorted in space according to the photographer, the date and the average tone of the image (Hochman and Manovich 2014). More traditional statistical figures, such as bar charts and scatterplots, are used to visualize the distribution of descriptive variables, such as time and date for the photo, or hashtags and other descriptions associated with them. The data can then be displayed as interactive figures on large ultra-high-resolution displays. Users can interact with this kind of visualization, and change the view from overview to detailed local views, all the way down to individual images.

To date, the publications from the projects have been mainly demonstrations of the visualizations the group has developed. New kinds of visualizations seem to be a research end in and of themselves in the current phase of the project, as in the study of Instagram photographs taken during the revolution in Kiev in 2014 where great care is taken to argue that the study does *not* aim to say anything about how the revolution was reported on Instagram, or the proportion of revolution-themed images to everyday photos from Kiev (Manovich et al. 2014). Graphs *are* used to show the distribution of images close to the Maidan (Independence Square) where demonstrations and fights between demonstrators and police took place, and where in central Kiev photos are posted from, but no conclusions are drawn from these figures.

The next frontier for cultural analytics will be to come closer to the interpretations of traditional art history and visual culture studies. Is it possible to let computers do the first interpretations, and then aggregate the results into new knowledge that is both convincing and interesting to the larger community of visual culture? Indeed, quantitative visual analysis is a promising field in digital humanities, and an area where new methods are developed constantly. At the time of writing, these methods are exploratory demonstrations of what can be done with digital tools and large corpora. It will be most interesting to follow over the years as these methods are coupled to the large collections that are being built in other areas of digital humanities, and as methods are linked to research questions to bring forward our knowledge of literature, art and history.

Standardized, shared models have for decades been called for in disciplines as diverse as archaeology and literature (Eiteljorg 2004; Renear 2004). When processing digital data or navigating through it, elements of encoding that make the data meaningful can be very useful, like the encoding standards of XML or TEI previously discussed. The idea of universalizing such encoded meaning for the entire web has become known as *the semantic web*. The semantic web is a notion of the web of *meaningful* data, which can itself be processed by computers and employs linked data as the mechanism for publishing structured data to the World Wide Web, where those data can be linked and integrated (Oldman et al. 2015). Indeed, the semantic web uses:

> the same HTTP protocol (Hypertext Transfer Protocol) and a similar way of identifying data (Uniform Resource Identifiers (URI) or 'web resources'), as that employed by web pages (W3C Technical Architecture Group et al., 2001). However, in contrast to an HTML (HyperText Markup Language) Web page, the Web of Data uses a simple meta-model called RDF (Resource Description Framework) consisting of only three elements; a subject, predicate and an object, commonly known as a 'triple'. (Oldman et al. 2015)[5]

The Semantic Web has strong alignment with the previously discussed notion of knowledge representation as a way of representing and encoding the world which enables it to be processed easily by computers (Oldman et al. 2015). In other words, 'linked data' is the notion of moving away from hierarchical taxonomies to graphs, or networks, which can model knowledge in a way that is able to capture the complexity of a knowledge domain, but also enables it to be re-organized, de-assembled and re-assembled as required for computational processing. So, when curating data, it can be a useful design principle to use these standards to enable the reuse and linking to other data sets, databases and technologies – especially in relation to open source and open access data.

The ability to connect to multiple datasources, and compare, process and reuse in sophisticated ways means that the notion of linked data has a lot of potential for the kinds of real-time (and historical) data science work that digital humanities is very adept at. (It also points to the use of linked data within data journalism and more activist-oriented notions of using data to effect change in politics and society.) In terms of critical digital humanities, there is a lot of work to be done on unpicking the normative values which underlie the kinds of schema and classification embedded within the algorithmic data structures of linked data. Indeed, the fragmentation of knowledge into chunks that can be composed and recomposed at will points to the nature of a computational episteme which privileges knowledge divided into non-narrative shards of information which are extremely difficult to read without the aid of a mediating application, code or algorithm. Additionally, the political economy of linked data, and linked open data, raises important questions for the way in which humanities knowledge is converted into data lakes that become a kind of oil for a postmodern capitalism (see Berry 2008; Cohen 2010). We return to these questions later in the book.

Here we want to draw attention again to what we might call the theoretical horizons of the digital humanities as a field. One such important new horizon of intellectual inquiry is the question of scale. It raises deep questions about the kinds of methods and approaches foregrounded in the humanities, as it is a complex process to design and implement digital methods for scaling up the work that humanities might undertake (see Hayles 2012; Rieder and Röhle 2012). A new interpretative paradigm for thinking about these issues requires careful design, thought, and both practical and theoretical reasoning. At these larger dimensions, scale is no longer a process of ad hoc improvisation in relation to both the technical and the work-flow characteristics of humanities work. Instead, the projective nature of humanities research itself needs to be scaled up while rethinking those corpora that make up the initial data set for a specific project. The old division, still much in evidence in talk about the digital humanities, around the notion of computers as good at counting and mechanically recognizing patterns, and humans as able to employ intuition, creativity and serendipity, is rethought. Machine learning is beginning to show results of a sort that earlier was thought impossible for computers to achieve. Indeed, a new interpretative paradigm around digital humanities constitutes new kinds of hybridity in research activities, which means that the moment of interpretation and creativity itself may be distributed around the project, not only between programmers and humanists, but also in the agencies deployed, such as minds, code, algorithms and systems.

The internet, combined with the raw power of computation, has also accelerated allowing extremely sophisticated processing of massive data sets (Big Data), and/or access to human processors (e.g. Mechanical Turk, taskrabbit, etc.). These new technologies also enable team-based working methods, offering the possibilities of new social ontologies in the humanities – 'Big Humanities'.

With the growth in power of computers, they are increasingly able to take on more functions. Some of these new capabilities of computational devices were thought to be 'human/cognitive' and not easily mechanized. This includes textual readings and sophisticated computational processes to categorize and order complex data (such as books, articles, papers, etc.). Indeed, the notion of intervention or experimentation drawn from the sciences has also been used provocatively to think about the kinds of tools developed by digital humanists as '"telescopes for the mind" that show us something in a new light' or 'thing theories' (Ramsay and Rockwell 2012: 80). Digital humanities has also been associated with posthumanism, as in computationalism, speculative realism / object-oriented ontology (SR/OOO), the nonhuman turn, and moves towards an 'inhumanities'. The research agenda of these varied approaches seem extremely problematic to humanities scholars, especially in their move to demote the 'human' from the centre of humanities research.

In some senses, debates in digital humanities over methodology echo the mid-nineteenth-century neo-Kantian Wilhelm Windelband, who proposed a distinction between Nomothetic research – the method of the natural sciences, which gathers particular examples under general laws (facts) – and Idiographic research – an interpretation of cultural and historical phenomena which were irreducibly and qualitatively individual and could not be reduced to general laws (values). The nomothetic vs idiographic distinction returns as a debate over patterns vs narrative, for example. It is also reflected in the perceived crisis of 'close reading', due to students 'not being interested' in practising this method. Something similar is occurring with the notion of modelling, where 'computing is [seen as] fundamentally a modeling activity. Any modeler must establish a correspondence between one domain and another. For the computational modeler, one domain is typically a phenomenon in the world or in our imagination while the other is typically a computing machine, whether abstract or physical' (C. L. Isbell, quoted in Ramsay and Rockwell 2012: 81).

This includes new kinds of work in the processes of academic research that is focused on interpretative practice, such as: hypothesis framing, observation, discovery, analysis, testing and reiterative hypothesis testing. Examples of the epistemological or disciplinary concerns of these include (Liu 2011): Linear vs hypertextuality, narrative vs database forms, permanent vs ephemeral writing, bound vs unbound forms, individual vs social reading/writing, deep vs shallow attention, focused vs distracted reading, close reading vs distant reading, fixed vs processual media, etc.

Indeed, this raises the question of what the research programmes relevant to a postdigital humanities might be – and this is a question of both research and practice, theoretical work and building things, technologically engaged work and critical technical practice (see Cecire 2011a, 2011b). This seems to resonate with the notion of speculative computing described by Drucker and Nowviskie, who argue:

> speculative computing extends the recognition that interpretation takes place from inside a system, rather than from outside. Speculative approaches make it possible for subjective interpretation to have a role in shaping the *processes*, not just the *structures*, of digital humanities. When this occurs, outcomes go beyond descriptive, generative, or predictive approaches to become speculative. New knowledge can be created. (Drucker and Nowviskie 2004: 442)

In this chapter, we have tried to give a rather rapid introduction to the questions raised by, and practice associated with, knowledge representations. Of course, in a book such as this we can only give a cursory overview of the key contours of the technologies and the debates. Nonetheless, there are many resources, both on the web and within text books, that can be consulted to deepen an understanding of the very important issues raised by this subject.

In the next chapter, we turn to look at the question of research infrastructures, both in terms of infrastructure as a condition of possibility for research in and of itself, and in terms of new possibilities created by specifically digital infrastructures.

5   Research Infrastructures

In this chapter, we want to spend some time thinking about the way in which research infrastructures support and make possible the research and teaching function of the university. As Parks argues, the word 'infrastructure' 'emerged in the early twentieth century as a collective term for the subordinate parts of an undertaking; substructure, foundation', that is, as what 'engineers refer to as "stuff you can kick"' (Parks 2015: 355). For example, at its most basic level, scholars and students need access to library facilities which act as a centrally provided set of research facilities to make research possible. How the library is structured, its funding, staff count, range of subjects, quantity of materials, organization and day-to-day operation can have profound effects on the conduct of research in the university. So research infrastructure, its provision, form and funding are hugely important to get right, and easy to get wrong. In the context of the digital humanities, and increasingly many other disciplines across the university, it is the provision of, particularly, digital resources and digital research infrastructures that have become important. But the decisions over the provision of these digital services can be controversial – not only can these services be expensive, they also shift money away from existing funding priorities and research infrastructures. They are also not risk-free and indeed can result in expensive failures, or white elephants, if they are not carefully developed.

But research infrastructures as a subject of analysis ranges wider than purely centralized research infrastructure provision might insinuate. For example, the department is a key research infrastructure that shapes and supports the creation of a shared environment for researchers working in the same field. Equally, the research centre within the university often acts as a specifically interdisciplinary structure that transcends both departmental and disciplinary boundaries. Digital humanities is therefore often located in different kinds of structures in different institutions, but also has different research infrastructure needs from its cognate fields in the humanities.

So one of the growing concerns for the digital humanities and for the university as a whole is the dependence on digital technology and the seemingly exploding proliferation of providers, systems, bespoke solutions and digital media platforms that have grown up in the university environment. These systems have become broadly understood as research infrastructures in themselves, and have been seen as digital research technologies that augment the already extant research infrastructures of the traditional university, research centres, archives, labs and hubs. Consequently, there has been some attempt not only to bring the new research infrastructures of the university into a closer relationship with existing provision, but also to develop policy – sometimes to centralize, and also to rationalize, this provision – across the university.[1] But, as Leon argues, 'one of the interesting things about this is that it points to a problem we have in digital humanities and the university writ large: the infrastructure of the university is not willing or does not have the capacity to support work that it claims to want and it claims to value' (Leon 2016).

The *European Roadmap for Research Infrastructures Report 2006* outlined the importance of infrastructure to the growing need for digital research in the twenty-first century. It argues that the 'definition of Research Infrastructures, including the associated human resources, covers major equipment or sets of instruments, as well as knowledge-containing resources such as collections, archives and databases'. So research infrastructures are defined as being '*single-sited, distributed,* or *virtual* . . . They often require structured information systems related to data management, enabling information and communication. These include technology-based infrastructures such as grid, computing, software and middleware' (EU 2006: 16).

We think the definition of 'research infrastructure' given by the European Social Fund (ESF) is particularly useful – it describes them as:

> facilities, resources and related services that are used by the scientific community to conduct top-level research in their respective fields and covers major scientific equipment or sets of instruments; knowledge-based resources such as collections, archives or structures for scientific information; enabling Information and Communications Technology-based infrastructures such as Grid computing, software and communication, or any other entity of a unique nature essential to achieve excellence in research. Such infrastructures may be 'single-sited' or 'distributed' (an organised network of resources). (ESF 2011: 5)

The way in which the discipline of digital humanities is bound up into its infrastructures – that is, the digital materiality that makes possible its computational base – is both constitutive of, and in need of, greater theoretical and critical attention in future iterations of the discipline.

But that is not to say that research infrastructures are wholly new to the humanities. Indeed, the humanities already have an infrastructure that has been built over many centuries and has become absolutely crucial to doing humanities scholarship, 'the infrastructure of libraries, archives, museums, galleries, and other sites of social and cultural heritage. These sites are deeply material but they are most certainly not invisible' (Anderson 2013: 10). They do, however, soon become backgrounded as part of the infrastructure provided by universities and research institutes, libraries and museum, and therefore many scholars do not pay enough attention to how they were formed, their sources of funding, and why they have the distinctive morphology, focus, content and thematic organization that they do.[2] Equally, in a time of digital infrastructure, these questions are raised anew, and need to be engaged with seriously by humanities scholars in relation to the kinds of work they already do, but also with an eye to the future work that is made possible through new forms of knowledge representation, mediation and access (see Verhoeven 2016).

The growing importance of infrastructure in the digital humanities, and its relationship to knowledge creation and explanation, broadly conceived, can be traced to the notion of digital infrastructure, in particular developed through the notion of research infrastructure or 'cyberinfrastructure' outlined by Atkins et al. (2003) and produced for the National Science Foundation (NSF). This report made an explicit link between knowledge production and productivity and investment in digital infrastructures and thereby to economic competitiveness (Atkins et al. 2003). This led to the recommendation for the NSF to set up, first, a division for science and engineering, but also prompted the National Endowment for the Humanities (NEH) to form the Office for Digital Humanities led by Brett Bobley.[3] This was a 'move of considerable symbolic power . . . the 2008 establishment of the Office of Digital Humanities at the National Endowment for the Humanities in the U.S.' (Svennson 2010). In effect, this shows the development of thinking around the building of facilities and infrastructures that made possible digital scholarship in the humanities.

For Bobley, the digital humanities 'include[d] topics like open access to materials, intellectual property rights, tool development, digital libraries, data mining, born-digital preservation, multimedia publication, visualization, GIS, digital reconstruction, study of the impact of technology on numerous fields, technology for teaching and learning, sustainability models, media studies, and many others' (Bobley, quoted in Smith 2009).[4] In Europe, the European Strategy Forum for Research Infrastructures (ESFRI) has made similar arguments in a European context, and has been active from 2002 in developing research tools and broad lines of development and supporting digital scholarship (Kaltenbrunner 2015: 6–7). But caution has to be exercised in relation to research infrastructure, which, due to its complexity and difficulty of implementation can result in projects that remain unfinished, or that do not achieve critical mass in usage. The common example given for a failed digital infrastructure is the Project Bamboo programme, which 'eventually failed to deliver a workable proof of concept at the end of the initial funding period, not to mention the longer term goal of a widely used infrastructure', which was blamed on capture by funding officers and computer scientists who disconnected from the needs of the scholarly community (Kaltenbrunner 2015: 11; Ramsay 2013a). Nonetheless, there are real institutional and political economic forces at play in relation to the digital humanities. For example, the NSF has continued to argue for the creation of what it called Cyberinfrastructure, and which it invests in through its support of the Advanced Cyberinfrastructure Division (ACI), which 'supports and coordinates the development, acquisition, and provision of state-of-the-art cyberinfrastructure resources, tools and services essential to the advancement and transformation of science and engineering. ACI also supports forward-looking research and education to expand the future capabilities of cyberinfrastructure. By fostering a vibrant ecosystem of technologies and a skilled workforce of developers, researchers, staff and users, ACI serves the growing community of scientists and engineers, across all disciplines, whose work relies on the power of advanced computation, data-handling, and networking' (NSF 2015; cf. Svensson 2010).

These reports and institutions tend to argue that the wider infrastructural transformations in platforms for data and computation produce new digital transformations that create opportunities for different disciplinary and interdisciplinary formations. This is to be linked to a political economy that makes it possible, usually through the funding provided by government, but also in terms of the outputs and research infrastructure to contribute to wider economic growth and international competitiveness.[5] These forces have been, and continue to be, hugely important for developing the infrastructures of the 21st-century university, but they do not fully capture the transformation that digital humanities is symptomatic of. In this chapter, we argue that digital humanities needs to be far more than the translation of old disciplines into new formats and infrastructures, e.g. paper to file, library to database (see also Klein 1996). Material change and new types of inscription technologies also necessarily take the humanities far 'beyond text', to encompass audio-visual, performance and the whole sensorium, while the internet potentially connects each work to any other work. This is key as often many of these funders appear to associate 'the development of digital infrastructures with the expectation that it will make research in the humanities more data-driven, and less hermeneutic' (Kaltenbrunner 2015: 7).[6] But also – and crucially – digital humanities cannot just be subservient to the economic needs of the nation, through being the conduit by which the 'humanities' are 'modernized' or 'rationalized'.

This explanatory model of digital infrastructures is clearly influenced by science inspired models of research work. The applicability of science for humanistic understanding is, of course, a long-standing debate. But where there are merits of 'big humanities'-type research programming, it cannot be denied that care is needed to avoid losing sight of the particularity and difference in the kinds of research undertaken in humanities, in contrast to the sciences. Fundamentally, humanities work has tended to be associated with understanding and therefore with specificity and particularity in actual artifacts. So the focus should be on research infrastructures that intensify and allow creative forms of humanities research for the twenty-first century, not their replacement by science as a hegemonic form of knowledge creation. See, for example, the Digging Into Data challenge which ran from 2009 to 2013 in three funding rounds that aimed 'to address how "Big Data" changes the research landscape for the humanities and social sciences'. It asked, if 'we have massive databases of materials available for research in the humanities and the social sciences – ranging from digitized books, newspapers, and music to information generated by Internet-based activities and mobile communications, administrative data from public agencies, and customer databases from private sector organizations – what new, computationally based research methods might we apply?', and argued that, 'as the world becomes increasingly digital, new techniques will be needed to search, analyze, and understand these materials. Digging into Data challenges the research community to help create the new research infrastructure for 21st-century scholarship' (ODH (Office of Digital Humanities) 2015).[7] Whilst not wishing to deny that Big Data and data science approaches offer new opportunities, it is hardly the only outcome possible from the application of computational techniques.[8]

Indeed, it may well be that this is the more minor of the digital methods that emerge in relation to the humanities, whereby the new opportunities of close reading assisted by various forms of augmented computation – such as 'really close reading' and micro-analysis, classification and desktop organization of fragmentary materials, combinatorial techniques of archive and real-time data, and new transformations in primary materials through computational techniques – will be made possible through research infrastructures (see Hancher 2016 for a discussion of this). For example, we might look at Stanford University's 'Mapping the Republic of Letters', Oxford University's 'Cultures of Knowledge' project, or the Dutch 'Circulation of Knowledge and Learned Practices in the 17th-century Dutch Republic', which, each in their own way, 'provide a forum for groups to join and discuss aspects of their work, whilst others are open for others to contribute content, annotations, and scholarly publications' (Anderson 2013: 14).[9]

These new forms of research infrastructure in the humanities challenge traditional distinctions between the humanities, texts, art and everyday life, and between archives and their relationship to both the institutions that curate them and to scholars who use them for research. As Hughes and Ell (2013: 38) argue, 'we must understand better the use of our digital collections and how they are part of research infrastructure[s] . . . which enables the development of new research questions'. Indeed, their implementation and use raise the question of what is it to read and write culture when computationally enabled distant reading techniques encourage abstraction and data visualization that delegates close reading to an algorithm. They also call us to think about what culture is when forms of representation and mediation proliferate beyond the screen into new forms of computational interface.

One of the most common research infrastructures associated with the digital humanities has been the research centre or lab.[10] This tends to be research focused at a higher level and may include postgraduate and post-doctoral researchers, but is nonetheless committed to work at a high level of intensity. It is notable that, in relation to the disciplinary identity of digital humanities, many of the main areas of activity argued for here in digital humanities take place in research centres either university- or departmentally organized; examples include: the King's Digital Lab (KDL) at King's College, London, the Institute for Advanced Technology in the Humanities (IATH) at the University of Virginia, the Sussex Humanities Lab at the University of Sussex, the Stanford Literary Lab, and the Maryland Institute for Technology in the Humanities (MITH) at the University of Maryland (Svennson 2012: 37).[11] As Fraistat argues, 'digital humanities centers are key sites for bridging the daunting gap between new technology and humanities scholars, serving as the crosswalks between cyberinfrastructure and users, where scholars learn how to introduce into their research computational methods, encoding practices, and tools and where users of digital resources can be transformed into producers' (Fraistat 2012: 282). There are also 'other digital humanities entities, such as HASTAC, the Humanities, Arts, Science, and Technology Advanced Collaboratory, [which] define themselves as collaboratories, virtual labs that exist without walls' (Earhart 2015: 392). Indeed, there are few departments of digital humanities and few examples of digital humanities in undergraduate provision, although this is changing. Digital humanities can be said to have emerged without the full development of undergraduate support and departmental structure in most cases.

Using the UK as an example, the continuing development of digital humanities there is perhaps represented by the innovations in relation to digital humanities understood as cross-disciplinary, and therefore often institutional forms that transcend a particular disciplinary area, for example: the Department of Digital Humanities at King's College, London, together with the King's Digital Lab (KDL);[12] the digitalHumanities@Oxford, a joint initiative by the Oxford e-Research Centre, IT Services, the Oxford Research Centre in the Humanities (TORCH), the Oxford Internet Institute and Oxford's Bodleian Libraries;[13] the Humanities Advanced Technology and Information Institute (HATII) at Glasgow University, which explores how information and communication technology can shape our knowledge and understanding in the arts, humanities and cultural heritage sector;[14] and finally, we might look at the Sussex Humanities Lab at the University of Sussex which has received £3 million of funding to develop an expanded digital humanities field.[15] There is ongoing institutional change related to digital humanities in universities – for example, some of these centres are undergoing change towards a more traditional departmental structure (often driven by concerns about the research excellence framework (REF) in the UK), so, for example the previous Centre for Computing in the Humanities (CCH) at King's College has become the Department of Digital Humanities at King's, which has subsequently divided into the King's Digital Lab and a separate department of digital humanities.

Indeed, the changing landscape of digital humanities means that the centre as the hub of digital humanities work may be shifting and practice is undergoing constant experimentation and change (see McCarty and Kirschenbaum 2003). But this is not evident everywhere, and in some institutions pockets of digital humanities work will continue to be done in fairly traditional subject area-led departments, such as in Schools of English. Sample argues that, in some sense, we might see a move from centres to 'camps' and that this, as a less institutionalized form of research practice, will encourage the seeking of affinities over affiliations, adding that: 'most of us working in the digital humanities will never have the opportunity to collaborate with a dedicated center or institute. We'll never have the chance to work with programmers who speak the language of the humanities as well as Perl, Python, or PHP. We'll never be able to turn to colleagues who routinely navigate grant applications and budget deadlines, who are paid to know about the latest digital tools and trends – but who'd know about them and share their knowledge even if they weren't paid a dime. We'll never have an institutional advocate on campus who can speak with a single voice to administrators, to students, to donors, to publishers, to communities about the value of the digital humanities' (Sample 2012). Indeed, this may well be true at an individual institutional level; however, at the level of higher education as a sector, it is clear that more formal institutional structures are emerging, together with subject-level groups, national subject associations and even proposed Learned Societies.

Nonetheless, it is certainly the case that change is underway for the digital humanities – even as some centres do indeed morph into departments, and some centres cease to exist, new ones continue to emerge that echo previous centre functions, or rethink them in interesting ways. As Friedlander has argued, 'centers offer interdisciplinary "third places" – a term sociologist Ray Oldenburg has used to identify a social space, distinct from home and workplace. Third places foster important ties and are critical to community life' (Friedlander, quoted in Fraistat 2012). Svennson (2010) offers a useful list of activities common to these groupings, which he adapts from Zorich (2008). Digital humanities centres (or similar research groupings) tend to help build digital collections as scholarly or teaching resources; create tools for authoring, building digital collections, analysing collections, data or research processes and managing the research process; use digital collections and analytical tools to generate new intellectual products; offer digital humanities training, lectures, programs, conferences or seminars on digital humanities topics; have their own academic appointments and staffing; provide collegial support for, and collaboration with, members of other academic departments at the home institution or other academic departments, organizations or projects outside the home institution; conduct research in humanities and humanities computing (such as digital scholarship and publication); create a zone of experimentation and innovation for humanists; serve as an information portal for a particular humanities discipline; serve as a repository for humanities-based digital collections; and provide technology assistance and advice to humanities departments.

Aspects of these activities show that physical space is a key consideration in developing and supporting new formative spaces around digital humanities. Whether through a research centre, institutional hub or the notion of a 'humanities lab', these spaces enable the concentration of technical and intellectual work to encourage experimentation, collaboration and the sharing of knowledge techniques for capacity-building around digital humanities, for both faculty and students. This doesn't mean to say that building these facilities is easy – it is important to take note of the 'difficulty of controlling and planning the spaces' (Svennson 2010) for digital humanities-type work. Digital humanities spaces and labs work best when they are multi-configurable and reusable, and encourage both research and social activities within their walls. An early commitment to a physical space by the university greatly assists the process of creating this 'third space' by granting both oversight and budget control to a unit that can focus energy and time on building capacity. Further, 'within the kind of "third place" typified by digital humanities centers, "technology is simultaneously a driver and an opportunity, and the centers, whether virtual or physical, effectively become safe places, hospitable to innovation and experimentation, as well as anchors from which to base the intellectual analog of civil society in which third places are vital parts'" (A. Friedlander, quoted in Fraistat 2012: 289). Another advantage where there is already an understanding of the relationship between theory and practice is that good technical facilities enable high-quality innovative theoretical and experimental digital humanities work to be undertaken.

Humanities laboratories or digital humanities centres are therefore exploratory laboratories that support new forms of research practice, whether in physical, digital or hybrid spaces (Svennson 2010). This can be in the form of a 'cultural laboratory' (Svennson 2010, quoted from Janlert and Jonsson 2000), a digital, controlled space – such as augmented reality, virtual world, real-time video conferencing space, etc. – and can also be used to facilitate and enhance cultural research work. Indeed, Svennson (2010) argues that 'participants in simulations could be humans or computer run entities [and] real-time interactive data can feed into digitally enhanced postdigital research spaces'. These new kinds of spaces enable, for example, data visualization techniques, which can offer 'a window to large data sets and possibilities to visualize or enact complex objects of analysis. Interactive tools can help the researcher to get an intuitive sense of objects of analysis and the model, and allow fast what-if analyses.' Moretti has argued that 'the solution for digital research is a lab attached to a department. That is to say with the department as its reference, but not exactly an organ of the department. The lab would have its own autonomy. It's clearly a precarious situation and honestly it would make sense to look to the sciences to see the ways in which a biology lab and the biology department function together. The way I see these labs is attached, but not co-extensive with the department – appendixes of the departments' (Moretti 2016). These ideas for fusing labs and departments are very suggestive and often productive if they are faculty-driven around shared research interests.

Labs also encourage experimentation with tools, methods, content, context and ideas, or what Ramsay has called an approach based on the 'hermeneutics of screwing around'. In other words, 'it's not a matter of replacing one with the other, as any librarian will tell you. It is rather to ask whether we are ready to accept surfing and stumbling – screwing around, broadly understood – as a research methodology' (Ramsay 2010). Indeed, Svennson further argues that 'on a more profound level, researcher interaction can change the models themselves, or their parameters, data and relations to allow the study of hypothetical correlations or comparison of outcomes from different models applied on the same object or situations. "Thick", qualitative models – of detailed environments, objects, processes and correlations, unstructured information – can be handled through use of technology, and complex qualitative correlations can be modeled by massive simulations' (Svennson 2010).

As previously mentioned, Ramsay calls on humanists to code (he refers to it as 'building'), and by this he gestures towards the programming and coding of software systems as part of a digital humanities project. In this book, we previously noted both the industrialization of knowledge that is a danger in digital humanities approaches that are not adequately critical, and the drive towards a permanent revolution in all forms of knowledge that the computational industries ceaselessly aim towards. That is, digital humanities has the potential to enable a reflexive approach to the question of its own representation (for example, the image, the imaginary and the imagined) and acknowledgement of the mass-produced temporal objects of the programming industries. This is important in thinking through the challenges computational culture poses for the shared research infrastructures, forms, and means of knowledge in society, and their mediation through algorithms and codes that construct new forms of reception and practices of reading for humanists as well as the general public. Indeed, in this chapter we acknowledge these issues but also place them in relation to critical questions of unbuilding software systems, offering critical interventions and standpoints on existing software structures through hacking, jamming and decoding already-extant infrastructures and logistics. Finally, we note that, like the humanities itself, the external funding environment is changing rapidly. Longer, larger grants from the research councils, large-scale collaborations in Europe and the US, and growing support for trans-disciplinary working from Science, Technology, Engineering and Mathematics (STEM) funders, all demand we move beyond the tradition of lone scholarship. This move to projects and teams causes us to rethink the technical and institutional support for producing work of the highest quality to build and rebuild humanities scholarship in the twenty-first century, so that it remains a critical field (see Boltanski and Chiapello 2005 for a discussion of projective models).

Nonetheless, the notion of research infrastructures has itself been contested, especially in relation to the large costs often involved in developing and maintaining them. As Anderson has noted, 'if research infrastructures are to contribute to the transformation of research then it is important that researchers working on histories, literature, culture and other aspects of what makes us human understand the value of these infrastructures for their own practices and how they operate to facilitate and to enhance the production of their research' (Anderson 2013: 7).

One of the ways we might start to think about this is to focus on the question of digital materiality, the actual stuff of digital research infrastructures. For example, software is increasingly constitutive of and increasingly constituting humanities work, archives, practices and publications. To think about this, we might first consider what software actually is. Software is often opposed to hardware. Hardware is the machine, the physical, tangible piece of technology, while software is the instructions that are written. Hardware is fixed, while the malleability of software is the fact that it can be changed – in fact, constant upgrading of software often becomes a chore. The distinction between physical hardware and ephemeral software blurs upon closer inspection, however – firstly, as code needs to be written in some kind of physical medium to exist at all. As the programmer types, the code is translated into an alphabet with only two characters, famously known as 0s and 1s.[16] The characters may be written in magnetized bits of iron in a hard drive, so the polarity of each magnetic part records a number or a letter, or as tiny bumps in a thin layer of polycarbonate plastic in a CD or DVD, or as electricity trapped inside tiny transistors in thumb drives and flash drives. Electricity and magnetism cannot be held in your hand, but anyone who has experienced an electric shock or seen a magnetic crane lift a car will know that both electricity and magnetism are very physical. Computer software is just as physical as a print book, although its materiality is different.

Of the three storage media considered above, the hard drive, the CD-ROM and the flash drive, only the CD is permanent, while the others can be wiped and rewritten, like chalk on a blackboard or pencil on paper. Since the beginning of writing, humans have used both ephemeral writing tools to support thought – such as the wax codex or the blackboard – and durable, fixed writing – such as stone and clay tablets – for accounting and legal and religious documents. Book culture (of which the academy is part) is mostly built upon permanent records, but in computers, software – writing that may be changed – is the norm.

So software seemingly has a physical presence, but it is present within hardware, as chalk is present on the blackboard. The computer's aluminium case holds many fixed parts: circuit boards printed in silicone, the flash drive, the battery, wires and a keyboard, not to mention all the parts needed for a high-resolution colour display. This is fixed when you buy a computer, and, while it is possible to replace some elements, it is becoming more difficult for each generation of machines, and most users never bother and throw old computers away. But to get all of these parts to function together, coded instructions are needed. There are algorithms that govern the performance of each of the constituent elements of the machine. Some of these are stored 'in hardware', for example by burning the 'zeroes' into the silicon of a PROM chip, but a large number of them are written in erasable forms of memory, and may be changed. It is a computer program, lines of code, that makes each transistor in a flash memory card trap electricity to store a 'one' or release it to store a 'zero'. Programmers call this *machine code*, which is what makes most of consumer electronics run, not to mention important parts of cars and aircraft. This middle state between hardware and software is regularly known as *firmware*. It is rarely changed, sometimes never, but most owners of computers and cell phones will upgrade firmware from time to time.

Much, if not most, of what programmers regularly regard as hardware thus appears to be software or firmware on closer inspection. And, conversely, when engineers create a new memory chip, they also program, by creating lines of code that will make the chip function as intended. This is where the field of software studies can contribute to a closer reading of these computational structures and widen and deepen digital humanities approaches to the understanding, and development, of research infrastructures and projects.

Software studies generally aims not to decide where the line between hardware and software *really* should be drawn, but rather to study and critique the outcomes of the many layers of code inside a computer. Any code relies on the performance of a set of processes that the code may invoke, and these processes are programmed on a lower level, all the way down to the smallest logical gates in a processor. The programmer only considers the possibilities, or affordances, of the language s/he is currently coding in, which we may call the *platform* of his/her code. The programmer will know the capabilities and limitations of the platform, and often of the lower-level platform that supports it, maybe even the platform below that.

Several scholars have used Gibson's term *affordances* to describe how technology has an influence on the final product. Gibson (1986) introduces the concept to explain human visual perception. We view our surroundings according to what can be done in them, as Gibson explains: 'if a surface is horizontal, flat, extended, rigid, and knee-high relative to a perceiver, it can in fact be sat upon. If it can be discriminated as having just these properties, it should look sit-on-able. If it does, the affordance is perceived visually. [. . .] an affordance is neither an objective property nor a subjective property; or it is both if you like. An affordance cuts across the dichotomy of subjective-objective and helps us to understand its inadequacy. It is equally a fact of the environment and a fact of behavior. It is both physical and psychical, yet neither. An affordance points both ways, to the environment and to the observer' (Gibson 1986: 128–9).

The notion of affordance was picked up and popularized by Donald Norman in *The Design of Everyday Things* (2002) in his descriptions of how we interact with various everyday technologies. What is important, Norman points out, is not what the technology can in fact do (or how it functions), but what the user thinks the technology can do. It is the 'perceived affordances' that matter, according to Norman (1999), critiquing those who leave human perception out, and use the concept of affordance to describe an attribute of a technology that persists also when no human is around to perceive it. Rex Hartson (2003) divides the concept of affordance into four types, related to how they support user paractice: (1) cognitive affordances, for cognitive actions such as learning or remembering; (2) physical affordances, for physical actions like clicking or moving; (3) sensory affordances, to assist in perception; and (4) functional affordances, to help users do what they intended. This assumes, of course, that the interface actually helps users accomplish what they intended, which is not always the case with the growth in behavioural programming, dark patterns and persuasive technologies. Indeed, Fuller has demonstrated that some of the most popular (in the meaning of 'widespread') interfaces have a greater range of functions than mere affordances. Fuller analyses Microsoft Word, and shows that the program's enormous range of features contains much more than what any user will ever need. Moreover, Fuller finds it difficult to determine what the program is actually for. It is made for writing, yes, but we write for so many reasons, and while Word supports many of them, there are some that obviously are made simpler, such as writing a formal letter, which is supported not only with ready-made sentences, but also with impressive letterheads. Other common uses are hardly supported at all, and while some esoteric uses, such as animated fonts, are possible for no obvious reason, other real-life uses have no support (Fuller's example is generative poetry, but also simple HTML coding is virtually impossible).

Microsoft Word is a useful example for highlighting another critical distinction, that between software, hardware and platform. 'Platform studies' is a movement mostly associated with the book series of the same name published by the MIT Press. In this series, a *platform* is defined as a system on which others can create new works. The first books in the series have been on game consoles, thus focusing on hardware rather than software. Software may also be platforms – think, for example, of Unity, a software creation suite, a file format, and a rendering and interaction engine for games. Unity allows authors to create 3D games (and other navigable spaces, such as Liestøl's SitSims) to be played back on mobile devices as well as computers. Understanding platforms like Unity is crucial if we want to understand how our contemporary culture evolves, as these are the media (or instruments) of our authors. Furthermore, Unity is a platform bridging other platforms (the devices), again demonstrating the perpetual layering of digital media.

The fluidity of software is often exemplified by showing that even Microsoft Word can act as a platform. It is a piece of software on which we can create other works, and while we are taught to think that it is made to create documents whose end state is ink on paper, we all increasingly read on screens, often in Word files read, commented and modified in the Word application – this is without mentioning the development of plug-ins, macros and automations. Platform studies is an important field in that it allows us to study hardware and software in combination, and shows the dividing line between hardware and software, platform and software, is fluid, and often dependent on the observer's perspective.

Software is collections of computer programs, chains of instructions the computer will perform in sequence, often at lightning speed, in order to manipulate *information* or *signs*. *Information* is the concept commonly used in computer science, while *signs* is used in semiotics. There are important theoretical differences between the two concepts, but these do not matter for our discussion here. A computer records, stores, manipulates, transmits and outputs to a user representations that are meaningful to a human observer. The digital is always about information, always about signs, and thus very often about human communication. Software is thus made up of procedures that can be used to manipulate signs to aid communication, memory or calculation and simulation. It is run by a machine that itself is made up of layers of procedures that may be rewritten. Software is instructions that are written (and can be rewritten) to regulate the flow of signs in a computer.

Chun (2011) and Manovich (2013) have also delved deep into the history of computing, looking for the ideologies that laid the foundation when digital computers were invented. Chun's starting point is that 'based on metaphor, software has become a metaphor for the mind, for culture, for ideology, for biology, and for the economy.' Chun wants to understand software better, and thus understand the metaphor better, and then turns to the early pioneers of computing. In detailed analysis, she maps how the concept of *software* changed from being anything in computing that wasn't hard wired, to a 'thing', an object that could be reused, sold and patented. She also shows in an intriguing analysis how computer programming was informed by contemporary ideas of how the brain worked, but the relationship was very quickly flipped, so software became a metaphor for how the mind functions. Manovich has similarly mapped the 'genealogy' of motion graphics from Alan Kay's early experiments to modern commercial software.

Knowing computer and software history is undoubtedly important, as it will shed light on how our current view of software is situated, and how other conceptualizations are possible. Chun's analysis (and, to a certain extent, Manovich's) runs the risk of being essentialist, however. Even if it is likely that a certain view of hardware, software and human memory was widespread in the 1940s, and even if the computers we have today in important ways are direct descendants of those systems, it does not follow that these views of computers and the human mind are still affecting our thoughts today. As Chun notes, following Lakoff and Johnson, to use a metaphor is to point out similarities between two separate objects. The two objects are not similar in all respects, however – that is much of the power of the metaphor as trope. When biologists or economists of today use software as a metaphor, they may very well have other similarities in mind than early computer pioneers had. Learning how developers thought during and immediately after World War II can only give a very limited insight into contemporary use of metaphor. To understand today's visions of computers and the rest of the world, we need to study contemporary use of language.

As the web is entering its third decade, more and more observe that it has a history that is worth studying, and it has become a research infra-structure in its own right. Unlike print, web sites can be very unstable as they are easily erased and replaced – in fact, they need to be kept available by running a web server 24/7. If the server's electric plug is pulled out, the site disappears. Indeed, as Anderson (2013: 19) observes, 'while use of the internet and web resources is relatively high, the awareness of the underlying computational mechanisms that act as the engine of engagement with digital information, digital resources, and computational processes is low'.

This is one of the areas of research around web archiving, which Brügger describes as 'any form of deliberate and purposive preserving of web material' (Brügger 2011). Libraries have kept books for centuries, and many national libraries now collect virtually all that is printed in the country. Collecting web sites in the same manner has proven difficult, however, for several reasons. The first issue is what and when to preserve. The web is dynamic, and any page may be changed at any time. Libraries keep newspapers every day, but news sites on the web add stories constantly, so when should the library save the site? In the morning? In the afternoon? At night? Every ten minutes? Add to this the fact that a modern web page is a melange of parts: although the main text may be stable and look the same each time it is opened, the commercials are likely to change as they are inserted by third parties, and will often be tailored to the user's browser history as captured by 'cookies' (small files stored in the user's computer). There will also often be links to stories on the front page, or panels with 'most emailed' or 'most shared' in the margins or at the bottom. Links to other stories may also be dynamically updated; readers who visit an old page on an earthquake may be served links to recent earthquake reports. Think then of stores like Amazon or music services like Spotify, which always recommend other books or songs to the users based on their previous history and the habits of others who have read or listened to the same. And we haven't even touched on social media sites like Facebook, where each user is served a unique, tailor-made flow of reports from other users. Many libraries automatically 'scrape' headlines and stories from thousands of sites at regular intervals, but commercials and other inserted elements are usually not kept. It is at any rate impossible to store the real experience of these texts. To preserve examples of the full experience, some libraries, such as the National Library of Denmark, have begun filming how popular sites look while a user reads it, to provide another perspective for future web historians.

Libraries' wish to preserve has also encountered the rights of privacy and protection of personal data. It is argued in many jurisdictions that personal web sites, blogs and social media are forms of private conversation, and not meant for the public, even if they are publicly available. Even when web sites dealing with sensitive personal informations, such as political opinion, religion, race or health issues, are written anonymously, the veil may be lifted if the information is coupled with other texts on the web. In Norway, written consent has been required for all harvesting of web sites, making it virtually impossible for the National Library to keep more than a fraction of the Norwegian Web space.

Even when harvesting and storage of web sites is unproblematic, there are forms of Web content that are difficult to store, such as audio and video streams, which is made impossible (or difficult) to record in order to protect the authors' intellectual property rights and avoid piracy. Other files may be downloaded and stored, but may be difficult to play back. As software formats become outdated, the necessary rendering software is not updated to new systems. It is now very difficult to play back VR files in the VRML format, or audio in the once-dominating Real Audio format. Other formats are changed and not made backwards compatible: old QuickTime films will not play back on modern computers. Adobe's Flash format, which in 2010 was the basis of millions of commercial web sites, seemed in 2015 to be doomed, rendered obsolete by HTML5 and Apple's decision not to allow Flash on their mobile devices. If historians a few decades from now are without Flash players in their computer systems, they will not be able to see how the fashion and music industries portrayed themselves on the web in the first decade of the third millennium.

Another question is the extent to which libraries are able to get data back out of the system in a form that is meaningful to human eyes. While the Internet Archive's WayBack Machine is a success in many ways, other libraries have yet to implement similar interfaces. In 2010, the US Twitter signed over its entire archive of tweets as a gift to the Library of Congress to make it available to researchers. In 2015, the archive was still not available to anyone (Scola 2015).

The problem of Flash is the latest concern in a much larger problem for computer historians. Katherine Hayles has called this the 'new dark ages', and warned that there may be no tangible evidence of the first fifty years of computing, as both the computer systems and their storage media are becoming obsolete. Within media and arts, the era of LaserDiscs is virtually lost for scholars: the discs are deteriorating, and there are very few working playback systems left. The products of the CD-ROM era, however popular in the early to mid-1990s, are facing the same problem. To play back one of Voyager's popular 'Expanded books', such as Robert Winter's successful disc *Beethoven's Ninth* (1994), one needs a vintage computer system, kept in the state of *c.* 1995, and with internal batteries replaced. Only a few libraries in the world keep such systems alive. It is the constant sorrow for teachers of Digital Literature that the founding classics of literary hypertext, such as *Afternoon* (Joyce 1990), *Victory Garden* (Moulthrop 1991) or *Patchwork Girl* (Jackson 1995), no longer can be read by their students. The files themselves are copyrighted and the property of the publisher Eastgate, but no rendering software exists for modern computers as of 2015. The Pathfinder project by Stuart Moulthrop and Nancy Kaplan aims to keep digital artworks from becoming lost to future scholars, by filming the authors while they read their digital works on a computer screen, and explain how the works are constructed and how they came into being. Similarly, the National Library of Denmark has, in addition to scraping web sites and storing them, begun filming gamers as they play computer games or navigate in 3D environments such as *Second Life*.

Conservation of digital works is also the concern of the Electronic Literature Organization, which in 2004 issued a set of guidelines titled 'Acid-free bits' (Montfort and Wardrip-Fruin 2004), recommending that authors use open formats (such as XML), and preserve source code, plans, original media files and descriptions of the works' construction. At the organization's 2015 conference, Leonardo Flores presented plans for a central repository for digital literature.

As repositories of web sites store many versions of each page, and these pages may easily be captured as 'screen shots' and inserted into a video editing program, a new form of academic practice has emerged, which Rogers

(2013) calls a *screencast documentary*. A screencast documentary is a short film consisting of screenshots, much like time-lapse photography of a web site over time. One of the first was Jon Udell's documentary of Wikipedia's article on 'the Heävy Mëtal Ümlaut' (Udell 2005), which showed graphically how an article that began as a joking aside grew into a scholarly article in the encyclopaedia genre. Since then, similar videos have been made of Google's development (Rogers et al. 2008). The importance of time-lapse films of web pages should not be understated. They are early examples of born-digital scholarly genres for disseminating the results of research on born-digital material. It is a format that is extremely effective in showing the results of long research, making the changes visible to the audience's eyes in ways other media just cannot, and something that current iterations of research infrastructures do not support.

One of the most interesting new territories opened up by digital humanities is the ability to take on much larger projects. Indeed, it could be argued that scale is an important new horizon of intellectual inquiry for the humanities. This raises deep questions about the kinds of methods and approaches foregrounded in the humanities, as it is a complex process to design and implement digital methods for scaling up the work that humanities might undertake. 'Big Data' projects in natural and social sciences are far from trivial: the enormous rise in computing power allows researchers to perform much more complex computations with far larger amounts of data. Careful consideration of methods and algorithms is required to reach a reliable conclusion. A tiny error or imprecision may become large when calculating with large numbers. Yet the sciences were already using quantitative methods throughout their discipline, so turning to Big Data is more a difference in scale than a difference in kind. Humanists are less used to dealing with numbers, big or small. Statistics have not been a staple in disciplines concerned with interpretation and meaning, but creative uses of large data sets show the way to a Big Data digital humanities.

First, numbers may be used to interpret culture. Musicologists at the University of Oslo have studied the use statistics of the music streaming service Wimp (now acquired by Tidal) over several years. Analysis of the patterns in the many millions of music streams has given unique insight into today's musical culture. By comparing playback to revenue streams, the research team has also been able to argue that a different and more egalitarian way of dividing the income would be possible. If adopted, this scheme could have significant impact for small and upcoming acts.

Computational linguistics also demonstrates that humanists do not need to deal with indirect measures of culture; it is possible to study frequencies and patterns in the actual humanist corpora and collections. The digital revolution in linguistics may be an inspiration for many other fields. One possible application, suggested by many, is style history in art, music or literature. Without computers, there is a limit to how many works a researcher will be able to study in a lifetime. By delegating the reading to computers, it is possible to find patterns of tonality, composition or thematics in much larger collections of historical works. Instead of discussing dozens of novels from a decade, one can discuss thousands.

To delegate interpretation to computers seems more distant, and, for most humanist scholars, also much more painful and problematic. Nuanced, careful interpretation and close reading is, after all, at the very core of most scholarly disciplines. But even if the humans are doing the actual interpretation, the access to much larger data provided by computers may be of great importance. We should remember here that the pioneer Busa himself argued that, in order really to interpret what a writer has meant, one needs to study his use of language in its totality. Only when considering each concept in its context and in relation to other concepts can one reach a reliable interpretation (Busa 1980). Indeed, it requires careful design, thought and both practical and theoretical reasoning to develop a new interpretative paradigm for thinking about these issues. At these larger dimensions, scale is no longer a process of ad hoc improvisation in relation to both the technical and the work-flow characteristics of humanities work. Scaling up the projective nature of humanities research itself, together with rethinking the corpora that make up the initial data set for a specific project, is needed. This requires that the old approach, still often maintained, which sees computers as being good at counting and mechanically recognizing patterns, and humans as able to profit from intuition, creativity and serendipity, is rethought. A new interpretative paradigm around digital humanities constitutes new kinds of hybridity in research activities, in which interpretation and creativity are distributed both throughout the project, with programmers and humanists being seen as creative and interpretative elements, and between different agencies, such as minds, code, algorithms and systems.

As we increasingly find that the world of computational abundance is normalized, the application of cheap digital technologies to manage or partially augment traditionally analogue experiences, technologies and practices will doubtless grow. That is, the power of compute is growing in both breadth and depth as it permeates society and culture (see Davies 2013). We are increasingly surrounded by new fields and flows of computation that co-construct and stabilize a new artifice for the human sensorium – streams, clouds, sensors and infrastructures. Not unlike previous moments in which media become part of everyday life, this new field is noticeable for its ability to modulate and transform itself through the use of algorithms and code – not just as a general plasticity but as a flexible structure that adapts to context and environment tailored to the individual – or, perhaps better, dividual – of the computational age. This new field of computation is not necessarily top-down and corporate-controlled either. Thus, we see, at a bottom-up level, the emergence of a market in cheap digital processors that enable the implementation of innovative new forms of culture and cultural experimentation – moments of part of the constellation we see as 'postdigital' (Berry and Dieter 2015).

Thus, as the historical distinction between the digital and the non-digital becomes increasingly blurred, to talk about the digital presupposes a conjunction in undertaking research that research infrastructures, and the design of these systems, have to take into account. And so, computation becomes spatial in its implementation, embedded within the environment and part of the texture of life itself which can be walked around, touched, manipulated and interacted with in a number of ways and means – research becomes mediated in and through the computal (Berry 2014). Indeed, in a similar way to how the distinction between 'being online' and 'being offline' has become anachronistic, with our always-on smartphones and tablets and widespread wireless networking technologies, so too, perhaps, the notion of a strong separation between physical and digital infrastructures needs to be reconsidered.

Today, the condition of possibility for the implementation of research infrastructures is increasingly linked to what we want to call compute, understood as an abstract quantity of computation. Compute as a concept exists in two senses: as the potential contained in a computational system, or infrastructure; and in the actuation of that potential in actual work, as such. Whilst always already a theoretical limit, compute is also the material that may be brought to bear on a particular computational problem – and now many problems are indeed computational problems, to the extent that the theoretical question posed by compute is directly relevant to the study of software, algorithms and code, and therefore the contemporary condition in computal society, because it represents the moment of potential in the transformation of inert materials into working systems. It is literally the computational unit of 'energy' that is supplied to power the algorithms of the world's systems. Compute then, is a notion of abstract computation, but it is also the condition of possibility for and the potential actuation of that reserve power of computation in a particular task. Compute becomes a key noetic means of thinking through the distribution of computation in the technological imaginary of computal society and a foundational concept for digital infrastructures.

In a highly distributed computational environment, such as we live in today, compute is itself distributed around society, carried in pockets, accessible through networks and wireless connections and pooled in huge computational clouds. Compute then is not only abstract but lived and enacted in everyday life – it is part of the texture of life, not just as a layer upon life but as a structural possibility for and mediation of such living. But, crucially, compute is also an invisible factor in society, partially due to the obfuscation of the technical condition of the production of compute, but also due to the necessity for an interface, a surface, with which to interact with compute.

In this sense, compute is the structural condition of possibility that makes the milieu possible by giving it place, in as much as it creates those frameworks within which technicity takes place. The question of compute then, both as a theoretical concept and as a technical definition, is crucial for thinking through the challenge of computation more broadly. But, in a rapidly moving world of growing computational power, comparative analysis of computational change is made difficult without a metric by which to compare different moments historically. This is made much more difficult by the reality that compute is not simply the speed and bandwidth of a processor as such, but includes a number of other related technical considerations such as the speed of the underlying motherboard, ram, graphics processor(s), storage system and so forth.

Compute then is a relative concept and needs to be thought about in relation to previous iterations, and this is where benchmarking has become an important part of the assessment of compute – for example, SPECint, a computer benchmark specification for a processor's integer processing power maintained by the Standard Performance Evaluation Corporation (SPEC 2014). Another, called GeekBench (2013), scores compute against a baseline score of 2,500, which is the score of an Intel Core i5–2520M @ 2.50 GHz. In contrast, SYSmark 2007, another benchmark, attempts to bring 'real world' applications into the processing measurement by including a number of ideal systems that run canned processing tasks (SYSmark 2007). As can be seen, comparing compute becomes a spectrum of benchmarks that test a variety of working definitions of forms of processing capacity. It is also unsurprising that as a result many manufacturers create custom modes within their hardware to 'game' these benchmarks and unfortunately obfuscate these definitions and comparators. For example, Samsung created a special 'white list' for Exynos 5–based Galaxy S4 phones which allows some of the most popular benchmarking apps to shift into a high-performance mode not available to most normal applications. These apps run the GPU at 532MHz, while other apps cannot exceed 480MH (Schwartz 2013).

As Kirschenbaum and Werner argue, 'a variety of scholars, theorists, and media arts practitioners now recognize that computers – by which we mean not only the tangible hardware, but also software and even the very algorithmic processes of computation – are material phenomena' (2014: 425). So, on a material register, the unit of compute can be thought of as roughly the maximum potential processing capacity of a computer processing chip running for a notional hour. In today's softwarized landscape, of course, processing power itself has become a service, and hence is more often framed in terms of virtual machines (VMs), rather than actual physical machines – a number of compute instances can be realized on a single physical processor using sophisticated software to manage the illusion. Amazon itself defines compute through an abstraction of actual processing, arguing, 'transitioning to a utility computing model fundamentally changes how developers have been trained to think about CPU resources. Instead of purchasing or leasing a particular processor to use for several months or years, you are renting capacity by the hour. Because Amazon EC2 is built on commodity hardware, over time there may be several different types of physical hardware underlying EC2 instances. [Amazon's] goal is to provide a consistent amount of CPU capacity no matter what the actual underlying hardware' (Amazon 2013).

Indeed, Amazon tends to discuss compute in relation to its unit of EC2 Compute Unit (ECU) to enable the discretization.[17] Google also uses an abstract quantity and measures 'minute-level increments' of computational time (Google 2013). The key is to begin thinking about how an instance provides a predictable amount of dedicated compute capacity and, as such, is a temporal measure of computational power, albeit seemingly defined rather loosely in the technical documentation.

The question of compute is then a question of the origin of computation more generally, but also of how the infrastructure of computation can be understood both qualitatively and quantitatively. Indeed, it is clear that the quantitative changes that greater compute capacity introduces make possible the qualitative experience of computation that we increasingly take for granted in our use of a heavily software-textured world. To talk about software, processes, algorithms and code is then deficient without a corresponding understanding of the capacity of compute in relation to them, and is a key issue for thinking about the conditions of possibility that computation make available for our lives today.

We now turn to how these research infrastructures, archives and encoded materials are used by thinking about the specific methods and approaches that may be applied to them. These, following general usage in the digital humanities, we are calling 'digital methods', but in addition we include a wide variety of techniques that are also hybrid in application.

6   Digital Methods and Tools

To be working within the field of humanities computing is already to be cognisant of the need to 'build' digital systems, to encode, and to be involved in a practice of a highly technical nature. Schreibman, Siemans and Unsworth explain that 'there is a clear and direct relationship between the interpretative strategies that humanists employ and the tools that facilitate exploration of original artifacts based on those interpretative strategies; or, more simply put, those working in the digital humanities have long held the view that application is as important as theory' (Schreibman et al. 2004: xxv).

This argument that digital humanities is oriented towards building rather than theory raises its own dangers for the field, however. Indeed, Galloway asks, 'is it the role of [digital] humanities researchers to redesign their discipline so that it is symmetrical with that [digital] infrastructure?' (Galloway 2014: 126). But the building of tools and systems highlights at a higher level that knowledge representation remains a fundamental problematic for digital humanities. This question becomes more pressing when we see that the Silicon Valley approaches and methods of using quantitative computational methods for creating new experiences and lifestyles have become strongly associated with the practices of humanities computing – e.g. Big Data. Nonetheless, there is a distinction between digital humanities and computer science. Humanities computing was what we might call applied computing, which was not about the research focus of computer science but rather with how humanities research questions might be answered through the application of computational technology. In the development of its early practices around encoding, archives and tools, digital humanities has provided foundational concepts and ideas which still inform the field, and which continue to draw from computer science, information and library studies, with far less attention to insights that might be drawn from media and communication, cultural studies, new media and other cognate disciplines.[1]

Consequently, digital humanities has a tendency towards scientistic notions of technology which owe more to engineering and computer science than to the humanities. This manifests itself in more mechanistic concerns with the construction of digital systems, and therefore towards what we might call explanation, rather than understanding, of technology. This, we think, in some senses explains the interest in digital humanities, in increasing quantification and discretization of the humanities, and the fetishization of large quantities of data as a result of these techniques. It also explains the warm welcome that the practices around Big Data have received in the digital humanities so far.

It is important to note that here we argue that this points to a need for a constellation of approaches within the digital humanities, informing both critical, methodological and empirical approaches that bring together different modularities of disciplinary expertise. Digital humanities is not, and should not be understood as, a one-size-fits-all discipline. So, by bringing together expertise from digital humanities and other disciplinary areas, interdisciplinary projects can address these major changes and offer cross-disciplinary perspectives and ideas in terms of the wider questions around culture and society – that is, both understanding culture, but also understanding culture that is produced, mediated, disseminated and controlled through digital technologies.

If we take seriously the question of *understanding* computational culture and technology, digital humanities is uniquely positioned to question how digital technologies structure, change and mediate humanities work more generally. Indeed, we are led to explore how computation itself is linked to a wider political economic context, which computation attempts to disassociate itself from in order to appear neutral and apolitical in relation to it.[2] This is a more general question of the deterritorializing power of computation, and its reterritorialization. But it is also a question of the wider social and political structures that make computation possible and inform its imaginaries, and how these are made possible by a political economy that not only funds and drives these digital systems, but actively encourages the more instrumental tendencies of the technologies. Indeed, 'the tendency for solutions to be cast in a technical register with software being the catalyst for change or resolution is also a striking feature in the growing computationalism of our societies' (Berry 2014: 24). It is also something that digital humanists can actively contribute to as a form of critique and as a thoughtful contribution to ensuring that critical, intellectual and hermeneutic specificities are defended, as well as being augmented, through new research infrastructures.

Now we want to turn to the question of digital methods in the digital humanities in order to highlight the importance of a deep understanding, rather than mere explanation – that is, to how these technologies operate to structure the world around them and in doing so transform humanities knowledge and practice. Boonstra, Breure and Doorn (2004: 22) describe the life cycle of information as creation, enrichment, editing, retrieval, analysis and presentation. These can be useful ways of classifying the various digital interventions that take place in digital humanities at different stages of a project or funding life cycle. They are also helpful for identifying the applicability of particular research projects or grant proposals within a larger digital humanities programme. They identify durability, usability and modelling as shared concerns across the life cycle. 'Durability' refers to the guarantee of long-term deployment of the produced digital information, 'usability' refers to the ease of use, efficiency and satisfaction experienced by the intended audience using the information produced. Finally, modelling refers in a broader sense to the more general modelling of research processes and historical information systems (see Boonstra et al. 2004: 22). It is notable that all of these life-cycle stages, together with the crosscutting concerns, raise opportunities for specifically critical interventions – for example, one might ask: 'usability' in what sense, for whom, under which conditions, who pays for it and what is the subject position that is privileged in this reading?

Indeed, this can sometimes be associated with a claim that theory is implicit in the building of computational structures, and therefore no longer theory in its own right separate from the building of computational systems (see Koh 2014: 99). Revealingly, in an interview in the *New York Times*, Scheinfeldt somewhat problematically argued that 'academia has moved into "a post-theoretical age". Thus we enter what he calls a "methodological moment", which he claims "is similar to the late 19th and early 20th centuries, when scholars were preoccupied with collating and cataloging the flood of information brought about by revolutions in communication, transportation and science". The practical issues of discipline building, of assembling an annotated bibliography, of defining the research agenda and what it means to be a historian "were the main work of a great number of scholars"' (Scheinfeldt, quoted in Cohen 2010). We might note that the claim that we have entered a post-theoretical age is itself a theoretical claim, but it also strangely echoes claims made by companies in Silicon Valley who argue that Big Data is sufficient in and of itself. Indeed, it appears to agree with Chris Andersen's argument that we no longer need theory, as the data will somehow be enough. This similarly should give us pause and indicate strongly that with a lack of critical reflexive foundation any discipline becomes a research and development department of industry, not a great future for the digital humanities.

Some of the key techniques that are deployed in the digital humanities but that also importantly raise questions for epistemology in relation to knowledge production and analysis are listed below. These can be grouped into approaches which include: distant reading (Moretti), short-form humanities+ (Liu), cultural analytics (Manovich) or digital methods (Rogers). There is also a scientist turn towards neuroscience (Hayles) or engineering (Ramsay) for epistemological or methodological innovation. They also produce outputs for the visual exploration of data, which can take many forms, for instance these examples drawn from Boonstra et al. (2004): Lifelines, The Lexis pencil, calendar view, concentric circles, visual analysis of texts, historical GIS, etc. For example, a technique we might think about using is *exploratory data analysis and data mining*, where data mining is a general term for a variety of techniques that are meant to gain insight into a data set. If the techniques employed are based on statistical formulas, data mining is often called 'exploratory data analysis'. Most often, its goal is to uncover the underlying structure of the data set, but it may also have the purpose of finding out what variables are the most important ones, or what cases are connected to each other, or what cases are the outliers in the data set. The way to present results from exploratory data analysis can take many forms, but often some complementary data visualization is used (Boonstra et al. 2004). Or we might consider using *cluster analysis* which seeks to identify homogeneous subgroups of cases in a population – that is, 'cluster analysis seeks to identify a set of groups in which within-group variation is minimised and between-group variation is maximised'. There are many different techniques for undertaking a cluster analysis, but many of them are hierarchical in structure (Boonstra et al. 2004). Alternatively, we can use *computer simulations* to help to evaluate behaviour within a 'specifically defined system, establish models and criteria, develop and analyse strategy, predict outcome, determine probability, and identify relational patterns'. In this case, a model is the starting point of simulation, and a 'correct operationalization of all variables and links between variables' in the model is a key requirement for satisfactory analysis. When the model has been established, a series of simulation runs can be performed to test various scenarios. During these runs, various computational techniques can be applied and tweaked to perform 'what-if' processing (Boonstra et al. 2004). Finally, we might consider using *content analysis*, which also dates back to the 1960s, when the 'famous Harvard program *The General Inquirer* was deployed in automatic analysis of political documents, folk tales and private correspondence, revealing secrets that could not be caught by the naked eye'. In this case, stylometry and content analysis can provide additional structure by adding a connection between text parts and a conceptual level (e.g. a list of topics, events or authors). Once established, these links can be used within a search and retrieval process or through experimentation in the search for new patterns (Boonstra et al. 2004).

The term 'digital methods' describes similar approaches that use digital tools to study both 'born digital' and traditional humanities texts. As we today live digital lives, most of the texts and images we create and consume are mediated through computers and digital cameras, and edited, distributed and presented to us on digital screens. In two decades, we have left behind an enormous quantity of writing and imagery, much of which is now available on the internet. Richard Rogers (2013) has concentrated on methods to approach specifically digital texts and has examined the data mining and large-scale processing techniques of companies such as Google, to develop a set of digital methods to contribute towards social science research. Indeed, Google established itself originally as the leading search engine by using algorithms that calculate statistics on links between web pages. Since then, the company has expanded out to a myriad of other services, all based on studying the actual behaviour of users (Levy 2011; Zuboff 2016).

In some ways, the phrase *digital methods* is misleading. In most sciences, a method is a procedure for sampling and registering data, and for analysing them with statistics. For most 'digital methods', the sampling procedure, the registering or the statistics are not unique to the digital realm. What is different is that the data tend to be born digital, collected from computer networks or digitized from archives and collections. Rogers (2013) describes studies in which data are collected from Google, Twitter and the Internet Archive, most often through their public APIs. We will, in the following, broaden the discussion somewhat, and include such major efforts towards understanding the born-digital humanities as software studies and web history. The demarcation line we will be using in understanding these approaches in this book is between collections of digitized objects and the 'born digital'. However, it is important to remember this comes with crucial caveats, namely that this division is artificial and introduced to help explain and understand the methodological issues involved in particular approaches. It is also important to remember that the broad overview of methods we introduce in this chapter can only be an example of the wide variety of approaches we find in the field. Indeed, there are many excellent resources available on the web and in printed format that can help gather a deeper understanding of the range and variety of approaches (see Deegan and Sutherland 2009; Rogers 2013; Arthur and Bode 2014).

Digital objects introduce a different challenge from that of analogue works. We may first consider the fact that a digital object exists in a certain file format, which in the last instance uses numbers to represent an object that to humans is presented in words, images, sound, or a combination thereof. It will often be necessary for a scholar to understand how this representation is done – that is, what file format is used and how it is constituted.

Different file formats limit and enable how the work can be studied with digital tools. Furthermore, software is necessary to view (or listen to) these files. The algorithms of this software will further limit and enable the scholar's work. For example, as Kirschenbaum has pointed out (1998), Photoshop's histogram representations are as accurate a rendition of a digital image file as the regular view, but they carry quite different meaning potential for the human viewer.

It is important to keep in mind that much digital humanities technical work is bespoke in terms of the implementation of the system. Whilst there have been attempts to create platforms as a form of research infrastructure in digital humanities, these have largely failed due to over-ambitious plans, lack of funding, a perceived lack of interest in the wider digital humanities field or technical problems. This has led to a growing realization that standards and protocols may be the best way of achieving some sense of interoperability or reuse in the humanities. This can be seen in the growing use of APIs to access underlying data, and of linked data as a means of aggregating and recombining data from different sources and databases.

Rogers usefully outlines three principles for digital methods. The first is to use 'methods embedded in online devices' – that is, to use for scholarly purposes the same techniques and methods that are used by major web commercial services (Rogers 2013: 29). His second principle is to devise algorithms to combine available digital data for research purposes. The third is to 'build upon the existing, dominant devices themselves, and with them perform a cultural or societal diagnostics'. His aim is, as often as possible, to ground research results solely in online data. As most social scientists studying internet users have found, 'cyberspace' is not a distinct sphere, but is increasingly postdigital, with a range of communication tools whereby people continue the communication and actions they do outside computer networks (see Berry and Dieter 2015). The traces left in digital networks are not distinct from wider society, but data that may be interpreted to learn about society as a whole. Indeed, internet data are just as valuable for humanities and social sciences as other knowledge forms. A main difference, however, is that the services 'embedded in digital tools' are not often in the right form for research, and their data, while rich, are often not directly suited to answering a researcher's questions.

Rogers lists an impressive range of projects built on top of existing services, such as Google's Search, Technorati's blog register, Internet Archive's Wayback Machine, Twitter's lists of tweets, and Facebook's lists of user interests. His procedure seems to be, first, to scan the services (and their APIs) for their capabilities, and then to search creatively for ways to use the capabilities for research purposes. Where common statistical methods dictate that you begin with a research question (and a hypothesis), and then decide on the method, Rogers reverses these so that when 'studying a web device, building a new tool, or making an interface on top of an existing one, the task is to list the elements at one's disposal, e.g., tweets, retweets, hashtags, usernames, user locations, shortened URLs, @replies, etc. (for Twitter, the microblogging platform). How may the digital objects be combined and recombined in ways that are useful not so much for searching Twitter but rather for social and cultural research questions?' (Rogers 2013).

Rogers claims that the effectiveness of Google's PageRank mechanism, whereby search queries are ordered so those sites that most other sites link to are presented as the most relevant results, led to a changed view of the web: both web designers and web researchers realized that web links may be viewed as a currency of authority. In web sites, it is now common to find links to those articles that are most shared, e-mailed or blogged by other readers, while researchers have utilized network analysis with good results.

Consequently, a large number of digital methods studies of the web are in the form of link analysis. Large collections of web sites are crawled (a procedure where a computer program begins with a web site, scans all its links, and then copies all the pages that the links lead to, and repeats the process for every page), and the links are analysed using network theory or 'small worlds theory'. Studies have found networks of bloggers confirming the idea of 'A-list' and 'B-list' bloggers, showing that aspirational blogs have links to the most popular blogs, while the popular blogs generally do not link back. Such studies, often using graphical visualizations in the form of maps of sites and links, can also show which sites are core to a topic, and which are peripheral. these kinds of studies have also found that the idea of the web as a public (debate) sphere, where anyone may join the discussion, is an inaccurate description of the majority of communicational practices one actually observes on this medium. Instead, researchers have found issue networks, where sites proclaiming similar views and opinions on a topic tend to link to each other, while links between camps holding different opinions on a topic are few and far between, just as there are few concrete examples of fora where opponents actively debate in good faith – this is often understood as a form of filter bubble.

In *The Language of New Media*, Lev Manovich wrote that, as software is found everywhere in media and society, we need a new discipline, a *software studies* (Manovich 2001), an idea later taken up by several other scholars and revisited by Manovich (Fuller 2008; Chun 2011; Bucher 2012; Manovich 2013). Software studies engages critically with any level or layer of software, but the focus has tended towards the 'high end', the highest level of abstraction and often that closest to the user interface. Following

Manovich's insight that software lays the premises for modern text (and image) production, several scholars have begun to study how the interface and functions of authoring software both enable and constrain what is being created. For example, as previously mentioned, Fuller (2001) has analysed how Microsoft Word and Photoshop both enable and constrain what is written or how images are edited, while Fagerjord has analysed the available templates in popular blog and video-editing software, arguing that it contains *prescripts*, pre-written instructions on how the final product should be (Fagerjord 2005b).

It is obviously important to understand and critique the affordances and limitations of the software we use to communicate and create knowledge and art, which Manovich (Manovich 2001) called *cultural interfaces*. Fuller goes further, however, pointing out both that it is possible (and, we would add, necessary) to map the underlying ideology beneath these kinds of software, and, interestingly, that there can be no single ideology determining Microsoft's bloated word-processor, which he calls an *amalgam*.

A core interest for software studies is to investigate how software forms contemporary culture by regulating what we see, hear and read. Amazon's recommender systems channel what we read, Spotify's 'related music' lists influence what music we hear, and Facebook's News Feed is part of our current sense of what goes on in the world. These lists are not edited by humans, but automatically made by algorithms based on each user's earlier use history, and the histories of others with similar consumption. Important as they are, these algorithms are also kept proprietary and therefore secret. Some of these systems, e.g., Amazon, can be studied via their APIs as described above, but often the researcher will have to retort to reverse engineering, trying to test out what input results in what output and then deduce how the system is made (see, for example, Berry et al. 2015). It would be a serious undertaking to understand and explain the details in modern recommender systems and social media algorithms, but it has been demonstrated that some important patterns may be learned. For example, Bucher (2012) has shown that in Facebook's News Feed, in order to be visible to others, users need to be actively contributing and sharing data. Users can be encouraged to adapt their behaviour through algorithmic nudges (see Berry 2011, 2014). Modern digital culture can be said to be 'programmed' by algorithms, both in terms of the mediation of creation, distribution and consumption but also in the shaping of behaviour of the users.

The technical questions mean there is a great deal of highly computational expertise, which can be contributed from the digital humanities, and which can provide an important foundation for its development as a field, linking both concerns with computation and more humanistic questions.

However, digital humanities tends to articulate its fears within the general rubric of tools and archives and how they are used and might be built (see Gold 2012). There is little connection with more general social and political questions within digital humanities, or, as Alan Liu has termed it, with cultural critique (see Liu 2012).

This way of organizing knowledge through ontologies and shards of data stored in databases and networks is in sharp contrast to the way in which knowledge tended to be organized in the nineteenth century and much of the twentieth, when narrative was a basic conceptual schema used to convey knowledge of many forms. Not only art, but also the popular forms of entertainment, used stories. It is not a coincidence that narratology, the study of narratives, evolved in the 1960s (Genette 1980; Todorov 1990; Barthes 1994), a time when all aspects of (capitalist or bourgeois) society were criticized. Narrative critique became an approach to understanding common culture and today the common culture is digital.

Manovich (2001) has argued that 'new' (digital) media have in common that they rely on databases, and the database is a cultural form that is in opposition to the narrative. Hayles (2005), in contrast, finds that Manovich's concept of database is too wide, and conflates database with data. She argues instead that it is the combinatorial possibilities, the 'possibility space', that challenges the narrative as the postdigital culture's dominant form. Across popular culture, it seems that both alternatives are widespread: databases are everywhere, especially in popular culture and art (and even narratives such as television and films are increasingly accessed from databases), while computer games, with their combinatoric simulations and quests, have long surpassed Hollywood's film industry in yearly turnover, and will for future historians be seen as the major cultural form of our current era. Also, the social media that have spurred the participatory revolution in the media are constructed from databases, and once registered in these, the 'productive users' are continually monitored and registered in other databases, mined for commercial purposes. It is understandably the case that not just for digital humanities, but also for humanities as a whole, understanding database logic will be increasingly important to understanding modern culture.

Digital collections have grown immensely over the decades, and it is not uncommon nowadays for the numbers of items in them to run into the millions. Large collections of high-definition images, sound and video may now also be treated computationally (see Manovich et al. 2014, Tifentale and Manovich 2015, for examples). This poses methodological challenges both for storage and retrieval of data, and for organizing and search facilities. At the same time, really large collections also open up the possibility of the analysis of extremely large data sets. 'Big Data' is currently a rally-ing cry in many of the sciences – as computers have become so powerful and quick, they can compute enormous amounts of data, such as complex meteorological data from millions of observation points, or the movements of millions of galaxies captured in real-time with different kinds of space instruments, or compute an individual's genome in just a few hours, while the first genome took ten years. Humanities researchers also compute con-siderably larger amounts of data than a decade ago – the most impressive scale is probably Google Books, which reportedly exceeded 25 million digi-tized books in 2015 (Heyman 2015).

Although Google Books appears to have largely given up its initial ambi-tion of making all printed books available to humanity, it still provides some access to the corpus via such services as the Ngram Viewer, which returns the frequency per publication year of any word. Pechenick et al. (2015) have, however, shown that Google Ngram Viewer has limited research value as the corpus is unweighted, and details of it are not known. Their analysis suggests that there is an overrepresentation of research lit-erature in the corpus, especially for the last 100 years. But libraries and scholarly collections are also increasingly being opened for study by outside researchers and the general public. The next phase in digital methods will be to combine such collections so analyses can be performed across many archives or corpora, which is precisely the approach that is used for many Big Data projects in medicine, biology and economics. A challenge is that collections have different formats and metadata, however. A recurring issue in digital methods is the need for standardized data models and the oppor-tunity of using linked data (an issue we touched on in chapter 4). Looking for possibilities of combining registers, and understanding the requirements of fields and metadata if a database is to be combined with another, is part of computational methods for the humanities.

Large collections open new possibilities for research, but also come with challenges. Working on such a large scale makes many established meth-ods impossible to use, as suggested by Manovich et al. (2012). Big Data requires a different kind of thinking and a different approach to analysis, and humanists need to turn to statistical methods created to cope with large numbers. Cross-disciplinary approaches are called for, as in earlier phases in the history of digital humanities. As we have shown examples of in chapter 2, there has always been healthy transfer of knowledge and methods between computer scientists (and researchers from other quantitative dis-ciplines, such as statistics) and humanists when building up new projects. The current leap in data power requires new alliances, however. Technical architecture is a first necessary hurdle to pass. The relational databases that traditionally have been used (see chapter 4) can be too slow for analysing really large data sets. Networks of parallel computers are required – what is called 'massively parallel software'. This is outside the scope of many digital humanities methods, both in competence, and, perhaps more importantly, in facilities and budgets. Large investments are necessary if the potential of Big Data is to be realized. To secure such gains, digital humanists need to learn the kind of methods required to design competitive research projects of massive scale, through thinking in terms of research infrastructures for the next century.

Computing large data sets makes it possible to approach much larger research problems, such as Moretti's initial distant reading challenge (2013): 'What does it mean, studying world literature? How do we do it? . . . the ambition is now directly proportional to the distance from the text: the more ambitious the project, the greater the distance must be'. The commonplace observation that there is never time for one person to read all books out there leads to a solution of delegation: the historian must delegate the reading to others. In his early work, Moretti delegates to other 'counting' historians, but later he delegates to the digital computer. What is often overlooked is his next insight on 'distant reading': that 'it allows you to focus on units that are much smaller or much larger than the text: devices, themes, tropes – or genres and systems'. This is a good example of digital methods. To consider a novel as a whole is a complex, major task that requires looking at the novel as a unique unit. To consider hundreds or thousands of novels, one needs to focus less on the unique, and more on the commonalities of the large set. This involves looking at larger patterns, such as genres or themes and epochs, or, again, to abstract, but on a smaller scale: looking at the patterns inside all the novels, such as the use of particular words or phrases, which computers can effectively be used to do.

In the next chapter, we bring some of these issues together to look at the question of the interface and how it relates to publishing. This is because many of the questions over hermeneutics and methods drawn from digital approaches rely on the mediation of interfaces that abstract away underlying computation, and, in some instances, the texts and materials themselves, through visualization techniques, dashboards and other specifically digital interface innovations.

7 Digital Scholarship and Interface Criticism

Humanities are concerned with the words and images of ages past and present. In a postdigital age, these are in digital format, not only the primary texts, images and archaeological finds that are represented in digital archives, but also the scholarly texts describing and discussing these, as well as all other contemporary mediated communication. Increasingly, we live our professional and private lives in constant interaction with information technology, using computer interfaces to read and watch, to research and compare, and to write and communicate. We have argued in this book that digital humanities needs to develop a deep understanding of computer technology, in dialogue with computer and information science, but rooted in the humanities tradition. Looking critically at the technologies we use is central to this understanding, including the interfaces in which we do most of our work. In this chapter, we discuss the possibility of a humanist critique of modern computer interfaces and the way they contribute to our thought and understanding. Computer systems designers strive to understand better how their systems influence the lives and works of their 'users', an influence for which aesthetic qualities such as 'look and feel' are increasingly important. Humanist approaches can without doubt help us to understand these effects. Indeed, we argue below that digital humanities should engage in critical design projects to create alternatives to the current computer systems. For many digital humanists, critical engagement in interface design may feel remote from their daily work, however. To put this argument into perspective, we will thus begin with something that is closer to home for any academic: digital scholarly publishing.

The fact that we all now search, find, read and publish research results digitally has opened the path for several new developments. We will first discuss open access (OA), which is the most widely known change, moving on to the discussion of peer review and open review, and then look at some new forms of scholarly argument in electronic form, hoping to demonstrate that digital interfaces have over the last decade become such an indispensable part of scholarly work that we should analyse how they work.

In the 1970s, Ted Nelson and Frederick W. Lancaster both published visions of research literature being stored and retrieved in a vast computer network (Nelson 1974; Lancaster 1978). Research repositories for computer texts were in fact built in the following decades, and Nelson's vision was also the direct inspiration for Tim Berners-Lee's World Wide Web, which was constructed as a library for science papers (Berners-Lee 1990, 1994). Berners-Lee's invention would, as we know, bring the internet to homes and workplaces all over the world, and it only makes sense that research writing also was moved to the web. The first web journals, such as *Journal of Digital Information, Postmodern Culture* and *First Monday* appeared in 1994 and 1995, the same year as the web became mainstream. A decade later, research publishing had moved online, with more than 90 per cent of journals being available on the web (Fagerjord 2014). This has led to profound changes in at least parts of the research publishing industry, perhaps most notably in some natural sciences and in humanities journals about digital culture, such as *Computers and Writing Studies*. These are changes that are slowly spreading to other disciplines as well. Journals are moving towards open access, experimenting with alternatives to blind peer review, and introducing new forms of research writing.

Most journals are still being published by large publishing houses, which require expensive subscription fees, making them available mostly to users of university research libraries. An increasing number follow *JoDI* and *First Monday* in being 'open access', however, and can be read for free by anyone with a browser. Many argue that publishers' fees are exploiting academic institutions, as electronic journals have no printing and shipping costs, and authors and reviewers are not paid. While publishers do have expenses for copy-editing, layout and, not to be overlooked, the work of managing how manuscripts flow between reviewers and authors, these cannot explain the sharp rise in subscription costs over the last decade. Some funding bodies, like the British research councils (such as ESRC and AHRC) now encourage the researchers they fund to publish open access and require them to make the articles available in public repositories, as they have already funded the research, and often the reviewers, too. Publishers are in most cases able to waive their access fees for those papers, indicating that the cost margins are negotiable. While this book is not the place to argue how scholarly publishing should be financed, we point to the obvious fact that open access allows a larger body of research results to be available for all, which is close to Nelson's and Lancaster's visions. But we want to emphasize that, even so, academic freedom to choose how one's work is published must be defended. Mandatory open access would, in our opinion, be a backwards step and undermine this freedom.

Open access is also a natural continuation of a trend where computer-savvy researchers have used electronic networks to spread their work electronically. Odlyzko (1999) documents how researchers used email to spread breakthroughs in mathematics before the web. On the web, many researchers have created web sites where they make their works available, either the 'preprint' manuscripts they submitted, or the printed works, frequently disregarding the copyright agreement with the journal in which they were published.[1]

This practice has become institutional: universities now routinely create repositories where employees can make their texts available to the extent the copyright agreement will allow. The latest development is the rise of social network sites for researchers, which automate the process even further. When authors sign up to a site like *Academia.edu*, its computers will crawl the web for their works, and copy them to their profile pages, to which other interested members can subscribe.

Open access has been an important rallying cry for the digital humanities. This has been manifested in concerns over both scholarly publishing (green/gold OA) and OA archives and data.[2] It has been a useful way for digital humanities to position itself as 'democratic' and 'radical' in relation to the traditional humanities and the relationship with the publishing industry's more questionable practices. However, digital humanities values towards open access and open source may clash with the norms of the academy (see Spiro 2012: 30).

Open access may also be important for digital humanities to contest attacks on its perceived neoliberalism. It also aligns the digital humanities with open source and the debates in technology circles over the value of 'open' vs 'closed' technologies. These also play out in relation to debates over the new economic world of Google vs Microsoft, for example. Google, naturally, has a political economic interest in OA work rather than traditional, inaccessible, publishers' journal catalogues. Google, etc., are also keen to support some digital humanities projects – particularly Big Data.

Electronic publishing also allows digital humanities to sidestep the problem of scholarly publication by creating fast and responsive OA journals, such as the *Journal of Digital Humanities*, *Vectors*, *Amodern*, etc. These new journals also allow the non-standard works to seek publication, e.g., technical books or Stanford Literary Lab's experimentation with 'Pamphlets'. We believe digital humanities is moving in the direction of the arXiv repository at Cornell University, where researchers in five quantitative disciplines deposit their work, often prior to publication. According to Fitzpatrick, 'a growing number of influential papers have *only* been published on the arXiv server, and some observers have suggested that arXiv has in effect replaced journal publication as the primary mode of scholarly communication within certain specialties in physics' (Fitzpatrick 2011). Books may also circulate before being printed: Manovich's *Software Takes Command* was circulated for several years as a Word manuscript before it eventually was published by the MIT Press in 2013. The Institute of the Future of the Book has developed 'CommentPress', a plug-in to the popular web publishing system WordPress, designed for book-length texts where readers can comment on any part of the text, from whole chapters down to individual paragraphs. Notable books that have been written in this system include McKenzie Wark's *Gamer Theory* (2007), Fitzpatrick's *Planned Obsolesence* (2011) and Jason Mittell's *Complex TV* (2015).

CommentPress and arXiv open up a practice in which publishing not only is open access, but also bypasses traditional peer review. There are many other examples. In the preparation of this book, we have consulted many documents on the web from authors' personal sites, where the provenance of the text can be difficult to discern. Most have been published in peer-review journals, but some are manuscripts or blog posts that never were published anywhere else. In these cases, we become the peers who review. Relying on our own judgement, we cite these pages because, in our opinion, their arguments are valid. We like to think that we exercise just as much judgement when reading these blog posts as we do when we review articles for journals (although, as the author of the blog post isn't anonymous like articles we are sent for review, it may be that the authors' *ethos* weighs in – we may trust a person based on her earlier work). While peer review is thought of by many as the backbone of the academic community, it may be under pressure.

In his overview of the history of the editorial peer review, Drummond Rennie finds that the idea of checking the quality of a scientific or scholarly report with a number of anonymous knowledgeable peers dates back to 1731 (Rennie 1999).[3] During the nineteenth century, many editors did not believe in the effectiveness of peer review, however, and it was not institutionalized in the majority of journals until the decades after World War II (Rennie 1999). Today, most researchers would consider peer review to be the best guarantee we have for the validity of research results. It is, then, remarkable when Jefferson et al. argue that the objectives of peer review (in medicine) are unclear. They suggest that the main objectives are '(1) selecting submissions for publication (by a particular journal) and rejecting those with irrelevant, trivial, weak, misleading, or potentially harmful content, and (2) improving the clarity, transparency, accuracy, and utility of the selected submissions', and then conclude that there are no studies that actually demonstrate that these two objectives are fulfilled by peer review (Jefferson et al. 2002b; Jefferson et al. 2002a). Rennie (1999) has accumulated a large number of studies to document that peer review often fails to uncover mistakes and errors, and frequently is unfair, unsystematic and idiosyncratic. While slow and costly, it is also conservative and stifles innovation and controversial results. Peer reviewers are often given more weight than the author, although they do not document their arguments the same way the author is required to. When rejected, authors ignore the comments. To Rennie, anonymous peer review is also unethical, as it leads to less responsible, often mean comments (see also Godlee 2000 for a similar view). Acknowledging this problem, the venerable *British Medical Journal* (BMJ) changed to open peer review in 2014, meaning that reviews are signed, and are available on the web site together with the editors' decision letter and all versions of the manuscript: 'Randomised controlled trials conducted at *The BMJ* since the turn of the millennium found that removing anonymity improved the tone and constructiveness of reviews without detriment to scientific and editorial value' (Groves and Loder 2014).

Rennie believes the BMJ's approach is the right way to go, while Fitzpatrick argues that, while open discussion is a requisite for a thriving research community, peer review before publishing has outplayed its role, as works are regularly made public in conferences, blogs and repositories like arXiv before peer review anyway. Her recommended solution is post-publication peer review. Interestingly, the BMJ has also opened for qualified comments in its online journal, where some articles (although a minority) may attract dozens of lengthy comments.

Fitzpatrick argues for a system of open publishing where authors and readers engage in lively debates, and algorithms sort and filter out the most interesting articles based on the number of comments, 'upvotes' (as in systems like Slashdot, Digg or Quora), links or other markers of interest. We believe systems like this are likely to be developed in the future, but hardly as *one* system in the way Fitzpatrick seems to argue. Already there are so many different research traditions, systems of credentials and rules for tenure and promotion, genres and publishing systems that it seems unlikely that they can all be held under one approach. And as the nature of the web is that anyone can publish whenever, new systems are likely to appear. CommentPress was a rarity with its ability to comment on each paragraph, a system created for academic debate and with a seemingly limited number of target users. Then *Medium* arrived, a network for authors of long-form writing, which quickly grew in popularity, with the very same possibility of paragraph-level comments.

The best and most important works are still likely to become visible, even at a time when there are so many researchers and publications that it is impossible for anyone to keep track just of a narrow field. Many different ways of floating to the surface and getting attention are indeed possible, not only publication in a world-famous journal that only the richest universities can afford to subscribe to. It is imperative that digital humanities recognizes this shift, and uses networked tools for better publishing, including open access, open review and open post-publication debate. Such systems will only work if the debates and reviews themselves are given credit, so, for example, a search committee for an academic position would also consider the reviews by candidates in online fora in their evaluation.

Electronic publishing has made open access and open review possible, but it has also inspired authors to rethink what it is they publish. Digital scholarship is more than methods of data collection and analysis. For much of the humanities, research is writing. Through argument and confrontation with and between earlier works, new insight emerges. As humanist research writing is now digital, we see the contours of a new writing method, a developed form of argument. We recognize the extent to which scholarly communication has changed. The 'born digital', and cultures of constant recombination have created an archive in motion – constantly changing and evolving. The nature of the conversation that is 'scholarship' has moved beyond just the journal article and monograph.

One example is the use of multimedia, such as audio-visual examples to document and illustrate. Print journals use drawings and photographs to a limited extent. Online journals have room for many more images, also in colour, and audio and video may be included too. Some online journals also use elements of graphic design to assist their arguments.

Kairos is 'a journal exploring the intersections of rhetoric, technology, and pedagogy', founded in 1996 (About Kairos n.d.). It is online only, and publishes 'webtexts', electronic writing with features that cannot be replicated in print. Its editors encourage both nonlinear hypertext writing and use of imagery and typography, meaning that no two articles look the same. As *Kairos* has run continuously for twenty years, it is a remarkable archive of experimental web writing, but also of how mainstream web design has changed, as many authors have made a point of making their works look similar to 'professional' contemporary web design. *Vectors* is another electronic journal that has published a large collection of nonlinear scholarly works. *Vectors* has in the past solicited works from select authors, and paired them with multimedia designers to create the 'projects', as the works are called.

Both *Vectors'* and *Kairos's* authors use illustration and graphic design to great effect. Typography, colour and placement are used both to communicate the works' structure, and to underscore the argument, through what James P. Purdy and Joyce R. Walker have described as 'formal enactment' and 'implicit association' (Purdy and Walker 2012). Formal enactment is to use form to demonstrate your argument. A piece about Facebook in the classroom may be designed so the text looks like a Facebook feed (Balzhiser et al. 2011); a study of 'stretchfilm', films that can be made longer or shorter, may be in the form of a 'stretchtext' (Fagerjord 2005a); while Melanie Swalwell's piece on computer games for *Vectors* must be 'played' like a computer game rather than read (Swalwell 2006). Another way of using layout and colour is to create a visual style that matches the topic, as in Scott Nelson et al.'s (2013) article about a pedagogical game in which part of the background story takes place in 1916. The article is set in typefaces typical of the second decade of the twentieth century, the background is paper turned yellow over the years, and it is illustrated with a board game and playing cards. By connotations, the article's visual design introduces both the historical period and the idea of using a game as a pedagogical tool.

Many humanist disciplines rely principally on monographs, and not journal articles, as we have discussed above. Academic book publishing is in crisis, however. A lot of monographs are published in runs of only a few hundred, scarcely bought, and hardly ever read. Pochoda (2013) has described academic publishing as a 'Procrustean bed' where works will have to be either a 6,000–8,000–word article, or an 80,000–plus-words monograph. In electronic systems, he argues, there is no need to choose between these two extremes, and authors can choose whichever length suits their topic and the treatment of it. It is too simplistic, however, to assume that the current formats are effects of the printing press only. One can print any number of pages and bind them, and there are a lot of thin books being printed – some of them are even quite well read. It is more likely that the widespread genres are effective solutions that often help to achieve a necessary balance between being short enough for people to find time to read them, and long enough for the topic to be treated in sufficient detail for the conclusions to be well supported. Where Pochoda is right is in the claim that we see other formats in electronic publishing. Science journals are increasingly making works shorter, and longer, at the same time. On the one hand, means like a 'visual abstract' suited for a PowerPoint slide (as used in *Cell*) or summaries of 'what is already known' and 'what this study adds' (as found in the BMJ) make it even quicker for a busy reader scanning for results. On the other hand, the same journals increasingly add large tables, figures and even data sets linked from the article, so readers can inspect the details (Fagerjord 2014). Visual abstracts and other forms of extreme compression can work in some disciplines, but would be very difficult in much of the humanities. Thompson has characterized the differences as two main kinds of writing: one is 'discrete results', which dominates in the sciences, and where journal articles are the main form of publishing. Standardized formats such as the Introduction, Materials and Methods, Results, and Discussion (IMRaD) outline are often found in these disciplines. 'Sustained argument' is the form in much of the humanities, especially sometimes sustained through an article, and often through a book of several hundred pages (Thompson 2005). It is rare that a philosophical treatise can be summarized in a 'this we knew, this is new' format. That does not mean that humanist scholars do not experiment with the possibilities opened by electronic media, however. Quite the contrary, humanities scholars embraced the web early on, and began to experiment with structure and multimedia.

In the 1990s, mainly before the advent of the web, hypertext scholars were full of hopes for a new, nonlinear scholarly writing (see, e.g., Bolter 1991; Landow and Delany 1991; Lanham 1993; Landow 2006). Notable works were also created as hypertexts published on the web, such as George P. Landow's *Victorian Web* (Landow 1994), a large collection of essays about the Victorian era, and *Sprawling Places*, a book-length hypertext by philosopher David Kolb (Kolb 2005). The two are examples of two different approaches to hypertext humanities. *Victorian Web* is a collection of short essays, in many ways akin both to digitized libraries and collections and to online journals with their possibilities of linking from article to article, but the standard length of each text is shorter than a journal paper. The collection is also curated; articles are placed in a hierarchy with navigation links. It will strike many as similar to Wikipedia (without the encyclopaedia-style prose), but it was created almost a decade earlier. *Sprawling Places*, on the other hand, is a coherent work by one author in the sustained argument tradition, but one in which the author refuses to follow only one line of thought, allowing the reader to follow different trajectories.

These projects are tiny compared to the digitized collections we have discussed in earlier chapters, but they point in an interesting direction: When archives, libraries and collections are digital, scholars may construct their research work on top of them, linking in the digital material in the text itself, and let the reader oscillate between the essay text and the items under discussion.

As previously mentioned, the World Wide Web was originally conceived as a hypertext repository for science papers, where hyperlinks between articles should make literature reviews lightning fast (Berners-Lee 1990). History has shown that the web proved useful for many other purposes, while copyright issues, economic interests and traditions of credentials and prestige delayed a true world-wide network of scholarly work. We are increasingly approaching it as a repository, and at least researchers in institutions with good research libraries now have most of the world's research journals and many of the monographs available from their web browsers. If open access publishing becomes the norm, as many believe, it will mean that literature references no longer need to link to a bibliography at the end of the article, they can instead bring up the cited work in its entirety.

One of the differences between the humanities and the sciences is that new humanist research does not necessarily replace earlier work. The natural sciences progress by being able to create increasingly more precise predictions and calculations of the world, and, while one respects earlier work, new work is meant to replace it. The humanities do not deal in calculations and predictions, but in interpretation and argument. We add to the body of knowledge, but not necessarily to replace it. Aristotle and Socrates are still relevant in philosophy, and humanists have always spent much time in libraries. A modern scholarly hypertext can now be created *in* the library, letting the readers follow links to the texts of earlier writers. This is likely to lead to a different writing style.

In a similar vein, it is increasingly the norm for researchers to make their data sets openly available for their readers. Even large data sets may be put online for others to download. With modern web technology, it is also possible to include the data sets in the main text of the article, so readers may perform calculations with the data while reading. Many of the *Vectors* projects we have studied earlier (Fagerjord 2014) are databases or collections created with Flash and XML, and readers are invited to navigate the collected objects with the interface tools provided. As research publishing, this could be characterized as 'showing' rather than 'telling'; at least in *Vectors*, many works do not have an explicit topic or a conclusion, but a central thematic that the reader gets to know. In an experimental online version of a review article published by Elsevier, Gardner et al. (2010) have read and coded 353 articles from *Leadership Quarterly*. The entire coded data set is available through the tables in the text: in a table of the different types of articles per year, each table cell is a hyperlink. If a reader chooses to click on the cell stating that, in 2000, there were 11 theoretical articles, a list with references and links to the 11 articles appear. Digital humanists have created and are creating huge digital online collections of works, examples and data. These will in the future be linked to our research articles and monographs, so readers can perform searches and aggregations in the databases through the illustrations and tables in the text.

At this point, we want to draw attention to what we might call the theoretical horizons of the digital humanities as a field. It is clear, for example, that in many ways we are at a critical inflection point in terms of the focus of digital humanities projects and their relationship with scale. Indeed, it could be argued that scale is an important new horizon of intellectual inquiry for the humanities. But scale is also operating in terms of access to research, literature and texts, not just data.

Electronic publishing has made possible profound changes in how research is disseminated, and it has inspired authors to develop new formats using semiotic modes beyond text, nonlinear and flexible-length formats, and arguments in the form of embedded databases of various scale and size. It is a recurring argument in this book that digital humanists need to understand and critique computer technology, and the technologies we use to create and publish our arguments should by no means be exempt from this critique.

We further need to acknowledge that what we have discussed above are changes in the appearance of text (here understood in an expanded sense, including sound and images, still and moving), and in how digital text may be rearranged by the reader, using computer controls. Both appearance and control resides in what in computer science is thought of as the interface. To consider the changes we have discussed above is thus to consider the interface(s) of digital scholarship. In chapter 3, we argued for a computer literacy, and this also implies an interface literacy, firmly based in the humanities and its tradition of theory and critique of text and visuals.

As the current mainstream view on user interfaces is that they should be simple, even intuitive, to use, it is important to acknowledge that, like anything else, they have a certain history, and could have been different. The Graphical User Interface (GUI) that we know today was based in the early work in the Augmentation Research Center Lab led by Douglas Engelbart, and developed by many of the same people at Xerox Palo Alto Research Laboratory (PARC) in California in the 1970s (Moggridge 2007). At its core is the principle of learning only a minimal set of commands. In written user interfaces, such as UNIX or LINUX, the user must learn a large vocabulary of commands, and type in the chain of commands that provide the desired result. In a GUI, the available commands are shown as lists of available actions and collections of available files in a 2D space, and the users select one of them with a pointing device, such as a mouse or, on a touch screen, their finger. Drop-down menus are examples of such lists. They function by a process of complex reduction, whereby the actions that can be performed on graphical entities are simplified to one function (click) or perhaps a couple more through the use of a modifier key such as ALT or Control.

GUIs are often described as 'intuitive' in computer literature. We humans 'instinctively' know how to use them – and the designer is taught not to accept any lower ambitions than the interface that does not have to be learned. This intuitiveness is an illusion, however. An interface is always a semiotic system to be learned, and anyone knows that this learning is sometimes much harder to acquire than others (the software salesman, your boss, your spouse) will tell you. At the very least, users need to learn to direct the pointing device, and to click (or tap) on a menu to open it, and again to select a menu item. Conventions such as the double click to open a folder, and, consequently, the idea that 'folders' may 'contain' 'documents', so documents may also be 'dragged' into folders or even 'programs', are all codes that must be learned.

Computer interfaces are semiotic codes communicating to users the possibilities and current state of computer programs, allowing the users to input data, and to view the results of computation. By inference, the interface forms an understanding of the underlying machinery. As Kirschenbaum argues:

> definitions of interface typically invoke the image of a 'surface' or a 'boundary' where two or more 'systems', 'devices', or 'entities' come into 'contact' or 'interact'. Though these terms encourage spatial interpretation, most interfaces also embody temporal, haptic, and cognitive elements. The steering wheel of a car, the control panel of a VCR, and the handle of a door are all examples of everyday interfaces that exhibit these dimensions. (Kirschenbaum 2004: 523)

This has both material and phenomenological dimensions.[4] Indeed, Norman argued that the 'real problem with interface is that it is an interface. Interfaces get in the way. I don't want to focus my energies on interface. I want to focus on the job' (Kirschenbaum 2004: 523).

The notion of the GUI as obvious, instinctive and even 'transparent' (cf. Bolter and Grusin 1999) does not hold up to further inspection. Manovich points out that, far from being transparent, the interface guides and governs our understanding of the computer and how it works, and also computer programs and what they can do (Manovich 2001: 65). To Manovich, there is no such thing as a neutral code, and any interface metaphor will always influence our perspective of the computer. Users will normally not be able to inspect the code, so whatever they know of the computer's workings, they will have to infer from the user interface. Via their use of the interface, they form mental models of how they assume the system works, models that may or may not be in concordance with the actual workings of the system (Norman 2002). A computer system is usually a 'black box', and, as with other black boxes, has to be reverse engineered to be scrutinized.

Manovich is quite clearly right, in that a GUI will assist the user in building a mental model of the computer and its program. The question is whether this model is sufficient to enable the user to operate the computer. The GUI is a modernist idea, Manovich points out, as it is believed to be efficient and obvious, and he seems to infer that this is an ideology that is worth less than a postmodernist logic (2001: 63). Manovich offers no alternative to the current GUIs, so it becomes less clear what a postmodernist interface would be. In modern GUIs such as, e.g., Windows, MacOS or Ubuntu, their file systems are represented as documents within folders, and folders within folders, sometimes also within other graphical representations of containers, such as the 'recycle bin' or a removable storage drive. This hierarchy of files is a quite iconic (see Peirce 1998) graphical representation of a file system similar to that on a UNIX machine with a command-line interface. It is hard to see how the desktop metaphor guides users to a different understanding of this hierarchy. GUIs offer the possibility of moving files by moving their icons on the screen and 'putting' files into 'folders'. UNIX offers far more powerful tools for moving, copying and deleting files, as well as changing which users have access to files, but these are used within a topography of files similar to that in Windows.

The computer interface therefore acts as a semiotic code, Manovich writes, 'that carries cultural messages in a variety of media. When you use the Internet, everything you access – text, music, video, navigable spaces – passes through the interface of the browser and then in turn, the interface of the OS' (2001: 76). Here, we need to be careful not to collapse interface, 'content' such as text and music, and the semiotic code. The three are quite distinct entities, and in fact need to be, in order to be comprehensible.

Consider reading a book on an electronic e-reader. To continue to the next 'page' (in fact, the next screenful of text), the user touches the right half of the screen. The interface the user interacts with is invisible, it is the glass itself, as a layer on top of the letters of the text. To a programmer, however, the text is also the interface, it is the result of a request, the request to fill the screen with a certain passage from the whole text. This passage may also have a link to another part of the book, signified by an underlined word. The underlined word is the interface to a command (to fill the screen with a certain passage of text), while, at the same time, it is part of the text the user reads – that is, the result of an earlier command. This double function is difficult to render in the interface/system-model, but easy to explain in semiotic terms: the underlined word is simultaneously coded as signifiers in two different codes (Fagerjord 2003). As a part of the text, the words are signifiers in English, while the underlining is a sign signifying the presence of a command, the possibility of replacing the current passage with another. But which other part? That is a third code: the words that are underlined are meant to explain what is found on the other end of the link. If it is an author's name, it is likely to be a link to the full bibliographic reference of her work. If it is the name of a chapter or a figure, the link will bring that part into view. At the same time as the words are meaningful as part of a phrase, they serve as a signifier for the passage linked. As readers, we cannot read the three codes at once, we have to oscillate between them, like when we watch the duck-rabbit figure Wittgenstein discusses (Wittgenstein 1997). In a sense the interface mediates a modal perspective on actions that are performed on the interface. Semiotics provides nuanced analytical tools and vocabulary to discuss details of user interfaces, which may be helpful for understanding what Manovich (2001) calls 'cultural interfaces'.

An interface instantiates what we could call *a computational imaginary.* This imaginary is important to consider if we direct our attention to ubiquitous computing and its important links between design, interface patterns and material technologies rather than its purely political economic drivers, for example in terms of lock-in, ecological ideas of digital media, and platform hegemony (see Maeda 2015 for discussion of the importance of design as a driver of industry growth and competitiveness). The materiality of technical devices remains crucial to understanding current technological imaginaries, however. As Drucker notes, 'graphs and charts reify statistical information. They give it a look of certainty . . . most humanists share with their social and natural science colleagues a willingness to accept the use of standard metrics and conventions without question in the production of . . . graphs' (Drucker 2012: 89). This applies equally to the deployment of interface techniques and practices that differ little from standard techniques used in the programming industries, many of which are developed from techniques of behavioural economics, psychology and persuasive technology, which have a diminished concept of the human.

It is tempting, when trying to think about digital humanities, to undertake analysis at either the surface or point of interaction (e.g. screen) or the level of the underlying machinery (e.g. database format, coding schema, etc.), a thinking about the multiple strata in design to draw an analytical distinction between the surface layer and the machinery layer. However, it is crucial that both layers are thought about in tandem, as software possesses an opaque machinery that mediates engagement, which may not be experienced directly, or through social mediations. Under the screen surface, there is a constant stream of processing, a movement and trajectory, a series of lines that are being followed and computed (see Berry 2014: 69).

In chapter 3, we wrote about layering as a central concept in computational thinking. Computer architecture is one example of this, thought of as systems on top of systems. The lower levels are the hardware, further up are the software layers. As we advance in the stack of systems, the code reads more like natural language, as many of the minute steps the computer needs to perform are taken care of by the lower-level functions. Scott Dexter (2012) reads this as an act of hiding; each level hides the functions of the lower. An alternative way of viewing it is as a shorthand: a command in a high-level language is a shorthand of writing a long series of steps in assembler code, and thus faster to do. This is the implication of Kittler's famous statement that 'there is no software' (1995) – that is, that each command is translated and translated again down to the logic ports in the silicon circuits.[5]

The surface, or interactional layer, of the digital is hugely important for providing the foundations through which we interact with these technologies. Not only are the interfaces responsive to our questioning via queries, searches, navigation and so forth, they are also designed, increasingly, to be both intuitive, intelligent and contextual, and aesthetic, stylish and pleasant. Modern interfaces often attempt not only to guess our intentions but also to invite extended use and shape the direction of our minds' travel. This is nonetheless a simplification of the architectural structure of the computer, allowing the fundamental dimensions of the relationship between the interface (commodity) and the code (mechanism) to be foregrounded. As Kirschenbaum (2004: 524) points out, the 'interface is often not only conceptually distinct, but also *computationally* distinct'. If we consider the interface *qua* interface, wishing to contribute to what could be interface criticism, it is beneficial to zoom in on the interface not only as a thin layer or surface upon computational machinery, but also as a discrete computational form in and of itself.[6] The interface may be thought of as a machine in its own right.

Another aspect of the interface/machinery split is that there can be rapid change in terms of both hardware and software. In a usual case, the user is unlikely to notice much difference in the usability of the device, however – the interface allows for a surface stability or at least a looser coupling between rapid technical change and the user experience of technology. Current mass-user systems are often kept under development, in what the industry calls a 'perpetual beta': a system is never finished, stabilized, or completed. As development techniques with shorter iteration cycles (e.g., 'agile computing') have become widespread, and through the use of 'service oriented architecture', systems are continually developed, even while they are open for thousands, even millions, of users. New features in Facebook are usually rolled out to groups of users, so your Facebook may look different from and have features other than mine. Google and other companies are known for their continuous 'A/B' testing experiments, in which users are assigned to different versions of the same service at random, and engineers study their use with statistical tools to decide which version performed best (Levy 2011).

The interface, often visualized as a thin membrane over computational devices is increasingly being stretched across computational devices, objects, practices and processes to create what we call *continuous interfaces* (see

Berry 2015b). We draw the notion of continuous interfaces from the concept of continuous computing, which has been deployed to talk about the increasing way in which ubiquitous computing is being embedded in devices which are in tension with their environment – for example, in Apple's new continuity technology (Apple 2015). The term continuity refers to the unbroken and consistent existence or operation of something over time, but also gestures towards a media notion of continuity of broadcast, in the maintenance of continuous action and self-consistent detail in the various scenes of a film or broadcast. Thomson, for example, argues that enabling a new area of continuous computing depends on three factors (adapted from Thomson 2015), including physical design, interaction models and the ability of the technical device to interact with its environment.

Interface experiences have intensified in recent years, as media for social and cultural life, but also as conceptual means for transcending institutional and technical boundaries between different spheres. This includes the micro-level of the individualized technologies, such as smartphones and other personal technologies, that stretch computation across lives, life histories and sociality. This is a problematic Berry has explored elsewhere (Berry 2011, 2014) and concerns questions of interoperability, of inter- or intra-computation and object-oriented paradigms of intercommunication between technical devices, which now appear to have begun to be augmented through a horizon of understanding provided by flat interfaces (Berry 2015a).[7] We might describe it as a 'thin computation' that tends to be optimized towards breadth rather than depth in its relationship to the functional properties of the computer, but also in a spatial dimension.[8]

The requirement for a shared constellation of representations, axiomatic concepts and grammars of interaction is a complex assemblage of technologies, articulated through code and design, that has characteristics of responsive design combined with a tight coupling between the materiality of the technical device and the articulation of the principles of the design language. The recent turn towards flat design has been manifested in the use of a double articulation of the geometric fundamentals of the primitives of the interface combined with a neo-materialist abstraction of fictional materials from which the interface is imagined to be constructed. The obduracy of the interface is guaranteed through technical restrictions built into the interface toolbox, in terms of both API functionality and the sophisticated deployment of integrated development environments (IDEs). But there is also a mythic reinforcement through the allegory of a material form that guarantees the conceptual and practical instantiation of interface design – so in the case of Google it is paper, and for Apple it is glass.

Continuous interfaces not only offer a conceptual means of thinking about a possible new phase in interface design, but also invite us to think about the way in which one can deploy interface criticism in the digital humanities. This helps to disrupt not just the traditional ways of thinking about computation, but also a growing tapestry of computational moments, objects, glances, notifications and complications that are weaved across the life-world and which we attend to continuously. Kirschenbaum (2004: 540) argued that digital humanists would have to design *for* interfaces and design interfaces themselves, but it is clear that they also have to learn to critique interfaces and the embedded forms of assumed knowledges, norms and politics that they have inscribed.

Berry (2014) has outlined a depth model of analysis that used the concepts of *commodity* and *mechanism* to describe the structure of computational systems. The *commodity layer* is accessible via the interface/surface and provides or procures a commodity/service/function, and furnishes a relative stability for the consumption of ends. The commodity is usually articulated at the level of the interface, usually visually, although other sensory interfaces exist. The *mechanism layer* is accessible via source code text, which contains the mechanisms and functions 'hidden' in the software. These are the 'means', and can be thought of as the substructure for the overlay of commodities and consumption. The mechanisms are usually delegated within the code layer, and thus hidden from the interaction. This is a useful starting point for an interface criticism for digital humanities.

Our society increasingly relies upon algorithms that deliver information to us in packaged form. Google's search engine, Amazon's recommendations and Facebook's News Feed are all examples of algorithmically selected information. This selection, however machinic, is also necessarily ideological and political. Where ideology critique of the 1960s concerned ideology embedded in mass communication, a similar critique of the 2010s would have to be of the algorithms of social media and of the surveillance algorithms of commercial providers, who track users over hundreds of sites and learn their habits and preferences. Indeed, as Mejias argues, 'it should not come as a surprise to most people that we are living in an era in which our online movements are recorded in logs that specify what web sites we visit, what we search for, what we buy, who we interact with, and so on' (Mejias 2013: 101). Some use this knowledge to send tailored advertising, while Google uses the knowledge to alter the results of users' searches, hoping to serve the users' needs even better, but it is also 'collected and analyzed for security purposes by governments and authorities' (Mejias 2013: 101). These algorithms are truly black boxes: most users hardly reflect on their existence, and fewer try to understand their mechanisms, even though they do influence what information any one of us gets when surfing the web or using our mobile apps.

So, interfaces are necessary to theorize because they are ever more present. They are where we live our digital lives, and we inhabit them and arrange them, not isolated from the offline world, but as a natural connection to it. As we have argued, the interface is not only a flat surface or skin to a system, but a deep zone in which users not only interact but reside and live with several systems. As an interface, it connects deeply into both the computer machinery and the life outside the screen, with few clear-cut borders in either direction.

Computers, television sets and mobile phones have followed the same trend: As our work, and our information, and our play move into the digital, physical outsides matter less and less, and are rapidly disappearing. This does not mean that form and style are less important than before – on the contrary: many would contend that Apple's enormous success in the consumer electronics market is due to its sense of style and ease. But it has moved inside the screen, and Apple was a pioneer in this. The company understood that the 'look and feel' of digital product is important to users – so important that they will make their purchase decisions based on this. This has several implications from how we think about digital media: 'look and feel' is the common term for the design of digital work, but can we actually 'feel' an intangible product? It must be the interaction, how the product responds to our input. This means that what was known as the interface is now more than a layer, a membrane, a mere conduit between man and machine: it is also the social field for aesthetics, identity and politics.[9] Moreover, the value of an interface is beyond performativity or ease of use, it must also be judged for its aesthetics, its interaction style, its look and feel. Interaction design has proven methods for usability design, but only blunt and ineffective strategies to develop pleasing and stylish user experience (UX) (Fagerjord 2015).

'Feel' is a word we use to describe the use of many senses: both the senses of touch, the skin's haptic senses, and 'to perceive, to be conscious', a product of any or all of the senses (*Oxford English Dictionary* 2015). We do not touch digital interfaces. We touch input devices, such as a keyboard, mouse or touch screen, and these do feel different, but we do not touch digital data. And while many experiments in 'haptic feedback' are made, these are digitally controlled analogue motors. What feeling we get from digital data is mainly from senses other than touch. Still, the feelings we are discussing are of a different kind from the feelings you may get from a novel (as in 'the book made me feel nostalgic'). It may be a feeling related to touch, a feeling of handling matter, although conveyed synaesthetically from our eyes and ears from our experience with physical handling of objects. Controls on touch screens are often made with inertia: if one spins a dial on an iPad, it continues to spin for a while after you lift your finger. If it moves slowly and stops quickly, it feels heavier than if it requires little movement from my finger on the touch screen to move the dial, and it continues to spin for a while after it is let go. It may also be a feeling of effectiveness (or the opposite: the feeling of losing track) when a system is made so one can do what one wants with ease. Purchasing something digitally or filing a registration may be a breeze, almost fun to do. Often it is not. The interaction, the work required, *feels* differently. Interestingly, the two may also combine: sometimes, a digital product is just pleasing to use, as if the care with which it was constructed shines through, and is perceived – *felt* – even if you use it for no particular purpose. Just as closing the door of an expensive car makes a sound that is heavy, but not loud, giving a sense of quality and meticulous and durable construction, or a mechanical dial on a machine may be so perfectly balanced that it just *feels* nice to turn it. We remember how we played with the wheel-shaped interface of the iPhone app 'Path' without using it for a purpose, just because it *felt* fun and pleasing (and we remember *feeling* disappointment when it was replaced by a more standard interface in a later release).

When Apple in 2013 launched iOS7, a new version of the operating system for its mobile devices, it based a lot of its marketing on the new 'flat' aesthetics of the user interface. The earlier versions had made heavy use of shadows and highlight to create illusions of depth, of reflections, and of diverse materials. iOS7 did away with shadows and highlights, instead using a flat look with bright colours. Backgrounds in apps were mainly white, and interaction elements for the user to press were no longer 'buttons', drawn with borders and shadows to look as though they protruded from the background, but 'links', that is, coloured text.

Apple's head designer Jonathan Ive said in interviews that this was a better, more 'logical' experience for users (again invoking the myth of the intuitive interface), and also that the earlier skeuomorphic imitation of 3D materials had always been a remedy for the low resolution of the first generations of mobile devices. His explanation hides the fact that Apple was a latecomer to the flat style, however. Microsoft's Windows 8, launched two years earlier, had a similar flat aesthetic, a look that had spread through Microsoft products since 2006 – seven years before iOS7. Rather than being a natural development, a sign of a more evolved medium or more educated users, the flat visual style is interface fashion. It is easy to demonstrate that the new flat style may in some cases be less intuitive or easy to use than the earlier skeuomorphic designs.

Fashion, look and feel are important to modern computer media, however. The computer industry knows this, but struggles with reliable methods for this kind of design, which often may clash with the ideology of intuitiveness and being easy to use. Usability methods were developed to make products usable, allowing users to do what they attempt to do effectively, with little learning and a minimum of mistakes. To create systems that are simple to use, Human Computer Interaction (HCI) designers use iterative methods, whereby early prototypes are tested with representative users, and their performance guides the development of the next iteration. At the base of this method is the test. Users are given a task, and test administrators watch their progress while recording the time spent and the number of critical mistakes. This method is proven to deliver usable systems effectively, as long as 'usable' is defined in quantifiable metrics.[10] What is much more difficult is to develop the right style, mood or feeling, the very qualities that speak to our identity and vanity. User Experience practitioners even have a hard time expressing what we are speaking of, calling it *hedonic quality* or *emotional impact*, trying to measure it through standardized surveys such as AttrakDiff (Hassenzahl 2001; Hartson and Pyla 2012: 453ff.). The problem with the measures, however, is that, while it is relatively simple to measure whether a product is positively received, it is difficult to find how to improve things when the responses are negative. Humanities, on the other hand, have long research traditions and nuanced vocabularies at hand to discuss styles of writing, of visual design and of imagery, and provide a theoretical resource that undoubtedly will help us understand and historicize these developments.

Alan Liu (2004) has treated a whole book to what he labels 'cool' aesthetics, claiming that this is the dominating visual style on the web, and that it is a reaction to the Western corporate culture of knowledge work. Most adolescents have at one time or another struggled to define what 'cool' is. On one hand, cool is a visual style indebted to modernist art and the International Style of graphic design; on the other hand, it is its opposite. 'No sooner do we see the unmistakeable imprint of modernist design in cool, however, than we immediately note its antithesis. Cool is also fundamentally antidesign' (2004: 216). To Liu, cool is a paradoxical movement of assimilating corporate culture tongue-in-cheek; seemingly bowing down to the values of knowledge work, the cool aesthetics is still counterproductive. It is only style, with no message. Liu's analysis is advanced and compelling.

Ida Engholm has taken a broader outlook in her doctoral thesis on the style history of the web from 1993 to 2003. In a mere decade from the web's inception, she is able to identify three distinct phases in web design, and nine major stylistic trends, including the Digital Modernism and Swiss Style discussed by Liu (Engholm 2003). There is a need to map and explore these visual styles. Later works in her spirit are analyses of the debate over 'skeuomorphic' or 'flat' interfaces (more on this below), and of the postdigital aesthetic in digital arts and design (see Berry and Dieter 2015).

Our argument is that aesthetics of the interface, its look and feel, is increasingly important as the outside of devices disappears, and the inside becomes the place to display identity, class and ideals. If we do not analyse the visuals and the interaction styles of digital media, we will never truly understand their place in the everyday lives of billions of people. It would be equally wrong, however, to focus only on the signifiers, and not the signifieds. The interface and the computation, the commodity and the mechanism, need to be thought of in tandem in the digital humanities.

We opened this chapter with a discussion of digital publishing, showing that modern forms of publishing turn into what might be called digital design. Steven Ramsay created quite a stir when he argued that all digital humanists should 'build things' (Ramsay 2011). However, it is difficult to imagine a humanist who does not write. In a postdigital age, writing might become building, just as empirical research and critical argument often will include the design and building of systems or digital works of criticism. To do this, one needs to understand the different, but interdependent, layers of interface and machinery. Building things may even be a way of understanding and/or critiquing modern interfaces as part of the computational cultures of a digital age.

For example, the artist Mark Madel has worked in building computer machinery that invites the audience to think about matters of life and death. In his 'Windows makeover', he created a theme for the Windows 95 operating system that replaced the original desktop with a completely new interface. The 'Start' menu became a 'Grope' menu, offering the applications 'Break-up, Intimacy, Love, Trust, Liaisons, Health, and Fault' (Madel 1998). Madel's hacked computer system makes both the interface and the underlying system come into vision, as the familiar computer has become uncannily unfamiliar. What is this computer system for? What can it do for us? Our everyday reliance on computers for all kinds of everyday tasks has made the technology become invisible for us. By the *Verfremdung*-effect of his interface to life, rather than to a computer system, Madel makes the computer technology come sharply into vision again.

Madel's artwork may be an answer to Liu's (2012) observation of the lack of cultural criticism in digital humanities. Madel could be said to engage in a critical design practice – a technically simple design project with huge potential regarding critical understanding of our relation to computers. This aesthetic move can be turned into a method: Stuart Moulthrop (2005) has called for what he terms 'interventions', works in digital media that are: (1) interfaces to a database with a generative logic; (2) made with commonly available tools; (3) critical, satirical or polemical; and (4) freely or widely distributed. Gregory Ulmer has in a similar way, for decades, pursued the use of poststructural theories for electronic writing and/or design (traditional terms for authorship fail to describe such activities) – first, in *Teletheory*, in which he asked how Derrida's grammatology could be applied to television; then, in *Heuretics* and later works, he has turned to computer (hyper)media (Ulmer, 1994, 2004).

With his idea of interventions, Moulthrop outlines how digital design can be used as an effective method of cultural critique. Most authors of interactive, multimodal texts find they spend more time than writers of traditional text on building complex digital forms, but sustained, refined argument that we know from earlier scholarly cultural criticism is difficult. There is a middle ground, however: the online journals we have discussed earlier in this chapter, such as *Kairos* or *Vectors*. These journals contain many examples of works arguing in text while their visuals pastiche other, well-known digital genres, such as a computer game, a blog, or a Facebook page (Purdy and Walker 2012; Fagerjord 2014). These authors may aspire to the form of cultural criticism called for by Moulthrop and Liu, but, just as much, they show how they are aware that interface style and design matter in today's digital culture.

Several scholars have used digital media to think through the relations between interface and text, and to demonstrate the applicability and power of their theories. Manovich first theorized how new media texts in essence are interfaces to databases, before he moved on to create 'database films' (Manovich 2001; Manovich and Kratky 2005). Another form of critical digital practice is to design humanist-based alternatives to current computer regimes. Peter Bøgh Andersen was a humanist computer scientist who proposed a semiotic approach to computer programming as an alternative to the widespread object-oriented approaches. Firmly based within the Scandinavian school of participatory design, Andersen's approach was to map the language used by workers in a workplace, then constructing the system by modelling not the workplace, but the language, in the computer system, using concepts from Hjelmslev's structuralist semiotics (Andersen, 1990).

To think about computer interfaces is to switch continuously between looking at the interface as a layer – a set of controls – and as a deep environment in which digital texts and digital media exist. To understand fully the materiality and the semiotics of digitized works, the very core of digital humanities, we need to develop the thoughts we have begun to trace here. We believe critical design will be an important method in this approach.

We now want to turn to think about how these strands that have been developed in the preceding chapters can be brought together to think about digital humanities in relation to the wider questions of cultural critique. The aim is to open the vista of digital humanities scholarship so that it can confidently widen its scope and focus to include cultural, material and social questions, particularly where it is able to contribute towards public culture. This is to continue the work of the humanities to raise the level of debate in public culture, not only through the traditional humanities approaches, but also through new means of reading and writing culture.

8   Towards a Critical Digital Humanities

In this final chapter, we move towards a more speculative and theoretical discussion of possible future directions for the digital humanities, particularly the notion of a digital humanities that links to the social, cultural, economic and political questions of a recontextualization and social re-embedding of digital technologies within a social field. This chapter seeks to connect the themes developed throughout the book in theorizing computational approaches within the arts and humanities and social sciences. As research continues to be framed in terms of computational categories and modes of thought, the digital becomes a potential research programme and the condition of possibility for research, something digital humanities should directly address as part of the research questions it investigates.

Throughout the book, we have attempted to provide a map of the digital humanities understood in some sense as a set of interlocking and inter-dependent parts that, whilst distinct and standing alone to some degree, nonetheless add up to make the whole greater than the sum of its parts. This is, in other words, to offer a notion of the digital humanities as a coherent, if nonetheless still contested, discipline. One of the key themes that we have reiterated is the need for a critical reflexivity in the digital humanities, and in this chapter we want to expand a little on this notion in relation to what we are calling a *critical* digital humanities.[1] In essence, the aim is to provide pointers towards a set of practices and ways of thinking rather than a comprehensive blueprint. Indeed, it is this gesture that we want to offer as a way of augmenting, and in some cases offering a pushback to, the sometimes instrumental tendencies within the digital humanities. Part of this has to be a focus on the socio-technical aspects of the technologies used, how they are assembled and made, and the possibility of making them otherwise.

Indeed, what we propose is to move beyond what might be called a 'technological sublime', and, through our theoretical and empirical projects, to develop 'cognitive maps' for thinking critically about digital culture (Jameson 1990). Part of the challenge in this approach is to bring the digital (software and computation) back into visibility for research and critique as both a material and an ideology. We argue that critical digital humanities starts with these premises in order to avoid the dangers of treating the computer as a 'truth machine' or allowing the technical issues of the research infrastructures and projects drive the kinds of questions that digital humanities is allowed to ask (see Berry 2011, 2014).

This would focus on the need to think critically about the implications of computational imaginaries, and raise some questions in this regard. This is also to foreground the importance of the politics and norms that are embedded in digital technology, algorithms and software. We need to explore how to negotiate between close and distant readings of texts and how micro-analysis and macro-analysis can be usefully reconciled in humanist work. As Liu (2011) argues, 'digital humanists will need to find ways to show that thinking critically about metadata, for instance, scales into thinking critically about the power, finance, and other governance protocols of the world', since, even though humanities engaged in cultural critique and even computing had its moments of social-justice activism and cyber-libertarianism, 'the digital humanities (initially known even more soberly as "humanities computing") never once inhaled' (Liu 2012: 419). Some key questions include: how do we make the invisible become visible in the study of software? How is knowledge transformed when mediated through code and software? What are the critical approaches to Big Data, visualization, digital methods, etc.? How does computation create new disciplinary boundaries and gate-keeping functions? What are the new hegemonic representations of the digital – 'geons', 'pixels', 'waves', visualization, visual rhetorics, etc.? How do media changes create epistemic changes, and how can we look behind the 'screen essentialism' of computational interfaces? Here we might also reflect on the way in which the practice of making-visible also entails the making-invisible – computation involves making choices about what is to be captured. Zach Blas's work, for example, is helpful in showing the various forms of race-, gender- and class-based exclusion in computational and biometric systems through his art practice, but we can imagine ways in which digital humanities can also work to make these kinds of exclusions and absences visible (Magdaleno 2014).[2]

From asking questions about the normative and political delegations into software/code to seeing how computational categories transform the historical constellation of concepts we associate with scholarly work, this would encourage us not just to 'build things' but to take them apart and critique them – making critical software to test our ideas and challenge our assumptions. And also to turn our hermeneutic skills on the very software and algorithms that make up these systems. Indeed, we would agree here with Grusin that 'digital media can help to transform our understanding of the canon and history of the humanities by foregrounding and investigating the complex entanglements of humans and nonhumans, of humanities and technology, which have too often been minimized or ignored in conventional narratives of the Western humanistic tradition' (Grusin 2014: 89).

Through exploring the digital humanities through a number of lenses, it has been extremely interesting to see how different disciplinary special-isms are transformed not just by their interaction, but also by the common denominator and limitations of computation – that is, how the constella-tion of concepts that is used within a disciplinary context are challenged and transformed within a computational frame. Hence, digital humanities needs to be critical of the 'digital' in digital humanities as much as of the 'humanities'. Indeed, there has already been some valuable work under-taken in this area, such as Alan Liu's work, but more needs to be done to deepen the digital humanities' theoretical and empirical approaches.

The aim of outlining a critical digital humanities here is not to offer a prescription for a final approach, rather it is to begin to enumerate the plurality of approaches within such a field, and more specifically a con-stellation of concepts related to a notion of 'digital humanities' and the softwarization of the humanities more generally. Indeed, critical digital humanities could help to reposition our traditional humanistic practices of history, critique and interpretation, so these humanistic traditions can help to refine and shape the direction and critical focus of digital humanities and its place in the academy. Thus, Liu asks, 'how [can] the digital humanities advance, channel, or resist today's great postindustrial, neoliberal, corporate, and global flows of information-cum-capital?', and how can we make sure that it is no longer 'a question rarely heard in the digital humanities associations, conferences, journals, and projects' (Liu 2012; see also Global Outlook 2015). Indeed, as Bianco argues, as digital humanists we must 'seriously question, maybe even interrogate . . . our roles in the legitimization and institutionalization of computational and digital media in the humanistic nodes of the academy . . . and not simply defend the legitimacy (or advocate for the "obvious" supremacy) of com-putational practices' (Bianco 2012: 100). This is echoed by Johnson, who argues, 'I think the 21st-century university has a lot of struggles and tensions that aren't about the digital being the new fancy tool, but are actually about the extent to which the university is or is not accountable to increasingly diverse *and* stratified communities' (Johnson 2016, origi-nal emphasis).

A critical digital humanities continues to map and critique the use of the digital but is attentive to questions of power, domination, myth and exploitation. This is what has been previously discussed as the dark side of the digital humanities (see particularly Chun 2013; Grusin 2013; Jagoda 2013; Raley 2013). As such, critical digital humanities can develop into an interdisciplinary approach which includes: critical theory; theoretical work on race, ethnicity, gender, sexuality, disability and class (see, for example, Earhart 2012; TransformDH 2013; Accessible Future 2015; Kim and Stommel 2015; Risam 2015); together with the historical, social, political and cultural contexts around digital transformations (Berry 2014) – that is, work that is both research- and practice-led, reflexive to its own historical context and theoretical limitations, and with a commitment to political praxis. Its theoretical work can be combined with 'building things' and other kinds of technologically engaged work, including drawing on approaches such as software studies, critical code studies, cultural/critical political economy and media and cultural studies, etc.

As such, critical digital humanities can seek to address the concerns expressed by Liu (2012) and others that digital humanities lacks a cultural critique (see Golumbia 2012). As Liu argues, 'while digital humanists develop tools, data, and metadata critically, rarely do they extend their critique to the full register of society, economics, politics, or culture' (2012). At this point, it is important to note that we are calling for a disciplinary constellation around these issues, rather than mandating that all scholars should produce the same kind of work. The aim is to open digital humanities to different forms of scholarly work and critical approaches that would widen the field and enrich its intellectual capacities.

Developing a critical approach to computation calls for the digital itself to be historicized. Focus on materiality of the digital draws our attention to the microanalysis required at the level of digital conditions of possibility combined with macroanalysis of scaling of digital systems – for example, real-time monitoring of streams of data, particularly communicative streams in the nascent public formation of knowledge, allows intervention from governments, security services and corporations. This idea of controlling not only the very possibility of engaging with culture, but also how it is understood, used, shared, discussed and reflected upon, is something that might have resemblances to a kind of Orwellian machinery but is in actuality of a terrifyingly greater intensity and higher resolution. Here culture is seen as data, both for corporations and for governments – something which is a complete anathema to the humanities. This results in a collapse of the public/private locus of opinion-formation and comprehension and, to follow Stiegler, creates 'short-chains' – fragmented knowledge that short-circuits the possibility of rational thought. It is also precisely this technical mediation, geared towards immediacy and reaction, that creates problematic conditions of apathy, disconnect and fatalism as well (but along with new potentials for authoritarianism).

In this book, we have already gestured to some of these issues, particularly in relation to thinking about digitality and computation in relation to the postdigital, but more remains to be done. Computation is a historical phenomenon and can be traced and periodized through historicization, but more work is needed here. Ignoring the hegemony of computational concepts and methods leads to a dangerous assumption, as it is a short step towards new forms of control, myth and limited forms of computational rationality. Digital humanities could be one of a number of cognate disciplines that should remain attentive to moments in culture where critical thinking and the ability to distinguish between concept and object become weakened (see Berry 2014). Digital humanities should not only map these challenges but also propose new ways of reconfiguring research and teaching to safeguard critical and rational thought in a digital age.

How then are we to embed the capacity for reflection and thought into a critically-oriented digital humanities and thus to move to a new mode of experience, a 'two dimensional experience responsive to the potentialities of people and things' (Feenberg 2013: 610). This requires a new orientation towards potentiality, or what Berry calls 'possibility' (Berry 2014), which would enable this new spirit of criticality – critical reason as such.[3] In other words, we need a reconfiguring of quantification practices and instrumental processes away from domination (Adorno, Horkheimer, Marcuse) and control (Habermas), towards reflexivity, critique and democratic practices. As Galloway argues, 'as humanist scholars in the liberal arts, are we outgunned and outclassed by capital? Indeed we are – now more than ever. Yet as humanists we have access to something more important . . . [to] continue to pursue the very questions that technoscience has always bungled, beholden as it is to specific ideological and industrial mandates' (Galloway 2014: 128). If we play in a digital sandbox, do we have to follow the rules of computation, or are there alternative models and theories of computation that we can move towards (cf. Drucker 2012: 88)? Indeed, as McPherson argues, 'politically committed academics with humanities skill sets must engage technology and its production not simply as an object of our scorn, critique, or fascination but as a productive and generative space that is always emergent and never fully determined' (McPherson 2012: 155; see also Berry 2014). Indeed, for Marcuse, 'critical analysis must dissociate itself from that which it strives to comprehend; the philosophic terms must be other than the ordinary ones in order to elucidate the full meaning of the latter. For the established universe of discourse bears throughout the marks of the specific modes of domination, organisation, and manipulation to which the members of a society are subjects' (Marcuse 1999: 193). The question then becomes the extent to which this totalizing system overwhelms the capacity for agency, and, as such, a critical consciousness. Indeed, related to this is the important question of the relationship between humanities and technology itself, in as much as one of the questions to be addressed is, are the humanities prior to technology and therefore a condition of possibility for it, or has the humanities become technologized to the extent that humanities is now itself subjected to a technological a priori? In other words, is humanities 'complicit with the system of domination that prevails under capitalism' (Feenberg 2013: 609)?

For Feenberg, this requires 'counter-acting the tendencies towards domination in the technological a priori' through the 'materialization of values' (2013: 613). This he argues can be found at specific intervention points within the materialization of this a priori, such as in design processes. Feenberg argues that 'design is the mediation through which the potential for domination contained in scientific-technical rationality enters the social world as a civilisational project' (2013: 613). Here digital humanities has the technical skills and cultural capital to make a real difference in how these projects are developed, the ways in which instrumental logics are embedded and interventions made possible. For example, digital humanities, through its already strong advocacy of open access, could push for and defend open source and copyleft licences for technical components and software.[4] Feenberg argues that the 'socialist a priori' should inform the processes of technical implementation and technical practice. That is, he explicitly asks us to contest particular forms of neoliberal and market-oriented logics that can be easily and unthinkingly incorporated into projects and their technical implementation. However, it seems to us that this underestimates the instrumentality implicit in design, and design practices more generally, which often tend to maximize instrumental values in their application of concepts of efficiency and organization and therefore are very difficult to resist. In contrast, we argue that it additionally requires a duty of care towards design, or a new form of critical design which is different from, and more rigorous than, the form outlined by Dunne and Raby (2013). Here we might start making connections to new forms of rationality that offer possibilities for augmenting or perhaps replacing instrumental rationalities, for example in the potentialities of critical computational rationalities, iteracies and other computational competences whose performance and practice are not necessarily tied to instrumental notions of efficiency and order, nor to capitalist forms of reification (Berry 2014).

Meanwhile, with the exploding quantity of information in society and the moves towards a digital economy, information is increasingly seen as a source of profit for capitalism if captured in an appropriate way. Indeed, data and information were said to be the new 'oil' of the digital age by

Alan Greenspan in 1971 (see Berry 2008: 41, 56). This highlights both the political and economic desire for data. Meanwhile, the digital enables exploding quantities of data that are increasingly hard to contain within organization boundaries. The increase in data affects not just massive corporations but also every one of us in our everyday life. Our activities generate a data exhaust that far exceeds our capacity to control it, let alone comprehend it. But this generates political possibilities as well as problems: from the growing contestation and awareness by individuals of the profound and shocking amounts of surveillance capacity held by corporations and governments, to the desire of populations to have some sense of ownership of their data lives at a national level. There is much potential for digital humanists, both pedagogically and in terms of research practice, to explore and communicate to a public these matters of concern. But to reiterate the argument of this book, we should no longer talk just about digital vs analogue (or online versus offline) but instead about modulations of the digital or different intensities of the computational. We must critically analyse the way in which cadences of the computational are made and materialized, and draw attention to a computational world and culture whilst transcending the distinction between digital and non-digital. Ironically, digital humanities is ideally located and has the intellectual and empirical capacity to do this.

For example, mega-leaks place raw data into the public sphere – usually as files and spreadsheets of data – and there is a growing problem with being able to read and comprehend them, hence the increasing need for journalists to become *data journalists*. Ironically then, 'opening the databanks' (Lyotard 1984: 67; Berry 2014: 178) creates a new form of opaqueness. Computational strategies are needed to read these new materials (e.g. algorithmic distant readings). Additionally, the politics of Wikileaks is connected to creating an informational overload within organizations, in terms of both their inability to cope with the release of their data, and the requirement to close communicational channels within the organization. So, information overload can become a political tactic for both control and resistance. Again, we can see how digital humanities could connect their methods and practices to examining these ways of working with data, both as cultural phenomena and to equip students with critical data skills and reflexive habits in their digital lives.

New methods for reading and writing will be required for the humanities to work with these new kinds of digital materials – what Berry (2011, 2014) has called *iteracy*. So we will need to attend to the ways in which culture (e.g. public/private) is materialized and fixed in forms specific to material digital culture – that is, to how culture is inscribed not just in moments of culture created by human actors but also in the technical devices, recording systems, trackers, web bugs and beacons of a digital age. One approach has been to reconstruct the idea of the methodological commons into a 'methodological infrastructure in which culturally aware technology complements technologically aware cultural criticism' (Liu 2012). Indeed, digital humanists will need to develop their powers of critique regarding sites of power, which include the instantiation of digital technologies, platforms and infrastructures.

The humanities need more than ever to communicate their vision of humanity (and so their own value) to the public, but also to reconstruct what the competences of a subject of computation can and should be. Liu argues that 'beyond acting in an instrumental role, the digital humanities can most profoundly advocate for the humanities by helping to broaden the very idea of instrumentalism, technological, and otherwise. This could be its unique contribution to cultural criticism' (2012). We agree, and this offers not a replacement for existing digital humanities work, but rather a widened and extended set of research questions. The field will be bigger, stronger and have more impact if it is able to engage with and accept a wider range of research approaches within its field.

At this point it is useful to note that introducing critical approaches into digital humanities projects often slows them down. This can be frustrating for other members of a research project, especially those from technical fields. Critical thinking can act as 'grit in the machine' and consequently can be difficult to justify under current calls for bids, rapid prototyping or what seem like fairly neutral digitization projects. However, we think that critical work offers a *productive* slowdown, forcing a project to reflect on its approach, method and goals, in the sense that Reuben Brower has in a different context called for 'reading in slow motion' (Brower, quoted in Hancher 2016)[5] – that is, to bring the slow, careful, critical thinking of the humanities not just to the 'content' of a software project, but also bring it to bear on the very technologies, methods and infrastructures that support the project.

In the limited space that remains, we would like to explore three possible sites for intervention that a newly radicalized and broadened notion of digital humanities might choose as areas of inquiry for critical approaches. First, we want to turn our attention to research infrastructure and how critical approaches can contribute to and offer methods for contesting the developments in and direction of this area. As we have discussed previously, research infrastructures provide the technical a priori for the support of and conditions of possibility for digital humanities projects. In thinking about this use, Liu (2016) has suggested the development of critical infrastructure studies, which would engage with both the theory and the practice of the critical making of infrastructure. In the context of the digital humanities, and the university more generally, the move to digital infrastructure within the university places a difficult series of technical decisions on the faculty and management of the university – not only technically complex, with the attendant implications for legacy systems, lock-in, future technical directions and so forth, but also having significant implications in terms of cost and ongoing maintenance fees. Additionally, the ways in which these aspects interrelate in terms of the 'space of work' is hugely important – that is, the functional capacity of the system is crucial – in as much as the range of humanities work may be adversely affected or inhibited by certain forms of technical system. For Liu, it is at this point that digital humanists can contribute, through committee work in the selection and promotion of particular technical solutions and standards that are conducive to the work of the wider humanities.

Whilst we think that Liu is right to connect the role of particular aspects of service to the range of contributions that can be made by digital humanists, we also think that the danger here is to offer only a prophylactic contribution by the digital humanities. We would like to suggest a more interventionist and activist role for the digital humanities, in terms not only of connecting research infrastructures to digital humanities work, but also more generally of how computation is the key mediator to and condition of possibility for management, accountancy and standardization in the academy. This critique is important as it posits a more general question about the university, what it is, where it is heading, and how computation aids or hinders the task of research and teaching in the university. Whilst this is beyond the scope of this book, we feel that the role of the university and digital humanities are deeply intertwined in terms of digital humanists in some sense acting as critical subjects for thinking about the future of the university.

In terms of infrastructures, we might consider the ways in which particular practices from Silicon Valley have become prevalent and tend to shape thinking across the fields affected by computation. For example, there has been a recent turn towards what has come to be called 'platformization' – that is, the construction of a single digital system that acts as a technical monopoly within a particular sector. The obvious example here is Facebook in social media. Equally, in discussions about digital research infrastructures, there is an understandable tendency towards centralization and the development of unitary and standardized platforms for the digitization, archiving, researching and transformation of such data. Whilst most of these attempts have so far ended in failure, it remains the case that the desire and temptation to develop such a system, whether in a single university or across a consortium of institutions, is very strong. Indeed, we would like to see the digital humanities working against such a move and instead developing either federated or network-based solutions and, as such, contributing to the re-decentralization of technical systems.[6]

Second, in relation to data, we might consider the more general societal implications of digital technology. Indeed, the notion that we leave behind 'digital breadcrumbs', not just on the internet, but across the whole of society, the economy, culture and even everyday life, is an issue that societies are just coming to terms with. Notwithstanding the recent Snowden revelations (see Berry 2014), new computational techniques demonstrate the disconnect between people's everyday understanding of technology and its penetration of life and the reality of total surveillance. Not just the lives of others are at stake here, but the very shape of public culture and the ability for individuals to make a 'public use of reason' without being subject to the chilling effects of state and corporate monitoring of our public activities. Indeed, computational technologies such as these described have little respect for the public/private distinction that our political systems have naturalized as part of a condition of possibility for political life at all. This makes it ever more imperative that we provide citizens with the ability to undertake critical technical practices, both in order to choose how to manage the digital breadcrumbs they leave as trails in public spaces, and to pull down the blinds on the postdigital gaze of state and corporate interests through the private use of cryptography and critical encryption practices.

Computation makes the collection of data relatively easy. This increases visibility through what Rey Chow (2012) calls 'capture'. Software enables more effective systems of surveillance and hence new capture systems. In thinking about the conditions of possibility that facilitate the mediated landscape of the *postdigital* (Berry and Dieter 2015), it is useful to explore concepts around capture and captivation. Chow argues that being 'captivated' is 'the sense of being lured and held by an unusual person, event, or spectacle. To be captivated is to be captured by means other than the purely physical, with an effect that is, nonetheless, lived and felt *as* embodied captivity' (Chow 2012: 48).[7]

To think about capture then is to think about the mediatized image in relation to reflexivity. For Chow, Walter Benjamin inaugurated a major change in the conventional logic of capture, from a notion of reality being caught or contained in the copy-image, such as in a repository, the copy-image becomes mobile, and this mobility adds to its versatility.

The copy-image then supersedes or replaces the original as the main focus; as such, this logic of the mechanical reproduction of images undermines hierarchy and introduces a notion of the image as infinitely replicable and extendable. Thus, the 'machinic act or event of capture' creates the possibility for further dividing and partitioning – that is, for the generation of copies, data and images – and sets in motion the conditions of possibility for a reality that is structured around the copy.

Thus the moment of capture or 'arrest' is an event of enclosure, locating and making possible the sharing and distribution of a moment through infinite reproduction and dissemination. So capture represents a techno-social moment but is also discursive in that it is a type of discourse that is derived from the imposition of power on bodies and the attachment of bodies to power. This Chow calls a heteronomy or heteropoiesis, as in a system or artifact designed by humans, with some purpose, not able to self-reproduce but which is yet able to exert agency in the form of prescription often back onto its designers. This essentially produces an externality in relation to the application of certain 'laws' or regulations usually drawn from pattern-analysis of Big Data.

Nonetheless, capture and captivation also constitute a critical response through the possibility of a disconnecting logic and the dynamics of mimesis. This possibility reflected through the notion of entanglements refers to what we might call 'derangements' in the 'organisation of knowledge caused by unprecedented adjacency and comparability or parity' (Chow 2012: 49). This is, of course, definitional in relation to the notion of computation which itself works through a logic of formatting, configuration, structuring and the application of computational ontologies (Berry 2011, 2014). Here we see the potential for digital humanities to think through and contest capture as a basic function of modern society: what is captured matters, and what matters is captured. However, this logic is limited within a historical context that calls for analysis beyond the limiting compressing and subtractive processes of computation.

This links to our final question about how visibility is made problematic when mediated through computational systems. The question is also linked to *who* is made visible in these kinds of systems, especially where, as feminist theorists have shown, visibility itself can be a gendered concept and practice, as demonstrated in the historical invisibility of women in the public sphere, for example (see Benhabib 1992). Thus, in what might be thought of as the postdigital – a term that Chow doesn't use but which we continue to think is helpful in thinking about this contrast – what is at stake is no longer this link between visibility and surveillance, nor indeed the link between becoming-mobile and the technology of images, but rather the collapse of the 'time lag' between the world and its capture. As Foucault argues, 'full lighting and the eyes of a supervisor capture better than darkness, which ultimately protected. Visibility is a trap' (Foucault 1991: 200).

This is when time loses its potential to 'become fugitive' or 'fossilized' and hence to be anachronistic. The key point is that the very possibility of memory is disrupted when images and text become instantaneous and therefore synonymous with an actual happening. This is a condition of the postdigital, whereby digital technologies make possible not only the instant capture and replication of an event, but also the very definition of the experience through its mediation both at the moment of capture – such as with the waving smartphones at a music concert or event – and in the subsequent recollection and reflection on that experience.

Here the visibility of certain sectors of a population may be intensified under the computational gaze: subjected to digital special measures, and interventions. Control of visibility is then a political moment in terms both of individual autonomy and collective representation and self-presentation. Who gets to control the very act of being visible, but also its resolution and the way in which it might be selectively applied across a population through digital technologies, are crucial issues. Here, by using 'visibility', we are talking not just about ocular ways of being visible, but also the making visible of computational techniques such as pattern-matching, machine learning, data visualization and so forth. Of course, related to this are the powers to make invisible, to hide or ignore people, problems or populations that the algorithmic gaze can be instructed to disregard.

The question then becomes how to 'darken' this visibility to prevent the totalizing nature of the full top-view that is possible in computational society? Using the metaphor of 'black boxes', how can we think about spaces that paradoxically enable democracy and the political, whilst limiting the reading of the internal processes of political experimentation and formation? Thus, how are we to create the conditions of possibility for 'opaque presence' to work on the edges or at the limits of legibility? We might call these spaces 'opaque temporary autonomous zones', which seek to enable democratic deliberation and debate. These should be fully political spaces, open and inclusive, but nonetheless opaque to the kinds of transparency that computation makes possible. As Rossiter and Zehle (2014) argue, we need to move towards a 'politics of anonymity', part of which is an acknowledgement of the way in which the mediation of algorithms could operate as a plane of opacity for various actors, opening critical zones for intervention.

It is important to note that this is not to create conditional and temporary moments – glitches in the regime of computational visibility. The idea is not to recreate notions of individual privacy as such, but rather to propose the creation of collective spaces of critical reflection for practices of creating a political response – that is, to draw on theory and 'un-theory' as a way of proceeding theoretically as 'an open source theory [and practice] in constant reformulation from multiple re-visions and remixings' (Goldberg 2014), what the Critical Theory Institute (CTI 2008) calls 'poor theory'. Indeed, we might argue that crypto practices can create spaces and shadows, thus tipping the balance away from systems of surveillance and control.[8]

By crypto practices, or crypto-activism, we mean the notion of 'hiding in plain sight', a kind of stenography of political practice. This is not merely a technical practice but a political and social one too. Here we are thinking of the counter-surveillance art of Adam Harvey, such as 'CV Dazzle', which seeks to design make-up that prevents facial recognition software from identifying faces, or the 'Stealth Wear' which creates the 'potential for fashion to challenge authoritarian surveillance' (Harvey 2014). Some examples in political practice can also be seen at the AntiSurveillance Feminist Poet Hair and Makeup Party. Additionally, Julian Oliver's work has also been exemplary in exploring the ideas of visibility and opacity. Here we are thinking in particular of Oliver's works that embed code executables, paradoxically, in images of the software objects themselves, such as 'Number was the substance of all things' (2012), but also 'PRISM: The Beacon Frame' (2013), which makes visible the phone radio networks, and hence the possibility of surveillance in real-time of networks and data channels (Oliver 2014).

These artworks develop the notion of opaque presence explored by Broeckmann (2010), who argues that in 'the society of late capitalism – whether we understand it as a society of consumption, of control, or as a cybernetic society – visibility and transparency are no longer signs of democratic openness, but rather of administrative availability'. The notion is also suggestively explored by the poet Edouard Glissant, who believes that we should 'agree not merely to the right to difference but, carrying this further, agree also to the right to opacity that is not enclosure within an irreducible singularity. Opacities can coexist and converge, weaving fabrics' (Glissant 1997: 190). Indeed, crypto practices have to be rethought as operating on the terrains of the political and technical simultaneously. Political activity, for example, is needed to legitimate these cryptographically enabled 'dark places' – both with the system (to avoid paranoia and attack), with the public (to educate and inform about them), and with activists and others.

We could think about these crypto-practices as (re)creating the possibility of being a crowd, in terms both of creating a sense of solidarity around the ends of a political/technical endeavour and of the means which act as a condition of possibility for it. Thus, we could say in a real sense that computer code can act to create 'crowd source', as it were, both in the technical sense of the computer source code, and in the practices of coming together to empower actors within a crowd, to connect to notions of the public and the common. But digital humanities could also help individuals to 'look to comprehend how things fit together, how structural conditions and cultural conceptions are mutually generative, reinforcing, and sustaining, or delimiting, contradictory, and constraining. [It] would strive to say difficult things overlooked or purposely ignored by conventional thinking, to speak critically about challenging matters, to identify critical and counter-interests' (Goldberg 2014). Again, by engaging with these practices both pedagogically and in terms of research projects, digital humanists can act as specific intellectuals who are able to bridge the world of words and new forms of datafication.

The question then becomes: what social force is able to realize the critique of computational society but also to block the real-time nature of computational monitoring? What practices become relevant when monitoring and capture become not only prevalent but actively engaged in? Tentatively, we would like to suggest embedding critical cryptographic practices made possible in what Lovink and Rossiter (2013) call OrgNets (organized networks) and linked to the wider research questions and approaches developed by the digital humanities.

Here, capture offers the possibility of a form of practice in relation to alienation, by making the inquirer adopt a position of criticism, the art of making strange. Chow has made links to Brecht and Shklovsky, and in particular their respective predilection for estrangement in artistic practice – such as in Brecht's notion of *Verfremdung* – and thus to show how things work, whilst they are being shown (Chow 2012: 26–8). In this moment of alienation, the possibility is thus raised of things being otherwise. This is the art of making strange as a means to disrupt everyday conventionalism and refresh the perception of the world – art as device. The connections between techniques of capture and critical practice, as advocated by Chow, and reading or writing the digital are suggestive in relation to computation more generally, not only in artistic practice but also in terms of critical theory. Indeed, capture could be a useful hinge around which to subject the softwarization practices, infrastructures and experiences of computation to critical thought, in terms of both their technical and social operations and the extent to which they generate a coercive imperative for humans to live and stay alive under the conditions of a biocomputational regime.

But so could what we might call crypto-activism, the creation of systems of inscription that enable the writing of opaque codes and the creation of 'opaque places'. This is not just making possible spaces of collectivity ('crowd source') but also the hacking and jamming of the real-time mediation of politics, dissent and everyday life (Deleuze 1992). As Glissant argues, 'we clamour for the right to opacity for everyone' (1997: 194). This, we think, calls for both a cartography of the hybridity of digital media (its postdigital materiality) and, importantly, the possible translation of crypto, as a concept and as a technical practice, into digital-activism tactics.

In contrast, to think for a moment about the other side of the antinomy, liberal societies have a notion of a common good of access to information to inform democratic citizens, whilst also seeking to valorize it. That is, the principle of visibility is connected to not only the notion of seeing one's representatives and the mechanisms of politics themselves, but also the knowledge that makes the condition of acting as a citizen possible. This is something that we believe digital humanities is well placed to explore and develop within the context of the historical traditions of the humanities as contributing to both reflexivity and a philosophy of life.

This book has documented how digital humanities has grown and developed and its potentialities and future possibilities. Although differences have emerged within the digital humanities between 'those who use new digital tools to aid relatively traditional scholarly projects and those who believe that digital humanities is most powerful as a disruptive political force that has the potential to reshape fundamental aspects of academic practice' (Gold 2012: x), it is still the case that as a growing and developing disciplinary area, it has much opportunity for growth and for these disparate elements to work together. As with differences between empirical and critical sociology, in a previous iteration of a contestation over knowledge, epistemology, disciplinary identity and research, digital humanities as a discipline will be richer and more vibrant with alternative voices contributing to projects, publications and practices. Indeed, the debates within digital humanities 'bear the mark of a field in the midst of growing pains as its adherents expand from a small circle of like-minded scholars to a more heterogeneous set of practitioners who sometimes ask more disruptive questions' (Gold 2012: xi). As Fitzpatrick argues, there is a 'creative tension between those who've been in the field for a long time and those who are coming to it today, between disciplinarity and interdisciplinarity, between making and interpreting, between the field's history and its future' (Fitzpatrick 2012: 14). This is a crucial part of the development of the digital humanities as a critical and humanistic area of inquiry and is the sign that it is indeed maturing from its earlier technical orientations towards a field of knowledge that deploys its own research questions, distinctive methodologies, practice-oriented research projects and theoretical contributions towards the humanities, but also to critical questions about humanity, citizenship, governance, knowledge and power.

Notes

1 Introduction

1 In this book, we have followed the suggestion of Liu (2016) that we treat digital humanities as a singular field as he argues that digital humanities is 'behaving linguistically as a collective noun characterized by what grammarians call *singular concord* (taking a singular verb)'. Further, he argues, 'concord in this sense need not imply consensus; it signals only that members of the field agree to participate in a common conversation' (Liu 2016: 1549).

2 We might equally note the emergence of digital sociology, computational social science, etc., as similar moves taking place in the social sciences.

3 It is interesting to contrast the approach in this book with that of Presner (2015), where he connects a critical approach through the digital humanities to a 'cultural-critical, *weakly* utopian possibility of the digital humanities' (2015: 65, original emphasis), particularly through the work of Pickering and Marcuse (2015: 58).

4 Sterne borrows a 'periodization from the history of sound recording, [and] refers to the "analog era" as the period dominated by analogue technologies of reproduction for print, images, video, and sound and the "digital era" as our present moment' (2015: 19).

5 This is where we differ from Sterne (2015: 20) who explains that 'there is no reason to think that digital humanities work is a radical break with the substance of questions that have spanned across centuries and generations of technical media simply because the tools are different'. Of course, this narrow definition of digital humanities as 'tools' avoids the wider question of how the historical constellation of knowledge is transformed through digital forms of storage, processing and dissemination, and depends on what Sterne means by a 'radical break' in this context. Sterne (2015: 29–31) prefers close reading practices used in conjunction with 'mundane tool adoption', rather than the possibilities opened up by distant reading extremely large data sets highlighted by, for example, Google Books' approximately 25–million-book database.

6 Market 1: national secondary school leavers (for undergraduate degree programmes); Market 2: local mature students who mostly study part-time (in the main for post experience programmes); and Market 3: international students (for both undergraduate and postgraduate study) (Veloutsou, et al. 2005).

7 As in Britain's new Teaching Excellence Framework (TEF) that will facilitate government monitoring for assessing the quality of teaching in England's

universities through a series of metrics which will be published to help prospective students to compare universities.

8 According to research from the University of Pennsylvania, only 4 per cent of enrolled students complete their chosen course; 80 per cent of students come from the richest 6 per cent of a population (*Forbes* 2013).

9 Busa further argues, 'using computers I had to realize that our previous knowledge of human language was too incomplete and anyway not sufficient for a computer program. Using computers will therefore lead us to a more profound and systematic knowledge of human expression; in principle, it can help us to be more humanistic than before' (Busa 1980: 89).

10 Colossus, one of the very first electronic computers, was constructed by British engineers during World War II to translate text, that is, to break German codes. Although the operations were mathematical and logical, they also relied on linguistics, and the desired outcome was readable text.

11 Jordan usefully links issues that are important in digital humanities to wider cultural critique through a notion of 'information politics', through which contestations over open access, open source, digital rights management and so forth create digital citizens, 'defined by their participation in digital culture [but which] also implies the often discussed collapse of the divide between production and consumption . . . because only when we have information in this form can we fully utilise it to produce further information that is always available to others for further making' (Jordan 2015: 199).

12 This has important links to a political economy of information, especially in relation to the internet, and is usefully explored by McChesney (2013), who argues: 'digital technologies can be deployed in ways that are extraordinarily inimical to freedom, democracy, and anything remotely connected to the good life. Therefore battles over the Internet are of central importance for all those seeking to build a better society. When the dust clears on this critical juncture, if our societies have not been fundamentally transformed for the better, if democracy has not triumphed over capital, the digital revolution may prove to have been a revolution in name only, an ironic, tragic reminder of the growing gap between the potential and the reality of human society' (2013: 232).

13 Koh reminds us that, as 'numerous postcolonial critics have noted, the ideas of *civilization*, *civility*, and their complement *civil society* continue to be dogged by their neocolonial dimensions' (Koh 2014: 95).

14 Scheinfeldt argues that digital humanists are the 'golden retrievers of the academy' (Scheinfeldt, quoted in Koh 2014: 95). But, as noted by goldenretrieverstraining.com, although golden retrievers 'aren't usually associated with aggression or aggressive behavior . . . they may growl, snap at another dog or individual, and sometimes even bite.'

15 Indeed Chun (2014: 4) argues, 'The humanities are sinking – if they are – not because of their earlier embrace of theory or multiculturalism, but because they have capitulated to a bureaucratic technocratic logic.'

16 Grusin further notes: '[neoliberalism] in higher education has itself been ena-

bled and intensified by the spread of networked digital technologies. This is not only true in higher education but also in the ways in which labor and employment have changed under a neoliberal regime that has been impacted by the spread of technology and the deskilling of labor' (Grusin 2016).

17 Chun (2014: 1) argues: 'the vapid embrace of the digital is a form of what Lauren Berlant has called "cruel optimism", [Berlant argues a] relation of cruel optimism exists when something you desire is actually an obstacle to your flourishing'.

18 Grusin (2013) has explained that we should think about this dichotomy in terms of the 'dark side of the moon', implying that we need to take account of and seek to understand the less illuminated elements of digital humanities.

19 Prescott further observes, 'I feel that the historical profession has become so internalized and cut off from wider intellectual cultures that it will prove to be beyond redemption, and we may need to look elsewhere to find the response that Tim [Hitchcock] seeks. Perhaps, dare I say it, it is the librarians and archivists who are already rising to this challenge and who will ensure that history has its Industrial Revolution' (Prescott 2014: 340).

20 We might note that the root of the word 'curate' is care, and care for the objects of study, digital or otherwise, is just the kind of approach we would want to propose for the digital humanities.

21 When we use 'computal', we are referring to the collective totality of computation as an abstract machine. We therefore need to develop critiques of the concepts that drive these processes of softwarization but also to think about what kind of experiences that make the epistemological categories of the computal possible. For example, one feature that distinguishes the computal is its division into surfaces, rough or pleasant, and concealed inaccessible structures.

22 Although GAFA (Google, Apple, Facebook, Amazon) is often used to represent high-technology Silicon Valley companies, it might be more accurate to direct attention to FANG (Facebook, Amazon, Netflix, Google), which more clearly denotes a special group of technology stacks concerning new models of computational media, such as streaming technologies (Berry 2011).

23 'Most computer technologists don't like to discuss it, but the importance of beauty is a consistent (if sometimes inconspicuous) thread in the software literature. Beauty is more important in computing than anywhere else in technology. . . . Beauty is important in engineering terms because software is so complicated. . . . Beauty is our most reliable guide to achieving software's ultimate goal: to break free of the computer, to break free conceptually. . . . But as we throw off the limits, what guides us? How do we know where to head? Beauty is the best guide we have' (David Gerlernter, quoted in Kirschenbaum 2004: 530).

24 Through the mediation of a tool – in this case, the macroscope – the digital humanist is able to move between different scales of data rapidly, creating a god's-eye view on history, literature, an epoch or a style, fulfilling the need for history of the *longue durée* but also the microhistory of social history and more

particularity in relation to the singularities that make up history itself. Whilst Hitchcock (2014) remains ambivalent about the possibilities that such a tool might hold – he writes 'if we are going to build a few macroscopes, . . . along with the blue marble views, we [should] keep hold of the smallest details' – it is still the case that the construction of tools and digital humanities are always closely related in the practices of digital humanists.

25 However, Pannapacker later changed his position, stating 'I regret that my claim about digital humanities as the nbt [next big thing] – which I meant in a serious way – has become a basis for a rhetoric that presents it as some passing fad that most faculty members can dismiss or even block when DH'ers come up for tenure' (quoted in Chun 2014: 5).

26 In fact, we think of basic coding skills as more akin to the humanities interpretative skills of reading and writing rather than as biased towards practical or vocational skills. For this reason, the notion of computational thinking is a helpful way of developing this capability for a new digital humanities subject.

27 For example, the Digital Methods Initiative at the University of Amsterdam, led by Richard Rogers, uses digital methods to study data that are 'born digital'. The software they create is used to find and extract data from Application Programming Interfaces (APIs) of large internet service providers, such as Wikipedia, Amazon, YouTube, Facebook and Google. The data extracted are then analysed using statistical and visualization methods, or through the use of network analysis software, such as Gephi, which has become the most recognizable output from the use of digital methods. The tools and methods that are developed are shared as open source software after successful testing. See https://wiki.digitalmethods.net/Dmi/WebHome.

2 Genealogies of the Digital Humanities

1 A series of monographs in the British Library Research series give a helpful overview of humanities computing up until the mid-1990s (Katzen 1990; Kenna and Ross 1995; Mullings 1996).

2 For the purposes of this discussion, digital history and digital humanities are somewhat conflated although they do have separate histories and trajectories in their own right (for example, see Thomas 2004; Gregory 2014). For a discussion of music and digital humanities, see Fujinaga and Weiss (2004). For performing arts, see Saltz (2004). See The Old Bailey Online (https://www.oldbaileyonline.org and https://www.londonlives.org, Hitchcock and Shoemaker 2015), The Atlantic Slave Trade and Slave Life in the Americas: A Visual Record project (http://slaveryimages.org) and Valley of the Shadow project (http://valley.lib.virginia.edu) for good examples of digital history, together with the History Harvest (http://historyharvest.unl.edu).

3 As Scheinfeldt (2014) explains, 'digital history [is] a natural outgrowth of long-standing public and cultural historical activities rather than a belated inheritance of the quantitative history experiments of the 1960s and 1970s. It is a story that begins with people like Allan Nevins of the Columbia Oral History

Office and Alan Lomax of the Library of Congress's Archive of American Folk-Song, especially with the man-on-the-street interviews Lomax coordinated in the aftermath of the Pearl Harbor attacks.'

4 'Recognizing a pattern implies remaining open to gatherings, groupings, clusters, repetitions, and responding to the internal and external relations they set up' (L. Hunter, quoted in Ramsay 2004: 195).

5 Kirschenbaum and Werner observe that 'software studies, critical code studies, and platform studies are each varyingly inflected methodologies for cultivating both the critical sensibility and the technical acumen necessary to swim deep into the cultural reservoirs of contemporary digital production' (Kirschenbaum and Werner 2014: 435).

6 Barnett (2014: 74) usefully asks what origin story of digital humanities would include the #AntiJemimas project, for example. For the project, Kismet Nuñez (*#AntiJemimas* Founder and Creative Director) 'deploys 21st century forms of art, autobiography, and performance against the discursive terrain of race, sex and personality. With the help of new media, [Nuñez] breaks herself into pieces to become more than her parts in a revolutionary act of defiance, affirmation & self-care.'

7 In a more complete history of digital humanities than we have space to outline here, we would include thinkers like G. W. Leibniz, who developed a method of calculation called the calculus raciocinator, an innovation his successors George Boole and Gottlob Frege extended, and, with the subsequent work of Georg Cantor, David Hilbert, Kurt Gödel, and Alan Turing, contributed to the computer that we know today (Davies 2000; see also McCarty 2013b). But we might also think of including Ada Lovelace, Charles Babbage, Christopher S. Strachey, Joseph Weizenbaum, Grace Murray Hopper, John von Neumann, Adele Goldberg and many others. We would also include systems like Strachey's Love Poetry Generator developed in 1953, and Weizenbaum's ELIZA software program in 1966, which demonstrated how text could be manipulated in and through computational systems.

8 The theological beginnings of digital humanities is also interesting in light of its conceptualization of world and words, as Busa himself commented, 'I am full of amazement at the developments [in digital humanities] since [1949]; they are enormously greater and better than I could then imagine. Digitus Dei est hic! The finger of God is here!' (Busa 2004).

9 However, one would note that art historical projects within digital humanities are also fundamentally concerned with visuality and the image.

10 Golumbia notes, however: 'despite its insistence on being only a set of methods, DH can be productively understood as a political intervention within literary studies, one of whose functions is to challenge the authority of "non-DH" literature scholars regarding our own discipline, in particular via a tendentious deployment of both the terms digital and humanities' (Golumbia 2014: 157).

11 Key journals within digital humanities include: *Digital Humanities Quarterly*, which is published by the Alliance of Digital Humanities Organizations as

a peer review and open access journal; *Digital Scholarship in the Humanities* (DSH) – originally titled *Literary and Linguistic Computing* (LLC), the journal has changed its name to reflect better the discipline of digital humanities and the content of publications; *Vectors: Journal of Culture and Technology in a Dynamic Vernacular,* an experimental journal that brings together multimedia texts; *Digital Studies / Le champ numérique,* sponsored by the Canadian Society for Digital Humanities (Société pour l'Étude des Médias Interactifs) (see also Kirschenbaum 2012b: 4).

12 It is also interesting to compare these debates with postcolonial critiques of the archive, such as that articulated by Mbembe (2015).

13 Kirschenbaum writes: 'To assert that digital humanities is a "tactical" coinage is not simply to indulge in neopragmatic relativism. Rather, it is to insist on the reality of circumstances in which it is unabashedly deployed to get things done – "things" that might include getting a faculty line or funding a staff position, establishing a curriculum, revamping a lab, or launching a center' (Kirschenbaum 2012b: 415). He continues this strategic sense of the term 'digital humanities' by arguing that 'DH is a means and not an end' (2012b: 427).

14 Sometimes this notion of community can be rather defensively deployed, for example Kirschenbaum argues 'so it is with digital humanities: you are a digital humanist if you are listened to by those who are already listened to as digital humanists, and they themselves got to be digital humanists by being listened to by others. Jobs, grant funding, fellowships, publishing contracts, speaking invitations – these things do not make one a digital humanist' (Kirschenbaum 2014: 55).

15 Koh argues, 'in all of these debates, technical knowledge is consistently emphasized or dismissed as an important condition of entry into the digital humanities community. Technical knowledge is linked to the concept of *building* and is cast as a means by which community members perform their civic duties' (Koh 2014: 99).

16 Hydraulic mining, also referred to as hydraulicking, is a technique used in mining that uses high-pressure jets of water to dislodge rock material or move sediment. In mining gold, for example, the resulting water–sediment slurry is filtered through sluice boxes that remove the gold ore. We are not sure that this is an appropriate metaphor for handling sensitive cultural artifacts as a form of knowledge-fracking, which appears exploitative and treats cultural history as a form of standing reserve.

3 On the Way to Computational Thinking

1 Wing attributes this definition to an unpublished 2010 manuscript.

2 We can only note here the problematics with various forms of labour used within the digital humanities, such as the digital microtask work that is generated by systems such as Amazon Mechanical Turk, or TaskRabbit. Also crowdsourcing efforts can, without a great deal of care, create ethical problems

in relation to the use of unpaid labour, unexpected exploitative situations and unfair intellectual property rights reassignments and contracts.

3 It is interesting to think about the computational imaginary in relation to the notion of 'work' that this entails or that is coded/delegated into the machine algorithms of our postdigital age. Campagna (2013) has an interesting formulation of this in relation to what Newman (2013) has called 'nothing less than a new updated *Ego and Its Own* for our contemporary neoliberal age' (2013: 93). Campagna writes, 'westerners had to find a way of adapting [a] mystical exercise to the structures of contemporary capitalism. What would a mantra look like, in the heart of a global metropolis of the 21st Century? What other act might be able to host its obsessive spirit, whilst functioning like a round, magic shield, covering the frightened believers from their fear of freedom? There was only one possible, almost perfect candidate. The activity of repetition par excellence: Work. The endless chain of gestures and movements that had built the pyramids and dug the mass graves of the past. The seal of a new alliance with all that is divine, which would be able to bind once again the whole of humanity to a new and eternal submission. The act of submission to submission itself. Work. The new, true faith of the future' (2013: 10). Here, though, we argue that it is not immaterial apparitions and spectres which are haunting humanity and which the Egoist can break free from, but the digital materiality of computers' abstractions formed of algorithms and code and which are a condition of possibility for individuation and subjectivity itself within cognitive capitalism.

4 Knowledge Representation and Archives

1 Later, McCarty has argued that *simulation* is a more fruitful term. We argue that *model* as defined by Minsky to be a useful concept, however (Minsky 1965; McCarty 2016).

2 www.archives.gov/exhibits/charters/declaration_history.html.

3 In fact, Hart's first version of the Declaration was typed in capital letters only, as the mainframe did not have lower-case at the time. Similarly, the Soviet counterpart, GOST, from the same era, could only encode Cyrillic characters.

4 For an excellent introduction to network analysis, see Golbeck (2013).

5 For 'HTTP', see http://en.wikipedia.org/wiki/Hypertext_Transfer_Protocol, www.w3.org/Protocols/rfc2616/rfc2616.html. The term 'URI' covers web resources that include URLs or webpage addresses: www.w3.org/TR/uri-clarification. For 'HTML', see http://en.wikipedia.org/wiki/HTML. A meta-model is the model of a model – the elements, properties and rules that a model can use. For 'RDF', see www.w3.org/RDF. RDF consists of only three elements, even though most systems employ another optional field, to identify a set of triples (named graphs) making a quad.

5 Research Infrastructures

1 That is to say that creating policies to aim for these ends is not the same as

actually developing the usually difficult technical solutions to do this. Not only are the difficulty and complexity of digital projects something that digital humanities has broad experience of, but also it understands well the relationship between good research infrastructure provision and good technical solutions.

2 A good example of the specificity, if not idiosyncrasy, of classification is demonstrated by the unique classification system of the Warburg Institute Library in the School of Advanced Study at the University of London. It has a 'unique classification system [in] the Library established by Aby Warburg and Fritz Saxl, and has been refined, extended and reorganised in particular sections by three generations of scholar librarians. It structures culture and expression under four categories: Image, Word, Orientation and Action, corresponding to the four floors of stacks above the Reading Room'. Indeed, it is claimed that 'detailed organisation of the Warburg Library makes inspired connections between different fields of endeavour and study. The open shelves lead readers to books which they might not otherwise find, while the unique arrangement of the sections aids intuitive connections' (Warburg 2016).

3 Kirschenbaum (2012a: 6) notes: 'That *the* major federal granting agency for scholarship in the humanities, taking its cues directly from a small but active and influential group of scholars, had devoted scarce resources to launching a number of new grant opportunities, many of them programmatically innovative in and of themselves, around an endeavor termed "digital humanities" was doubtless the tipping point for the branding of DH, at least in the United States.'

4 On the subject of multimedia, see Rockwell and Mactavish (2004), who argue that various forms of born-digital content, made popular particularly with the rise of the internet, are amenable to digital humanities methods and approaches. See also Kolker (2004: 383).

5 The contradictory logics of building research capacity for the university to exercise research leadership in terms of each of its disciplinary specialisms and to encourage intellectual curiosity, whilst also being chained to the political economic needs of the nation, is something very common to these documents. Whilst we do not have space to develop this issue further, contradictions are also located in aspects of digital humanities' own self-justifications that draw from these discourses.

6 See, for example, UK e-Science programme (Hey and Trefethen 2002).

7 A further 'digging into data' challenge was also announced in 2016 as part of the ODH-led Trans-atlantic Platform (see www.transatlanticplatform.com).

8 It also remains unsettling that research infrastructures might sometimes be seen as a means for engendering top-down change in both the higher education sector and individual universities. Whilst it is not always the case that digital infrastructure projects are mobilized in this way, nonetheless they sometimes lean towards a desire for bureaucratic control of certain research practices, but also indirectly of the research approaches that individual scholars might undertake. This is something that digital humanists should act to contest, and they

should seek to ensure that research priorities in the use of digital technologies for humanities are led by humanists and their need for research infrastructures.

9 See http://republicofletters.stanford.edu, http://emlo.bodleian.ox.ac.uk/home and http://ckcc.huygens.knaw.nl.

10 As Moretti explained in 2004, 'My little dream . . . is of a literary class that would look more like a lab than a Platonic academy' (Moretti, quoted in Eakin 2004). To which, 'Harold Bloom, the Yale English professor famous for his prodigious command of canonical literature, was more dismissive. Interrupting a description of the theory, he pronounced Mr. Moretti "an absurdity"' (Eakin 2004).

11 We could also add the Scholar's Lab at the University of Virginia, Digital Scholarship Lab at the University of Richmond, the Humanities and Critical Code Studies Lab at the University of California, the Humanities Lab at Duke University, the Electronic Textual Cultures Lab at the University of Victoria, HUMlab at Umeå University, the CulturePlex Lab at Western University, the Digital Humanities Lab at Aarhus University, Alfalab at the Royal Netherlands Academy of Arts and Sciences (KNAW) and many others.

12 www.kcl.ac.uk/artshums/depts/ddh/index.aspx.

13 http://digital.humanities.ox.ac.uk.

14 www.gla.ac.uk/subjects/informationstudies.

15 The Sussex Humanities Lab links digital humanities, media and cultural studies, performance, history and sociology together in order to broaden the field and generate new opportunities for cross-disciplinary work.

16 The characters are not just 1 or 0, they may also represent 'false' and 'true', 'no' and 'yes', 'off' and 'on' and other binary oppositions (Finneman 1999).

17 Amazon used to define the ECU directly, stating: 'We use several benchmarks and tests to manage the consistency and predictability of the performance of an EC2 Compute Unit. One EC2 Compute Unit provides the equivalent CPU capacity of a 1.0–1.2 GHz 2007 Opteron or 2007 Xeon processor. This is also the equivalent to an early-2006 1.7 GHz Xeon processor referenced in our original documentation' (Berninger 2010). They appear to have stopped using this description in their documentation (see Amazon 2013).

6 Digital Methods and Tools

1 Galloway argues, 'Few things will cripple the humanities more than the uncritical "adoption of tools" or the continued encroachment of positivistic research methods borrowed from cognitive science, neuroscience, computer science, or elsewhere' (Galloway 2014: 128).

2 The extent to which digital humanities is linked to a favourable political economic climate as well as generous funding is something that does not receive enough attention and disciplinary reflexivity in the field.

7 Digital Scholarship and Interface Criticism

1 One example may be Bruno Latour's web site, which seems to contain the final

version of almost every article this prolific author has written, including those from journals that normally do not allow open access.

2 Nearly every open access policy at a university or funding agency is a 'green' policy – that is, a policy requiring deposit in an open access repository often with an embargo of 18–24 months – rather than submission as 'gold' to unrestricted open access journals (*Guardian* 2013). Note that the UK funding councils require publications in gold for sciences and green for social science and humanities as a condition of their funding.

3 Fitzpatrick (2011) argues that peer review originates in book censorship predating scientific journals, however.

4 Maeda (2015) argues: 'I predict large tech companies will place greater attention on design. This is not dissimilar to the automobile industry as it began to mature – the famous point when Henry Ford refused to sell variations in the only color that mattered, compared with GM, which diversified its designs to appeal to larger populations across multiple brands like Chevrolet, Buick and Cadillac with differing emotional appeal. We see it already with Google's efforts around Android's enhanced "Material" visual language led by Matias Duarte, eBay's design leadership efforts led by John Donahoe and IBM's resurgence in the design space with its new Austin center led by Phil Gilbert.'

5 If we are to be consistent, we should follow Kittler's argument and realise that the code the geeks read is also a user interface; a programming language is a shorthand for humans to make it possible to create complex programs with less effort, opening up to creative uses. We could program in assembler code, yet hardly any programmers do. Today, instead, we tend to program in what are called 'high-level languages' and use text editors which are themselves specialized interfaces for using the computer. In this chapter, we will be concerned with the interfaces of running programs, aimed at users when they are not programming.

6 The production of a series of subjectivities constantly overloaded and reinforced through the interface as a temporal object which mediates experience can be captured in the idea of a subjectivity specific to a condition on contextual computing, continuous interfaces and flat design, what we might term *flat dasein*. That is a minimal subjectivity augmented through environmental and non-conscious cognition from machinic faculties produced via the programming industries, and particularly the cognitive-software-design complex of Silicon Valley.

7 Design as a theoretical limit for the reconciliation of a highly fragmented computation experience, but also life in postmodern capitalism, are interestingly reflected on by Latour (2008), when he argues: 'today everyone with an iPhone knows that it would be absurd to distinguish what has been designed from what has been planned, calculated, arrayed, arranged, packed, packaged, defined, projected, tinkered, written down in code, disposed of and so on. From now on, "to design" could mean equally any or all of those verbs. Secondly, it has grown in extension – design is applicable to ever larger assem-

blages of production. The range of things that can be designed is far wider now than a limited list of ordinary or even luxury goods.'

8 Tactics which might be deployed in a continuous interface criticism might include disrupting the bluetooth and WiFi antennas that enable the continuity experience, connecting and disconnecting new devices into the fabric of continuity technologies, connecting devices across platforms, e.g. across material and flat design paradigms, and overloading the data or computational power to cause glitches to be surfaced in terms of the continuous interface. Treating continuity transfers as a logistics network, and selectively slowing down and speeding up the continuity computational objects would be an interesting example of playfully demonstrating the continuity system. An example of a hack of Apple's instantiation of continuous computing is the Continuity Activation Tool, see https://github.com/dokterdok/Continuity-Activation-Tool/

9 The interface might also be thought of as a 'gift' or, in Lewandowska and Cummings's terms, have the 'potential to contest the economising of culture, the reduction of all exchange to financial calculation' (Lewandowska and Cummings 2005: 85). This points to the possibility of developing interface criticism as part of the field of digital humanities.

10 See Hartson and Pyla (2012) for an extensive overview of this tradition.

8 Towards a Critical Digital Humanities

1 The notion of a critical digital humanities has been previously explored in Berry (2013, 2014).

2 We could start with some detailed surveys of the digitization and archive projects already undertaken and reflect on the likelihood that they privilege particular race, gender and class actors not only in their content, but also in the decisions over which archives are selected and which are funded.

3 Drucker notes that her colleagues were fond of remarking that 'humanists came into those conversations [about digital projects] as relativists and left as positivists out of pragmatic recognition that certain tenets of critical theory could not be sustained in that environment' (Drucker 2012: 88). It is this digital hollowing-out of the humanities that needs to be resisted and highlighted.

4 Here we see links with a broadly ethical framework that can be drawn from and strengthened through, for example, deontological approaches. We also see the possibility for more politically oriented contestation through certain kinds of advocacy, in terms both of engagement with or support for, say, the Free Software Foundation, and policy interventions, open-sourcing projects, refusing to work with 'closed' providers and educating fellow scholars, etc.

5 Reuben Brower further calls for 'slowing down the process of reading to observe what is happening, in order to attend very closely to the words, their uses, and their meanings' (Brower, quoted in Hancher 2016). Of course, similarly we would argue that attending to the way in which digital humanities projects are funded, designed, assembled, implemented and disseminated, by slowing down the process and creating what we might call 'humanities interventions' at

points in each stage, would enable us to reflect on the process and the decisions being made – for example, regarding an assumption about a presumed gendered user, the use of certain case studies, or an underlying computationalism in the epistemology of the project.

6 It is here that we are supportive of attempts to use technologies promoted by the Indyweb, for example, but also open standards through linked data and licence-free formats.

7 Chow further notes: 'The French word *captation*, referring to a process of deception and inveiglement [or persuading (someone) to do something by means of deception or flattery] by artful means, is suggestive insofar as it pinpoints the elusive yet vital connection between art and the state of being captivated. But the English word "captivation" seems more felicitous, not least because it is semantically suspended between an aggressive move and an affective state, and carries within it the force of the trap in both active and reactive senses, without their being organised necessarily in a hierarchical fashion and collapsed into a single discursive plane' (Chow 2012: 48).

8 Of course, paradoxically, these opaque spaces themselves may draw attention from state authorities and the intelligence community who monitor the use of encryption and cryptography – demonstrating again the paradox of opacity and visibility.

References

About Kairos (n.d.) *Kairos: A Journal of Technology, Rhetoric, and Pedagogy*, http://kairos.technorhetoric.net/about.html

Accessible Future (2015) Building an Accessible Future for the Humanities Project, www.accessiblefuture.org.

Acevedo, D., Vote, E., Laidlaw, D. H. and Joukowsky, M. S. (2001) Archaeological data visualization in VR: analysis of lamp finds at the great temple of Petra, a case study. *IEEE Visualization*, 493–6.

Acord, S. K. and Harley, D. (2013) Credit, time, and personality: the human challenges to sharing scholarly work using Web 2.0. *New Media & Society*, 15:3, 379–97, doi:10.1177/1461444812465140.

Agrawai, R., Imielinski, T. and Swami, A. (1993) Mining association rules between sets of items in large databases. In *Proceedings of the 1993 ACM SIGMOD International Conference on Management of Data*, Washington, DC: ACM, 207–16.

Agre, P. E. (1997) Toward a critical technical practice: lessons learned in trying to reform AI. In *Social Science, Technical Systems, and Cooperative Work: Beyond the Great Divide*, ed. G. Bowker et al. Hillsdale, NJ: Erlbaum, pp. 131–58.

Algorithm (2015) *Encyclopædia Britannica Online*, global.britannica.com/topic/algorithm.

Allen, J. (2013) Critical Infrastructure, http://post-digital.projects.cavi.dk/?p=356.

Allington, D., Brouillette, S. and Golumbia, D. (2016) Neoliberal Tools (and Archives): A Political History of Digital Humanities, https://lareviewofbooks.org/article/neoliberal-tools-archives-political-history-digital-humanities.

Amazon (2013) Amazon EC2 FAQs, http://aws.amazon.com/ec2/faqs/#What_is_an_EC2_Compute_Unit_and_why_did_you_introduce_it.

Amoore, L. and Piotukh, V. (2015) Life beyond big data: governing with little analytics. *Economy and Society*, 44:3, 341–66, http://dx.doi.org/10.1080/03085 147.2015.1043793.

Andersen, P. B. (1990) *A Theory of Computer Semiotics*. Cambridge: Cambridge University Press.

Anderson, S. (2013) Thinking infrastructure: what are research infrastructures? *International Journal of Humanities and Arts Computing*, 7:1–2, 4–23.

Apple (2015) Connect your iPhone, iPad, iPod touch, and Mac using Continuity, https://support.apple.com/en-gb/HT204681.

Argamon, S. (2008) Interpreting Burrows's delta: geometric and probabilistic foundations. *Literary and Linguistic Computing*, 23, 131–47.

Arthur, P. L. and Bode, K. (2014) *Advancing Digital Humanities: Research, Methods, Theories*. London: Palgrave.

Atkins, D., Droegemeier, K. K., Feldman, S. I., Garcia-Molina, H., Klein, M. L. and Messina, P. (2003) *Revolutionizing Science and Engineering Through Cyberinfrastructure: Report of the National Science Foundation Blue-Ribbon Advisory Panel on Cyberinfrastructure*. Washington: National Science Foundation, www.nsf.gov/cise/sci/reports/atkins.pdf.

Balzhiser, D., Grover, M. and Lauer, E. (2011) The Facebook papers. *Kairos*, 16, http://kairos.technorhetoric.net/16.1/praxis/balzhiser-et-al.

Barnett, F. (2014) The brave side of digital humanities. *differences*, 25:1, 64–78.

Barthes, R. (1994) Introduction to the structural analysis of narratives. In *The Semiotic Challenge*. Berkeley: University of California Press, pp. 95–135.

Benhabib, S. (1992) *Situating the Self: Gender, Community and Postmodernism in Contemporary Ethics*. London: Routledge.

Benjamin, W. (2002) The work of art in the age of its technological reproducibility. In *Walter Benjamin: Selected Writings*, ed. H. Eiland and M. W. Jennings. Cambridge, MA: Harvard University Press.

Berardi, F. (2012) *The Uprising: On Poetry and Finance*. London: Semiotext(e).

Berners-Lee, T. (1990) Information Management: A Proposal, May, www.w3.org/History/1989/proposal-msw.html.

Berners-Lee, T. (1994) A Brief History of the Web, www.w3.org/DesignIssues/TimBook-old/History.html.

Berninger, D. (2010) What the Heck is an ECU?, http://cloudpricecalculator.com/blog/hello-world.

Berry, D. M. (2008) *Copy, Rip, Burn: The Politics of Copyleft and Open Source*. London: Pluto Press.

Berry, D. M. (2011) *The Philosophy of Software: Code and Mediation in the Digital Age*. Basingstoke: Palgrave.

Berry, D. M. (2012a) *Understanding Digital Humanities*. Basingstoke: Palgrave Macmillan.

Berry, D. M. (2012b) The social epistemologies of software. *Social Epistemology*, 26:3–4, 379–98.

Berry, D. M. (2013) Critical digital humanities. *Stunlaw*, http://stunlaw.blogspot.co.uk/2013/01/critical-digital-humanities.html.

Berry, D. M. (2014) *Critical Theory and the Digital*. New York: Bloomsbury.

Berry, D. M. (2015a) Flat theory. *Boundary 2*, http://boundary2.org/2015/01/27/flat-theory.

Berry, D. M. (2015b) Continuous interfaces. *Stunlaw*, http://stunlaw.blogspot.co.uk/2015/06/continuous-interfaces.html.

Berry, D. M. and Dieter, M. (2015) *Postdigital Aesthetics: Art, Computation and Design*. Basingstoke: Palgrave.

Berry, D. M. Borra, E., Helmond, A., Plantin, J. C. and Walker Rettberg, J. (2015)

The data sprint approach: exploring the field of digital humanities through Amazon's Application Programming Interface (API). *Digital Humanities Quarterly*, 9:4, ISSN 1938–4122.

Besser, H. (2004) The past, present and future of digital libraries. In *A Companion to Digital Humanities*, ed. S. Schreibman, R. Siemans and J. Unsworth. London: Wiley-Blackwell.

Bianco, J. (2012) This digital humanities which is not one. In *Debates in Digital Humanities*, ed. M. K. Gold. Minneapolis: University of Minnesota Press, pp. 96–112.

Bilansky, A. (2016) Search, reading, and the rise of database. *Digital Scholarship in the Humanities*, doi:10.1093/llc/fqw023.

Boltanski, L. and Chiapello, E. (2005) *The New Spirit of Capitalism*. London: Verso.

Bolter, J. D. (1976) *Turing's Man: Western Culture in the Computer Age*. Chapel Hill: University of North Carolina Press, 1984.

Bolter, J. D. (1991) *Writing Space: The Computer, Hypertext, and the History of Writing*. Hillsdale, NJ: Erlbaum.

Bolter, J. D. and Grusin, R. (1999) *Remediation: Understanding New Media*. Cambridge, MA: MIT Press.

Boonstra, O., Breure, L. and Doorn, P. (2004) Past, present and future of historical information science. *Historical Social Research*, 29:2, www.ahc.ac.uk/docs/pastpresentfuture.pdf.

Börner, K. (2011) Plug-and-play macroscopes. *Communications of the ACM*, 54:3, 60–9.

Bratton, B. (2014) The black stack. *e-flux*, www.e-flux.com/journal/the-black-stack.

Brecht, B. (2007) Popularity and realism. In *Aesthetics and Politics*. London: Verso, pp. 79–85.

Broeckmann, A. (2010) *Opaque Presence / Manual of Latent Invisibilities*. Berlin: Diaphanes Verlag.

Brügger, N. (2011a) Web archiving – between past, present, and future. In *The Handbook of Internet Studies*, ed. M. Consalvo and C. Ess. Oxford: Wiley-Blackwell, pp. 24–42.

Brust, A. (2012) Cloudera's Impala brings Hadoop to SQL and BI, www.zdnet.com/clouderas-impala-brings-hadoop-to-sql-and-bi-7000006413.

Bucher, T. (2012) Want to be on the top? Algorithmic power and the threat of invisibility on Facebook. *New Media & Society*, 14:7, 1164–80.

Busa, R. (1980) The annals of humanities computing: the Index Thomisticus. *Computers and the Humanities*, 14:2, 83–90, www.jstor.org/stable/30207304.

Busa, R. A. (2004) Foreword: perspectives on the digital humanities. In *A Companion to the Digital Humanities*, ed. S. Schreibman, R. Siemens and J. Unsworth. Oxford: Blackwell, pp. xvi–xxi.

Campagna, F. (2013) *The Last Night: Anti-Work, Atheism, Adventure*. London: Zero Books.

Cecire, N. (2011a) Introduction: theory and the virtues of digital humanities.

Journal of Digital Humanities, 1:1, http://journalofdigitalhumanities.org/1–1/ introduction-theory-and-the-virtues-of-digital-humanities-by-natalia-cecire.

Cecire, N. (2011b) When digital humanities was in vogue. *Journal of Digital Humanities*, 1:1, http://journalofdigitalhumanities.org/1–1/ when-digital-humanitieswas-in-vogue-by-natalia-cecire.

Chow, R. (2012) *Entanglements, or Transmedial Thinking about Capture*. London: Duke University Press.

Chun, W. (2013) The Dark Side of the Digital Humanities, www.c21uwm. com/2013/01/09/the-dark-side-of-the-digital-humanities-part-1.

Chun, W. H. K. (2011) *Programmed Visions: Software and Memory*. Cambridge, MA: MIT Press.

Chun, W. H. K. (2014) Working the digital humanities: uncovering shadows between the dark and the light. *differences*, 2:1, 1–25.

Codd, E. F. (1970) A relational model of data for large shared data banks. *Communications of the ACM*, 13, 377–87.

Cohen, P. (2010) Digital keys for unlocking the humanities' riches. *The New York Times*, 16 November, www.nytimes.com/2010/11/17/arts/17digital.html?_r=0.

Cordell, R. (2014) On Ignoring Encoding, http://ryancordell.org/research/dh/ on-ignoring-encoding.

Cowen, T. (2013) *Average Is Over: Powering America Beyond the Age of the Great Stagnation*. London: Dutton Books.

CTI (2008) Poor theory notes: toward a manifesto. *Critical Theory Institute*, https://www.humanities.uci.edu/critical/poortheory.pdf.

Dahl, O.-J. and Nygaard, K. (1966) SIMULA: an ALGOL-based simulation language. *Communications of the ACM*, 9, 671–8.

Davidson, C. (2012) Humanities 2.0: promise, perils, predictions. In *Debates in Digital Humanities*, ed. M. K. Gold. Minneapolis: University of Minnesota Press, pp. 476–89.

Davies, J. (2013) Compute Power with Energy-Efficiency, http://developer.amd. com/wordpress/media/2013/06/Compute_Power_with_Energy-Efficiency_ Jem_AMD_v1.1.pdf.

Davies, M. (2000) *The Universal Computer: The Road from Leibnitz to Turing*. London: W. W. Norton & Company.

Deegan, M. and Sutherland, K. (2009) *Text Editing, Print and the Digital World*. London: Ashgate Publishing.

Deegan, M. and Tanner, S. (2004) Conversion of primary sources. In *A Companion to Digital Humanities*, ed. S. Schreibman, R. Siemans and J. Unsworth. London: Wiley-Blackwell, pp. 488–504.

Deleuze, G. (1992) Postscript on the societies of control. *October*, 59, 3–7, https:// files.nyu.edu/dnm232/public/deleuze_postcript.pdf.

DeRose, S. J., Durand, D. G., Mylonas, E. and Renear, A. H. (1990) What is text, really? *Journal of Computing in Higher Education*, 1:2, 3–26.

Dexter, S. (2012) The esthetics of hidden things. In *Understanding Digital Humanities*, ed. D. M. Berry. New York: Palgrave Macmillan, pp. 127–44.

Drucker, J. (2012) Humanistic theory and digital scholarship. In *Debates in Digital Humanities*, ed. M. K. Gold. Minneapolis: University of Minnesota Press, pp. 85–95.

Drucker, J. and Nowviskie, B. (2004) Speculative computing: aesthetic provocations in humanities computing. In *A Companion to Digital Humanities*, ed. S. Schreibman, R. Siemans and J. Unsworth. London: Wiley-Blackwell, pp. 431–47.

Dunne, A. and Raby, F. (2013) Critical Design FAQ, www.dunneandraby.co.uk/content/bydandr/13/0.

Eakin, E. (2004) Studying literature by the numbers. *The New York Times*, 10 January, www.nytimes.com/2004/01/10/books/studying-literature-by-the-numbers.html?_r=0.

Earhart, A. (2012) Can information be unfettered? Race and the new digital humanities canon. In *Debates in Digital Humanities*, ed. M. K. Gold. Minneapolis: University of Minnesota Press, pp. 309–18.

Earhart, A. (2015) The digital humanities as a laboratory. In *Between the Humanities and the Digital*, ed. P. Svennson and D. T. Goldberg. Cambridge, MA: MIT Press, pp. 391–400.

Eastgate (2015) Hypertext Fiction, www.eastgate.com/catalog/Fiction.html.

Eco, U. (1976) *A Theory of Semiotics*. Bloomington: Indiana University Press.

Economist (2014) Coming to an office near you. *The Economist*, www.economist.com/news/leaders/21594298–effect-todays-technology-tomorrows-jobs-will-be-immenseand-no-country-ready.

Eiteljorg, H. (2004) Computing for archaeologists. In *A Companion to Digital Humanities*, ed. S. Schreibman, R. Siemans and J. Unsworth. London: Wiley-Blackwell, pp. 20–30.

Elliott, J. (2015) Whole genre sequencing. *Digital Scholarship in the Humanities*, http://dx.doi.org/10.1093/llc/fqv034.

ELMCIP (2015) http://elmcip.net.

Engholm, I. (2003) WWW's designhistorie: Website utviklingen i et genre- og stilteoretisk perspektiv. Ph.D. thesis, IT University of Copenhagen.

ESF (2011) Research Infrastructures in the Digital Humanities, European Science Foundation, www.esf.org/fileadmin/Public_documents/Publications/spb42_RI_DigitalHumanities.pdf.

EU (2006) *European Roadmap for Research Infrastructures Report 2006*. Luxembourg: European Strategy Forum on Research Infrastructures, Office for Official Publications of the European Communities.

Facebook (2011) EdgeRank Magic revealed in F8 Conference, https://www.facebook.com/notes/edgerank-algorithm/edgerank-magic-revealed-in-f8–conference/206484249362078.

Fagerjord, A. (2003) Rhetorical convergence: earlier media influence on web media form. Ph.D. thesis, University of Oslo.

Fagerjord, A. (2005a) Editing stretchfilm. In *Proceedings from Hypertext '05*, Salzburg, Austria, 6–9 September. New York: ACM, p. 301. DOI: 10.1145/1083356.1089507.

Fagerjord, A. (2005b) Prescripts: authoring with templates. *Kairos*, 10.1, http://kairos.technorhetoric.net/10.1/binder2.html?coverweb/fagerjord/index.html.

Fagerjord, A. (2014) Databases and covert conclusions: new patterns in research publishing on the web. ECREA 2014, 13 November, Lisbon, Portugal, http://fagerjord.no/blog/ecrea2014.

Fagerjord, A. (2015) Humanist evaluation of locative media design. *The Journal of Media Innovation*, 2(1), 107–122.

Feenberg, A. (2002) *Transforming Technology: A Critical Theory Revisited*. Oxford: Oxford University Press.

Feenberg, A. (2013) Marcuse's phenomenology: reading chapter six of 'One-Dimensional Man'. *Constellations*, 20:4, 604–14.

Feeney, M. and Ross, S. (1993) *Information Technology in Humanities Scholarship: British Achievements, Prospects, and Barriers*. British Library R&D Report 6097. London: The British Library and The British Academy.

Finneman, N. O. (1999) *Hypertext and the Representational Capacities of the Binary Alphabet*. Aarhus: Centre for Cultural Research.

Fish, S. (2012) The digital humanities and the transcending of mortality. *The New York Times*, 9 January, http://opinionator.blogs.nytimes.com/2012/01/09/the-digital-humanities-and-the-transcending-of-mortality.

Fitzpatrick, K. (2011) *Planned Obsolescence: Publishing Technology and the Future of the Academy*. New York: New York University Press.

Fitzpatrick, K. (2012) The humanities done digitally. In *Debates in Digital Humanities*, ed. M. K. Gold. Minneapolis: University of Minnesota Press, pp. 12–15.

Flanders, J. (2011) 'You work at Brown. What do you teach?' *#alt-academy: a media commons project*, http://mediacommons.futureofthebook.org/alt-ac/pieces/you-work-brown-what-do-you-teach.

Flanders, J. (2012) Time, labor, and 'alternate careers' in digital humanities knowledge work. In *Debates in Digital Humanities*, ed. M. K. Gold. Minneapolis: University of Minnesota Press, pp. 292–308.

Folsom, E. (2007) Database as genre: the epic transformation of archives. *PMLA*, 122:5 (October), 1571–9.

Forbes (2013) Are MOOCs really a failure? *Forbes*, www.forbes.com/sites/susanadams/2013/12/11/are-moocs-really-a-failure?

Foucault, M. (1991) *Discipline and Punish*. London: Penguin Social Sciences.

Fox, A. and Patterson, D. (2014) *Engineering Software as a Service: An Agile Approach Using Cloud Computing*. California: Strawberry Canyon LLC.

Fraistat, N. (2012) The function of digital humanities research centers at the present time. In *Debates in Digital Humanities*, ed. M. K. Gold. Minneapolis: University of Minnesota Press, pp. 281–91.

Franzosi, R. (1998) Narrative as data: linguistic and statistical tools for the quantitative study of historical events. *International Journal of Social History*, 43, 81–104.

Fujinaga, I. and Weiss, S. F. (2004) Music. In *A Companion to Digital Humanities*, ed. S. Schreibman, R. Siemans and J. Unsworth. London: Wiley-Blackwell, pp. 97–107.

Fuller, M. (2001) It looks like you're writing a letter. *Telepolis*, 7 March, www.heise.de/tp/r4/artikel/7/7073/1.html.

Fuller, M. (ed.) (2008) *Software Studies: A Lexicon*. Cambridge, MA: MIT Press.

Galloway, A. R. (2014) The cybernetic hypothesis. *differences*, 25:1, 107–29.

Gardner, W. L., Loweb, K. B., Mossa, T. W., Mahoney, K. T. and Coglisera, C. C. (2010) Scholarly leadership in the study of leadership: a review of The Leadership Quarterly's second decade, 2000–2009. *The Leadership Quarterly*, 21, 922–58.

GeekBench (2013) GeekBench Processor Benchmarks, http://browser.primatelabs.com/processor-benchmarks.

Genette, G. (1980) *Narrative Discourse*. Ithaca, NY: Cornell University Press.

Gibson, J. J. (1986) *The Ecological Approach to Visual Perception*. Hillsdale, NJ: Erlbaum.

Gilmour-Bryson, A. (1987) Computers and medieval historical texts. In *History and Computing*, ed. P. Denley and D. Hopkins. Manchester: Manchester University Press, pp. 3–9.

Glissant, E. (1997) *The Poetics of Relation*. Michigan: The University of Michigan Press.

Global Outlook (2015) Global Outlook: Digital Humanities, www.globaloutlookdh.org.

Godlee, F. (2000) The ethics of peer review. In *Ethical Issues in Biomedical Publication*, ed. A. H. Jones and F. McLellan. Baltimore, MD: Johns Hopkins University Press, pp. 59–84.

Golbeck, J. (2013) *Analyzing the Social Web*. Amsterdam: Morgan Kaufmann.

Gold, M. K. (2012) *Debates in the Digital Humanities*. Minneapolis: University of Minnesota Press.

Goldberg, D. T. (2014) Afterlife of the Humanities, http://humafterlife.uchri.org.

Golumbia, D. (2012) Why Digital Humanities Hates Literary and Cultural Studies: The Secret History, and What to Do About It, http://wp.vcu.edu/english/2012/02/25/dr-golumbia-and-why-digital-humanities-hates-literary-and-cultural-studies.

Golumbia, D. (2013) 'Digital humanities': two definitions. *uncomputing*, www.uncomputing.org/?p=203.

Golumbia, D. (2014) Death of a discipline. *differences*, 25:1, 156–76.

Google (2013) Compute Engine – Google Cloud Platform, https://cloud.google.com/products/compute-engine.

Greenhalgh, M. (2004) Art history. In *A Companion to Digital Humanities*, ed. S. Schreibman, R. Siemans and J. Unsworth. London: Wiley-Blackwell, pp. 31–45.

Greenwald, G. (2013) 30c3 Keynote, Chaos Computer Club, http://media.ccc.de/browse/congress/2013/30C3_-_5622_-_en_-_saal_1_-_201312271930_-_30c3_keynote_-_glenn_greenwald_-_frank.html.

Gregory, I. (2014) Challenges and opportunities for digital history. *Frontiers in Digital Humanities: Digital History*, http://dx.doi.org/10.3389/fdigh.2014.00001.

Groves, T. and Loder, E. (2014) Prepublication histories and open peer review at The BMJ. *British Medical Journal*, 349, www.bmj.com/content/349/bmj.g5394.

Grusin, R. (2013) The Dark Side of the Digital Humanities, www.c21uwm. com/2013/01/09/dark-side-of-the-digital-humanities-part-2.

Grusin, R. (2014) The dark side of digital humanities: dispatches from two recent mla conventions. *differences*, 25:1, 79–82.

Grusin, R. (2016) The digital in the humanities: an interview with Richard Grusin, interview by Dinsman, M. *Los Angeles Review of Books*, https://lareviewofbooks. org/article/digital-humanities-interview-richard-grusin.

Guardian (2013) Open access: six myths to put to rest. *The Guardian*, www. theguardian.com/higher-education-network/blog/2013/oct/21/open-access-my ths-peter-suber-harvard.

Hagen, A. N. (2015) The playlist experience: personal playlists in music streaming services. *Popular Music and Society*, 38, 625–45.

Hancher, M. (2016) Re: search and close reading. In *Debates in the Digital Humanities 2016*, ed. M. K. Gold and L. F. Klein. Minneapolis: University of Minnesota Press, pp. 118–38.

Hart, M. (2008) The history and philosophy of project Gutenberg, https://www. gutenberg.org/wiki/Gutenberg:The_History_and_Philosophy_of_Project_ Gutenberg_by_Michael_Hart.

Hartson, R. (2003) Cognitive, physical, sensory, and functional affordances in interaction design. *Behaviour & Information Technology*, 15, 315–38.

Hartson, R. and Pyla, P. S. (2012) *The UX Book: Process and Guidelines for Ensuring a Quality User Experience*. Amsterdam: Morgan Kaufmann.

Harvey, A. (2014) Stealth Wear, http://ahprojects.com/projects/stealth-wear.

Hassenzahl, M. (2001) The effect of perceived hedonic quality on product appealingness. *International Journal of Human–Computer Interaction*, 13:4, 481–99.

Hayles, N. K. (2005) *My Mother Was a Computer: Digital Subjects and Literary Texts*. Chicago: University of Chicago Press.

Hayles, N. K. (2012) How We Think: Transforming Power and Digital Technologies, in Berry, D. M. (ed.) *Understanding Digital Humanities*, Basingstoke: Palgrave Macmillan, pp. 42–66.

Hayles, N. K. (2015) Final commentary: a provocation. In *Between the Humanities and the Digital*, ed. P. Svennson and D. T. Goldberg. Cambridge, MA: MIT Press, pp. 503–6.

Hey, T. and Trefethen, A. E. (2002) The UK e-Science Core Programme and the grid. *Future Generation Computer Systems*, 18:8, 1017–31, http://users.ecs.soton. ac.uk/ajgh/FGCSPaper.pdf.

Heyman, S. (2015) Google Books: a complex and controversial experiment. *The New York Times*, International Arts, 28 October.

Higgenbotham, S. (2010) How Caffeine Is Giving Google a Turbo Boost, http://

gigaom.com/2010/06/11/behind-caffeine-may-be-software-to-inspire-hadoop-2–0.

Hitchcock, T. (2013) Confronting the digital. *Cultural and Social History*, 10:1, 9–23, http://dx.doi.org/10.2752/147800413X13515292098070.

Hitchcock, T. (2014) Big Data, small data and meaning. *Historyonics*, http://histo ryonics.blogspot.co.uk/2014/11/big-data-small-data-and-meaning_9.html.

Hitchcock, T. and Shoemaker, R. (2015) *London Lives: Poverty, Crime, and the Making of a Modern City, 1690–1800*. Cambridge: Cambridge University Press.

Hochman, N. and Manovich, L. (2014) A view from above: exploratory visualisations of the Thomas Walther collection. In *Object:Photo: Modern Photographs: The Thomas Walther Collection 1909–1949. An Online Project of The Museum of Modern Art*. New York: The Museum of Modern Art.

Hockey, S. (2004) The history of humanities computing. In *A Companion to Digital Humanities*, ed. S. Schreibman, R. Siemans and J. Unsworth. London: Wiley-Blackwell, pp. 3–19.

Holmevik, J. R. (1994) Compiling SIMULA: a historical study of technological genesis. *Annals of the History of Computing, IEEE*, 16, 25–37.

Hoover, D. L. (2004) Testing Burrows's delta. *Literary and Linguistic Computing*, 19 (1 November), 453–75.

Hughes, L. M. and Ell, P. (2013) Digital collections as research infrastructure. In From Evolution to Transformation: Research Infrastructures and Scholarly Research. Special issue of the *International Journal of Humanities and Arts Computing*, September (Edinburgh University Press).

Iqbal, M. T. (2013) Google Spanner: The Future Of NoSQL, www.datascience-central.com/profiles/blogs/google-spanner-the-future-of-nosql.

Jackson, S. (1995) *Patchwork Girl*. Watertown, MA: Eastgate Systems.

Jagoda, P. (2013) The Dark Side of the Digital Humanities, www.c21uwm. com/2013/01/09/the-dark-side-of-the-digital-humanities-part-3.

Jameson, Fredric (1990) Cognitive mapping. In *Marxism and the Interpretation of Culture*, ed. N. Cary and K. Grossberg. Urbana: University of Illinois Press, pp. 347–60.

Janlert, L. E. and Jonsson, K. (2000) Kulturlaboratoriet ('The Culture Laboratory'). *Tvärsnitt*, 22:1, 54–61.

Jefferson, T., Alderson, P., Wager, E. and Davidoff, F. (2002a) Effects of peer review: a systematic review. *The Journal of the American Medical Association*, 287.

Jefferson, T., Wagner, E. and Davidoff, F. (2002b) Measuring the quality of editorial peer review. *The Journal of the American Medical Association*, 287.

Jockers, M. (2013) *Macroanalysis: Digital Methods and Literary History*. Illinois: University of Illinois Press.

Johnson, J. M. (2016) The digital in the humanities: an interview with Jessica Marie Johnson, interview by Dinsman, M. *Los Angeles Review of Books*, https:// lareviewofbooks.org/article/digital-humanities-interview-jessica-marie-johnson.

Johnson, S. (1999) *Interface Culture*. New York: Basic Books.

Jordan, T. (2015) *Information Politics, Liberation and Exploitation in the Digital Society*. London: Pluto Press.

Joyce, M. (1990) *Afternoon, a story*. Watertown, MA: Eastgate Systems.

Kaltenbrunner, W. (2015) Reflexive inertia: reinventing scholarship through digital practices. Doctoral dissertation manuscript, Leiden University.

Katzen, M. (1990) *Scholarship and Technology in the Humanities*. London: Bowker Saur.

Kenna, S. and Ross, S. (1995) *Networking in the Humanities*. London: Bowker Saur.

Kim, D. and Stommel, J. (2015) Disrupting the Digital Humanities, www.disrupt ingdh.com.

Kirschenbaum, M. (1998) A White Paper on Information, www2.iath.virginia. edu/mgk3k/white/frames.html.

Kirschenbaum, M. (2004) 'So the colors cover the wires': interface, aesthetics, and usability. In *A Companion to Digital Humanities*, ed. S. Schreibman, R. Siemans and J. Unsworth. London: Wiley-Blackwell, pp. 523–42.

Kirschenbaum, M. (2008) *Mechanisms: New Media and the Forensic Imagination*. Boston, MA: MIT Press.

Kirschenbaum, M. (2010) What is digital humanities and what's it doing in English departments? *ADE Bulletin*, 150.

Kirschenbaum, M. (2012a) Digital humanities as/is a tactical term. In *Debates in Digital Humanities*, ed. M. K. Gold. Minneapolis: University of Minnesota Press, pp. 415–28.

Kirschenbaum, M. (2012b) What is digital humanities and what's it doing in English departments? In *Debates in Digital Humanities*, ed. M. K. Gold. Minneapolis: University of Minnesota Press, pp. 3–11.

Kirschenbaum, M. (2013) 'What is digital humanities and what's it doing in English departments? *ADE Bulletin*, 150 (2010), http://mkirschenbaum.files. wordpress.com/2011/03/ade-final.pdf.

Kirschenbaum, M. (2014) What is 'digital humanities', and why are they saying such terrible things about it? *differences*, 25:1, 46–63.

Kirschenbaum, M. and Werner, S. (2014) Digital scholarship and digital studies: the state of the discipline. *Book History*, 17, 406–58.

Kittler, F. (1995) There is no software. *Ctheory*, www.ctheory.net/articles.aspx?id= 74.

Kladstrup, R. (2015) Philadelphia Social History Project (PSHP), http://philadel phiaencyclopedia.org/archive/philadelphia-social-history-project.

Klein, K. T. (1996) *Crossing Boundaries: Knowledge, Disciplinarities, and Interdisciplinarities*. Charlottesville: University of Virginia Press.

Knuth, D. E. (1973) *The Art of Computer Programming: Fundamental Algorithms*. Reading: Addison-Wesley.

Koh, A. (2014) Niceness, building, and opening the genealogy of the digital humanities: beyond the social contract of humanities computing. *differences*, 25:1, 93–106.

Kolb, D. (2005) Sprawling Places, 10 October, www.dkolb.org/sprawlingplaces.

Kolker, R. (2004) Digital media and the analysis of film. In *A Companion to Digital Humanities*, ed. S. Schreibman, R. Siemans and J. Unsworth. London: Wiley-Blackwell, pp. 383–96.

Lakatos, I. (1980) *Methodology of Scientific Research Programmes*. Cambridge: Cambridge University Press.

Lancaster, F. W. (1978) *Toward Paperless Systems*. New York: Academic Press.

Landow, G. P. (1994) Victorian Web, www.victorianweb.org.

Landow, G. P. (2006) *Hypertext 3.0*. Baltimore, MD: Johns Hopkins University Press.

Landow, G. P. and Delany, P. (1991) Hypertext, hypermedia and literary studies: the state of the art. In *Hypermedia and Literary Studies*, ed. P. Delaney and G. P. Landow. Cambridge, MA: MIT Press, pp. 3–50.

Lanham, R. A. (1993) *The Electronic Word*. Chicago: University of Chicago Press.

Latour, B. (2008) A Cautious Prometheus? A Few Steps Toward a Philosophy of Design (with Special Attention to Peter Sloterdijk), www.bruno-latour.fr/sites/default/files/112–DESIGN-CORNWALL-GB.pdf.

Lebert, M. (2008) *Project Gutenberg (1971–2008)*. Chapel Hill, NC: Project Gutenberg.

Leon, S. M. (2016) The digital in the humanities: an interview with Sharon M. Leon, interview by Dinsman, M. *Los Angeles Review of Books*, https://lareviewofbooks.org/article/the-digital-in-the-humanities-an-interview-with-sharon-m-leon.

Levy, S. (2011) *In the Plex: How Google Thinks, Works, and Shapes Our Lives*. New York: Simon & Schuster.

Lewandowska, M. and Cummings, N. (2005) An economy of love. In *Economising Culture*, ed. G. Cox, J. Krysa and A. Lewin. London: Autonomedia, pp. 75–87.

Liestøl, G. (2014) Along the Appian way: storytelling and memory across time and space in Mobile Augmented Reality. In *8740*, ed. M. Ioannides et al. Switzerland: Springer International Publishing, pp. 248–57.

Liu, A. (2004) *The Laws of Cool: Knowledge Work and the Culture of Information*. Chicago: University of Chicago Press.

Liu, A. (2011) The State of the Digital Humanities: A Report and a Critique, www.sms.cam.ac.uk/media/1173142 [video].

Liu, A. (2012) Where is cultural criticism in the digital humanities? In *Debates in Digital Humanities*, ed. M. K. Gold. Minneapolis: University of Minnesota Press, pp. 490–509.

Liu, A. (2016) Is digital humanities a field? – an answer from the point of view of language. *Journal of Siberian Federal University, Humanities and Social Sciences*, 7 (2016 9), 1546–52.

Lothian, A. (2011) Marked bodies, transformative scholarship, and the question of theory in digital humanities. *Journal of Digital Humanities*, 1:1, http://journalof digitalhumanities.org/1–1/marked-bodies-transformative-scholarship-and-the-question-of-theory-in-digital-humanities-by-alexis-lothian.

Lovink, G. (2012) What is the social in social media? *e-flux*, www.e-flux.com/journal/what-is-the-social-in-social-media.

Lovink, G. and Rossiter, N. (2013) Organised networks: weak ties to strong links. *Occupy Times*, http://theoccupiedtimes.org/?p=12358.

Lyotard, J. F. (1984) *The Postmodern Condition: A Report on Knowledge.* Manchester: Manchester University Press.

Maasø, A. (2014) Surviving streaming: how insight into listening patterns and the streaming model provide maps for the future. Presented on *Berlin Music Week*, www.hf.uio.no/imv/english/research/projects/cloudsandconcerts/publications/surviving_streaming_berlin_maaso_050914.pdf.

Madel, M. (1998) Windows Makeover [Digital installation]. New York: Postmasters.

Maeda, J. (2015) Weekend read: why design matters more than Moore. *The Wall Street Journal*, http://blogs.wsj.com/accelerators/2015/05/22/weekend-read-why-design-matters-more-than-moore.

Magdaleno, J. (2014) Is facial recognition technology racist? *The Creators Project*, http://thecreatorsproject.vice.com/blog/is-facial-recognition-technology-racist.

Manovich, L. (2001) *The Language of New Media.* London: MIT Press.

Manovich, L. (2009) How to follow global digital cultures, or cultural analytics for beginners, Manovich.net.

Manovich, L. (2013) *Software Takes Command.* New York: Bloomsbury Academic.

Manovich, L., Douglass, J. and Zepel, T. (2012) How to compare one million images. In *Understanding Digital Humanities*, (ed. D. M. Berry. New York: Palgrave MacMillan, pp. 249–78.

Manovich, L. and Kratky, A. (2005) *Soft Cinema* [DVD]. Cambridge, MA: MIT Press.

Manovich, L., Tifentale, A., Yazdani, M. and Chow, J. (2014) The Exceptional and the everyday: 144 hours in Kiev. 2014 IEEE International Conference on Big Data, Washington DC, 27–30 Oct., www.the-everyday.net.

Marcuse, H. (1999) *One-dimensional Man.* London: Routledge.

Mbembe, A. (2015) Decolonizing knowledge and the question of the archive, https://africaisacountry.atavist.com/decolonizing-knowledge-and-the-question-of-the-archive.

McCarty, W. (2003) Humanities computing. In *Encyclopedia of Library and Information Science*, ed. M. Drake. New York: M. Dekker, pp. 1224–35.

McCarty, W. (2004) Modeling: a study in words and meanings. In *A Companion to Digital Humanities*, ed. S. Schreibman, R. Siemans and J. Unsworth. London: Wiley-Blackwell.

McCarty, W. (2005) *Humanities Computing.* London: Palgrave.

McCarty, W. (2010) Industrialisation of the digital humanities? *Humanist*, 24:422, http://lists.digitalhumanities.org/pipermail/humanist/2010–October/001644.html.

McCarty, W. (2012) A telescope for the mind? In *Debates in Digital Humanities*, ed. M. K. Gold. Minneapolis: University of Minnesota Press, pp. 113–23.

McCarty, W. (2013a) Getting there from here: remembering the future of digital humanities, 2013 Roberto Busa Award lecture, DH2013, University of Nebraska (Lincoln).

McCarty, W. (2013b) What does Turing have to do with Busa? Keynote for ACRH-3, Sofia, Bulgaria, www.mccarty.org.uk/essays/McCarty,%20Turing%20and%20Busa.pdf.

McCarty, W. (2016) Fictions of possibility: simulation and 'the course of ordinary terrestrial experience'. *Journal of Siberian Federal University, Humanities & Social Sciences*, 7 (2016 9), 1553–61.

McCarty, W. and Kirschenbaum, M. (2003) Institutional models for humanities computing, EADH – The European Association for Digital Humanities, http://eadh.org/publications/institutional-models-humanities-computing.

McChesney, R. W. (2013) *Digital Disconnect: How Capitalism is Turning the Internet against Democracy*. New York: The New Press.

McGann, J. (2004) Marking texts of many dimensions. In *A Companion to Digital Humanities*, ed. S. Schreibman, R. Siemans and J. Unsworth. London: Wiley-Blackwell, pp. 198–217.

McGann, J. (2014) *A New Republic of Letters: Memory and Scholarship in the Age of Digital Reproduction*. Boston, MA: Harvard University Press.

McGann, J. (n.d.) The Ivanhoe Game, http://www2.iath.virginia.edu/jjm2f/old/Igamesummaryweb.htm.

McGee, M. (2013) EdgeRank is dead: Facebook's new algorithm now has close to 100K weight factors. *MarketingLand*, http://marketingland.com/edgerank-is-dead-facebooks-news-feed-algorithm-now-has-close-to-100k-weight-factors-55908.

McPherson, T. (2012) Why are the digital humanities so white? Or thinking the histories of race and computation. In *Debates in Digital Humanities*, ed. M. K. Gold. Minneapolis: University of Minnesota Press, pp. 139–60.

Meeks, E. (2012) The Curmudgeon Club, https://dhs.stanford.edu/natural-law/the-curmudgeon-club.

Mejias, U. A. (2013) *Off the Network: Disrupting the Digital World*. London: University of Minnesota Press.

Melnik, S., Gubarev, A., Long, J. J., et al. (2010) Dremel: interactive analysis of web-scale datasets. *Proceedings of the 36th International Conference on Very Large Data Bases*, pp. 330–9.

Minsky, M. L. (1965) Matter, mind and models. *Proceedings of the International Federation of Information Processing Congress*, vol. 1, 45–9, http://groups.csail.mit.edu/medg/people/doyle/gallery/minsky/mmm.html.

Mittell, J. (2015) *Complex TV: The Poetics of Contemporary Television Storytelling*. New York: NYU Press.

Moggridge, B. (2007) *Designing Interactions*. Cambridge, MA: MIT Press.

Montfort, N. and Wardrip-Fruin, N. (2004) Acid-free Bits: Recommendations for Long-lasting Electronic Literature, https://eliterature.org/pad/afb.html.

Moretti, F. (2013) *Distant Reading*. London: Verso.

Moretti, F. (2016) The digital in the humanities: an interview with Franco Moretti, interview by Dinsman, M. *Los Angeles Review of Books*, https://lareviewofbooks. org/interview/the-digital-in-the-humanities-an-interview-with-franco-moretti.

Moulthrop, S. (1991) *Victory Garden*. Watertown, MA: Eastgate Systems.

Moulthrop, S. (2005) After the last generation: rethinking scholarship in the days of serious play. Digital Arts and Culture, IT University of Copenhagen, 2015, https://pantherfile.uwm.edu/moulthro/essays/dac2005.pdf.

Mullings, C. (1996) *New Technologies for the Humanities*. London: Bowker Saur.

Nelson, S., et al. (2013) Crossing battle lines: teaching multimodal literacies through alternate reality games. *Kairos*, 17, http://kairos.technorhetoric. net/17.3/praxis/nelson-et-al/index.html.

Nelson, T. H. (1974) *Computer Lib / Dream Machines*. Self-published, www.new mediareader.com/book_samples/nmr-21-nelson.pdf.

Newman, S. (2013) Afterword. In F. Campagna, *The Last Night: Anti-Work, Atheism, Adventure*. London: Zero Books, pp. 92–5.

Norman, D. A. (1999) Affordances, conventions and design. *Interactions*, 6, 38–43.

Norman, D. A. (2002) *The Design of Everyday Things*. New York: Basic Books.

Nowviskie, B. (2010) #alt-ac: Alternate Academic Careers for Humanities Scholars, http://nowviskie.org/2010/alt-ac.

NSF (2015) About advanced cyberinfrastructure, National Science Foundation: Advanced Cyberinfrastructure (ACI) Division, www.nsf.gov/cise/aci/about.jsp.

Nyhan, J. (2012) Hidden histories: computing and the humanities c. 1965–1985, *Digital Humanities Quarterly*, 6:3, www.digitalhumanities.org/dhq/vol/6/3/ index.html.

ODH (2015) What is the Digging Into Data Challenge? http://diggingintodata. org/about.

Odlyzko, A. (1999) Peer and non-peer review. In *Peer Review in Health Sciences*, ed. F. Goodlee and T. Jefferson. London: BMJ, pp. 309–11.

Oldman, D., Doerr, M. and Gradmann, S. (2015) ZEN and the Art of Linked Data: New Strategies for a Semantic Web of Humanist Knowledge, https:// lirias.kuleuven.be/handle/123456789/485765.

Oliver, J. (2014) Julian Oliver, http://julianoliver.com/output.

Oliver, J., Savičić, G. and Vasiliev, D. (2011) Critical Engineering Manifesto, http://criticalengineering.org.

Oxford English Dictionary (2015) Feel. Oxford: Oxford University Press, www.oed. com/view/Entry/68977#eid4572147.

Pannapacker, W. (2013) Stop calling it 'digital humanities'. *The Chronicle of Higher Education*, http://chronicle.com/article/Stop-Calling-It-Digital/137325.

Parks, L. (2015) 'Stuff you can kick': towards a theory of media infrastructures. In *Between the Humanities and the Digital*, ed. P. Svennson and D. T. Goldberg. Cambridge, MA: MIT Press, pp. 355–73.

Patterson, M. (2015) Edgerank: a guide to the Facebook news feed algorithm. *SproutSocial*, http://sproutsocial.com/insights/facebook-news-feed-algorithm-guide.

Pechenick, E.A., Danforth, C.M. and Dodds, P. S. (2015) Characterizing the Google Books corpus: strong limits to inferences of socio-cultural and linguistic evolution. *PLoS ONE*, 10, e0137041– .

Peirce, C. S. (1998) Sundry logical conceptions. In *The Essential Peirce: Selected Philosophical Writings*, ed. N. Houser and C. J. W. Kloesel. Bloomington: Indiana University Press, pp. 267–88.

Pitti, D. V. (2004) Designing sustainable projects and publications. In *A Companion to Digital Humanities*, ed. S. Schreibman, R. Siemans and J. Unsworth. London: Wiley-Blackwell, pp. 471–87.

Pochoda, P. (2013/05/01) The big one: the epistemic system break in scholarly monograph publishing. *New Media & Society*, 15, 359–78.

Prescott, A. (2014) I'd rather be a librarian. *Cultural and Social History*, 11:3, 335–41, http://dx.doi.org/10.2752/147800414X13983595303192.

Presner, T. (2015) Critical theory and the mangle of digital humanities. In *Between Humanities and the Digital*, ed. P. Svennson and D. T. Goldberg. Cambridge, MA: MIT Press, pp. 55–67.

Purdy, J. P. and Walker, J. R. (2012) Scholarship on the move: a rhetorical analysis of scholarly activity in digital spaces. In *The New Work of Composing*, ed., D. Journet, C. E. Ball and R. Trauman. Illinois: Computers and Composition Digital Press.

Raley, R. (2013) The Dark Side of the Digital Humanities, www.c21uwm. com/2013/01/09/the-dark-side-of-the-digital-humanities-part-4.

Ramsay, S. (2004) Databases. In *A Companion to Digital Humanities*, ed. S. Schreibman, R. Siemans and J. Unsworth. London: Wiley-Blackwell, pp. 177–97.

Ramsay, S. (2010) The Hermeneutics of Screwing Around; or What You Do with a Million Books, www.leeannhunter.com/digital/wp-content/uploads/2014/08/RamsayBooks.pdf.

Ramsay, S. (2011) Who's in and who's out, Stephen Ramsay, http://stephenram say.us/text/2011/01/08/whos-in-and-whos-out.

Ramsay, S. (2013a) Bambazooka, http://stephenramsay.us/2013/07/23/bamba zooka.

Ramsay, S. (2013b) DH types one and two, http://stephenramsay.us/2013/05/03/ dh-one-and-two.

Ramsay, S. and Rockwell, G. (2012) Developing things: notes toward an epistemology of building in the digital humanities. In *Debates in Digital Humanities*, ed. M. K. Gold. Minneapolis: University of Minnesota Press, pp. 75–84.

Reid, A. (2012) Graduate education and the ethics of the digital humanities. In *Debates in Digital Humanities*, ed. M. K. Gold. Minneapolis: University of Minnesota Press, pp. 350–67.

Renear, A. H. (2004) Text encoding. In *A Companion to Digital Humanities*, ed. S. Schreibman, R. Siemans and J. Unsworth. London: Wiley-Blackwell, pp. 218–39.

Rennie, D. (1999) Editorial peer review: its development and rationale. In *Peer*

Review in Health Sciences, ed. F. Goodlee and T. Jefferson. London: BMJ, pp. 1–13.

Rieder, B. and Röhle, T. (2012) Digital methods: five challenges. In *Understanding Digital Humanities*, ed. D. M. Berry. Basingstoke: Palgrave, pp. 67–84.

Risam, R. (2015) Revise and Resubmit: An Unsolicited Peer Review, http://roopi karisam.com/uncategorized/revise-and-resubmit-an-unsolicited-peer-review.

Rockwell, G. and Mactavish, A. (2004) Multimedia. In *A Companion to Digital Humanities*, ed. S. Schreibman, R. Siemans and J. Unsworth. London: Wiley-Blackwell, pp. 108–20.

Rogers, R. (2013) *Digital Methods*. Cambridge, MA: MIT Press.

Rogers, R., van der Vlies, L., de Groot, K., Weltevrede, E. and Borra, E. (2008) Google and the politics of tabs, Govcom.org, https://movies.digitalmethods.net/google.html.

Rossiter, N. and Zehle, S. (2014) Toward a politics of anonymity: algorithmic actors in the constitution of collective agency and the implications for global justice movements. In *The Routledge Companion to Alternative Organization*, ed. M. Parker, G. Cheney, V. Fournier and C. Land. London: Routledge, pp. 151–62.

Rouvroy, A. (2009) *Governmentality in an Age of Autonomic Computing: Technology, Virtuality and Utopia*, http://works.bepress.com/antoinette_rouvroy/26.

Ryle, G. (1945) Knowing how and knowing that. *The Aristotelian Society*, 46, 1–16.

Saltz, D. Z. (2004) Performing arts. In *A Companion to Digital Humanities*, ed. S. Schreibman, R. Siemans and J. Unsworth. London: Wiley-Blackwell, pp. 121–31.

Samuels, L. and McGann, J. (1999) Deformance and interpretation. *New Literary History*, 30:1, 25–56.

Scheinfeldt, T. (2008) Sunset for ideology, sunrise for methodology? *Found History*, http://web.archive.org/web/20150219145840/http://foundhistory.org/2008/03/sunset-for-ideology-sunrise-for-methodology.

Scheinfeldt, T. (2014) The dividends of difference: recognizing digital humanities' diverse family tree/s. *Found History*, http://foundhistory.org/2014/04/the-dividends-of-difference-recognizing-digital-humanities-diverse-family-trees.

Schnapp, J. and Presner, P. (2009) Digital Humanities Manifesto 2.0, www.humanitiesblast.com/manifesto/Manifesto_V2.pdf.

Schreibman, S., Siemans, R. and Unsworth, J. (2004) *A Companion to Digital Humanities*. London: Wiley-Blackwell.

Schwartz, R. (2013) The Dirty Little Secret About Mobile Benchmarks, http://mostly-tech.com/tag/geekbench.

Scola, N. (2015) Library of Congress' Twitter archive is a huge #FAIL. *Politico*, www.politico.com/story/2015/07/library-of-congress-twitter-archive-119698.html.

Selby, C. and Woollard, J. (2013) Computational Thinking: the Developing Definition, http://eprints.soton.ac.uk/356481.

Shrager, J. (2015) The Genealogy of Eliza, http://elizagen.org.

Smith, A. (2004) Preservation. In *A Companion to Digital Humanities*, ed. S. Schreibman, R. Siemans and J. Unsworth. London: Wiley-Blackwell, pp. 576–91.

Smith, K. (2009) Q&A with Brett Bobley, Director of the NEH's Office of Digital Humanities (ODH). *HASTAC*, www.hastac.org/node/1934.

Sowa, J. F. (2000) *Knowledge Representation: Logical, Philosophical, and Computational Foundations*. Pacific Grove: Brooks/Cole.

SPEC (2014) The Standard Performance Evaluation Corporation (SPEC), www. spec.org.

Spencer, M., Bordalejo, B., Wang, L. S., Barbrook, A. C., Mooney, L. R. and Robinson, P. (2003) Analyzing the order of items in manuscripts of The Canterbury Tales. *Computers and the Humanities*, 37, 97–109.

Spiro, L. (2012) 'This is why we fight': defining the values of the digital humanities. In *Debates in Digital Humanities*, ed. M. K. Gold. Minneapolis: University of Minnesota Press, pp. 75–84.

Stark, T. (2012) 'Cinema in the hands of the people': Chris Marker, the Medvedkin Group, and the potential of militant film. *OCTOBER*, 139 (Winter), 117–50.

Sterne, J. (2015) The example: some historical considerations. In *Between Humanities and the Digital*, ed. P. Svennson and D. T. Goldberg. Cambridge, MA: MIT Press, pp. 17–33.

Stiegler, B. (2009) *Acting Out*. Stanford: Stanford University Press.

Stiegler, B. (2012) Call for Digital Studies, https://digital-studies.org/wp/call-for-digital-studies.

Stiegler, B. (2013) *What Makes a Life Worth Living: On Pharmacology*, trans. D. Ross. Cambridge: Polity.

Sudahar, S. et al. (2015) Network analysis of narrative content in large corpora. *Natural Language Engineering*, 21, 81–112.

Svennson, P. (2010) The landscape of digital humanities. *Digital Humanities Quarterly*, 4:1, http://digitalhumanities.org/dhq/vol/4/1/000080/000080.html.

Svennson, P. (2012) Envisioning the digital humanities. *Digital Humanities Quarterly*, 6:1, http://digitalhumanities.org/dhq/vol/6/1/000112/000112.html.

Svennson, P. and Goldberg, D. T. (2015) *Between Humanities and the Digital*. Cambridge, MA: MIT Press.

Swalwell, M. (2006) Cast-offs from the golden age. *Vectors*, 2, www.vectorsjournal. net/projects/index.php?project=66.

SYSmark (2007) SYSmark 2007 Preview, http://bapco.com/products/sysmark-2007#details-product-info.

Terranova, T. (2014) Red stack attack! Algorithms, capital and the automation of the common. *EuroNomade*, www.euronomade.info/?p=2268.

Text Encoding Initiative (2015) www.tei-c.org.

Thomas, W. G. (2004) Computing and the historical imagination. In *A Companion to Digital Humanities*, ed. S. Schreibman, R. Siemans and J. Unsworth. London: Wiley-Blackwell, pp. 56–68.

Thompson, J. B. (2005) *Books in the Digital Age: The Transformation of Academic and Higher Education Publishing in Britain and the United States*. Cambridge: Polity.

Thomson, B. (2015) Apple Watch and continuous computing. Stratechery, https://stratechery.com/2015/apple-watch-and-continuous-computing

Tifentale, A. and Manovich, L. (2015) Selfiecity: exploring photography and self-fashioning in social media. In *Postdigital Aesthetics: Art, Computation and Design*, ed. D. M. Berry and M. Dieter. London: Palgrave Macmillan, pp. 109–22.

Todorov, T. (1990) *Genres in Discourse*. Cambridge: Cambridge University Press.

TransformDH (2013) #TransformDH: Transformative Digital Humanities: Doing Race, Ethnicity, Gender, Sexuality and Class in DH, http://transformdh.org.

Udell, J. (2005) Heavy metal umlaut. *Jon Udell*, http://jonudell.net/udell/gems/umlaut/umlaut.html.

Ulmer, G. L. (1994) *Heuretics: the Logic of Invention*. Baltimore, MD: Johns Hopkins University Press.

Ulmer, G. L. (2004) *Teletheory: Grammatology in the Age of Video*. New York: Atropos.

Unsworth, J. (2001) A Master's Degree in Digital Humanities: Part of the Media Studies Program at the University of Virginia. Lecture given to the 2001 Congress of the Social Sciences and Humanities, Université Laval, Québec, Canada, 25 May, http://people.lis.illinois.edu/~unsworth/laval.html.

Unsworth, J. (2002) What is Humanities Computing and What is Not? http://computerphilologie.uni-muenchen.de/jg02/unsworth.html.

Vaughan-Nichols, S. J. (2013) Drilling into Big Data with Apache Drill, http://blog.smartbear.com/open-source/drilling-into-big-data-with-apache-drill.

Verhoeven, D. (2016) As luck would have it: serendipity and solace in digital research infrastructure. *Feminist Media Histories*, 2:1 (Winter), 7–28.

Veloutsou, C., Paton, R. A. and Lewis, J. (2005) Consultation and reliability of information sources pertaining to university selection: some questions answered? *International Journal of Educational Management*, 19:4, 279–91.

Waltzer, L. (2012) Digital humanities and the 'ugly stepchildren' of American higher education. In *Debates in Digital Humanities*, ed. M. K. Gold. Minneapolis: University of Minnesota Press, pp. 335–49.

Warburg (2016) The Warburg Institute Library: Description and Services, http://warburg.sas.ac.uk/library/description-services/#c307.

Wark, M. (2007) *Gamer Theory*. Cambridge, MA: Harvard University Press.

Warwick, C. (2004) Print scholarship and digital resources. In *A Companion to Digital Humanities*, ed. S. Schreibman, R. Siemans and J. Unsworth. London: Wiley-Blackwell, pp. 366–82.

Weizenbaum, J. (1966) ELIZA: a computer program for the study of natural language communication between man and machine. *Communications of the ACM*, 9, 36–45.

Wing, J. M. (2006) Computational thinking. *Communications of the ACM*, 49, 33–5.

Wing, J. M. (2008) Computational thinking and thinking about computing. *Philosophical Transactions of the Royal Society*, 366, 3717–25.

Wing, J. M. (2011) Research Notebook: Computational Thinking – What and Why? http://link.cs.cmu.edu/article.php?a=600.

Winter, T. N. (1999) Roberto Busa, S.J., and the invention of the machine-generated concordance. *The Classical Bulletin*, 75, 3–20.

Wittgenstein, L. (1957) *Philosophische Untersuchungen*. London: Basil Blackwell.

Zorich, D. M. (2008) *A Survey of Digital Humanities Centers in the United States*. Washington, DC: Council on Library and Information Resources, www.clir.org/pubs/abstract/pub143abst.html.

Zuboff, S. (2016) The secrets of surveillance capitalism. *Frankfurter Allgemeine*, www.faz.net/aktuell/feuilleton/debatten/the-digital-debate/shoshana-zuboff-secrets-of-surveillance-capitalism-14103616.html.

Index